The Committee

---

*The Committee* is based on a political journal kept by Bruce Wolpe, who served as a senior adviser to Rep. Henry A. Waxman (D-CA), chair of one of the most powerful committees in Congress, the House Committee on Energy and Commerce. For three years (February 2009–2012), Wolpe recorded an inside view of how a powerful committee and the House look and feel as legislation is developed and processed. Using the insider view of the rough-and-tumble politics of cap-and-trade, health care reform, tobacco, oversight, and the debt ceiling agreement, *The Committee* uniquely frames how politics and policymaking are practiced on Capitol Hill within the theory and literature of political science. The themes align with political scientists' questions relating to committee power, partisanship, and the political strategies used to build winning policy coalitions in the Committee and on the floor of the House. *The Committee* will appeal to those teaching in the area of American politics and those interested in the formulation of major policies, and its insights continue to reverberate within the context of today's partisan conflicts. The strategies and politics of moving legislation through Congress, including internal and external coalition building as well as the committee chair's role in framing policy narratives, will captivate both novice and die-hard readers of politics.

**Bryan W. Marshall** is the Paul Rejai professor and chair of the Department of Political Science at Miami University.

**Bruce Wolpe** has served as chief of staff to Julia Gillard, Australia's twenty-seventh Prime Minister, and as senior adviser to Representative Henry A. Waxman (D-CA), chair of the US House Committee on Energy and Commerce.

LEGISLATIVE POLITICS & POLICY MAKING

*Series Editors*

Janet M. Box-Steffensmeier, Vernal Riffe Professor of Political Science,
The Ohio State University

David Canon, Professor of Political Science, University of Wisconsin, Madison

RECENT TITLES IN THE SERIES:

For a complete list of titles in this series, please see www.press.umich.edu.

# THE COMMITTEE

*A Study of Policy, Power, Politics, and Obama's Historic Legislative Agenda on Capitol Hill*

Bryan W. Marshall and Bruce C. Wolpe

University of Michigan Press
Ann Arbor

Copyright © 2018 by Bryan W. Marshall and Bruce C. Wolpe

Published in the United States of America by the
University of Michigan Press


2021   2020   2019   2018     4   3   2   1

A CIP catalog record for this book is available from the British Library.

Library of Congress Cataloging-in-Publication Data

Names: Marshall, Bryan W., author. | Wolpe, Bruce C., 1951– author.
Title: The committee : a study of policy, power, politics, and Obama's historic legislative
   agenda on Capitol Hill / Bryan W. Marshall and Bruce C. Wolpe.
Description: Ann Arbor : University of Michigan Press, 2018. | Series: Legislative politics
   and policy making series | Includes bibliographical references and index. | Identifiers:
   LCCN 2017059952 (print) | LCCN 2018012637 (ebook) | ISBN 9780472123957
   (e-book) | ISBN 9780472073832 (hardcover : alk. paper) | ISBN 9780472053834 (pbk. :
   alk. paper) | ISBN 9780472123957 (ebook)
Subjects: LCSH: United States. Congress (111th : 2009-2010) | United States. Congress.
   House. Committee on Energy and Commerce. | United States—Politics and
   government—2009–2017. | MESH: Public Policy—United States.
Classification: LCC JK1059 111th (ebook) | LCC JK1059 111th .M37 2018 (print) |
   DDC 328.7309/0511—dc23
LC record available at https://lccn.loc.gov/2017059952

# Contents

# Foreword

*About the Authors: Two Beginnings,*
*One Old Political Hand and One New*

Bryan Marshall

In 2008–9, I served as the American Political Science Association's Steiger Congressional Fellow. Although a longtime avid student of Congress, this was my first real experience in that great institution. I was a political novice, a brand-new albeit willing political hand. I was incredibly fortunate to land what proved to be a jewel of a position as a policy adviser for the House majority whip, Representative James E. Clyburn (D-SC). I remain very grateful to the congressman, his staff, and the many friends I met along the way. My time working for the majority whip truly transformed how I think about Congress and thus how I teach my students about congressional politics.

I have always maintained that the historic legislative record of the 111th Congress and thus much of President Obama's policy legacy resulted in no small part to Jim Clyburn, his extraordinary talents, and the skills and tenacity of his staff. Congressman Clyburn had an unassuming and down-to-earth leadership style. He preferred the velvet glove over the iron fist in persuading colleagues to support the party line. But this is not to say he didn't possess (and use) a hammer from time to time. On occasion, his deep baritone voice could immediately silence a raucous crowd of hundreds of members of Congress and their staffers in a basement room in the Capitol. (After all, he started out as a teacher!) The majority whip was a gracious southern-style representative; he was and is today deeply respected by members on both sides of the aisle and was uniquely suited to bring together the disparate factions of the Democratic caucus. He was elected to Congress in 1994 and chosen by his peers as president of his congressional freshman class. From there, his leadership role grew: he served as chair of the Congressional Black Caucus (1999–2001), vice chair and chair of the Democratic caucus (2003–6), majority whip (2007-10). With the loss of Democratic control of the House, he now serves as the assistant Democratic leader.

I worked in the whip's "policy shop," part of a larger team in a position that demanded considerable flexibility, as we handled all the critical policy and political issues on the leadership's agenda. I was responsible for an extensive policy portfolio that included defense, veterans affairs, homeland security, intelligence and national security, and children's welfare, to name a few. I was stationed with other staff in one of the whip's offices directly off Statuary Hall in the Capitol, only about fifty paces from both the House floor and the Speaker's office. It was prime real estate—literally the hub of congressional action. It doesn't get any better than that for a Congress jock.

The experience provided me with a rare opportunity to understand the intricate relationships the party leadership needs to foster and maintain with the caucus rank and file, committees, and the executive branch. I spent much of my time learning about how the leadership builds coalitions. The ingredients of real sausage making are political jockeying and legislative compromise, whipping and counting votes, and then corralling votes on the House floor. I watched and learned how the party leadership put together support for President Obama's historic first budget resolution. Much like the stimulus package, the passage of the budget was a buffet of individual compromises. On some key votes, I worked with the White House Legislative Affairs staff, who brought presidential resources to bear on fence-sitters and coaxed them to support the leadership's position. When I was not on the House floor, I spent considerable time following legislation through the legislative process, attending committee hearings and markups to report about issues or potential conflicts to the leadership. The Rules Committee and leadership staff meetings were especially insightful in terms of learning about political strategy and how the leadership used procedures to advantage party priorities.

My time in the corridors of the Capitol was invaluable—irreplaceable, really—in terms of learning about politics and how Congress works. There were so many lessons to be learned: the "forty-minute meeting" rule, the art of careful listening for asks from members to lock in their support on a measure, even the necessity of speed walking (often running) up and down the hidden corridors of the Capitol. I was the low staffer on the totem pole—and deservedly so—but there are no inconsequential positions with the whip: every task and role is important. With every person I met, at every meeting I attended, I was an extension of the Whip's Office, representing the boss. I was part of a small, highly professional network that served as the eyes and ears for the whip and the party leadership. But my first lesson on my very first day in January 2009 proved one of the most important. As I trailed along behind a senior staffer, trotting down a vast hallway to an early morning meeting, he looked back and coolly explained the key to success: "We have 256 members in this caucus, and you're part of the whip team and need to learn to treat each and every member's priority as if it was your own." For the leadership, this advice was the key to gaining trust and building effective relationships. I know it sounds clichéd, but it doesn't make it any less true. The Hill runs on relationships and trust. Getting things done in Congress requires building relationships, and relationships in Congress don't work well or for long without trust. His advice proved prescient.

I also vividly remember that sunny brisk day after the election in November when I left my wife and three young children (and our dog) to start my new position in Washington, D.C. I visited home only sporadically for about the next year, and that time away from my family was very difficult. But I got to take an incredible journey on the Hill, in a historic place at a unique political moment of time. None of it would have been possible without my loving and supportive wife, Candace. So, I dedicate this book to her and to our children, Autumn, Evan, and Dylan.

I also thank my coauthor, Bruce Wolpe, who has been wonderful to work with, a top-notch partner in shaping this manuscript. When I first read Bruce's journal, I wondered at his cogent thoughts and clarity, his grasp of detail and meaning in the context of the monumental dynamics at work every day—and those days on the Hill were long bone-tiring days. My colleagues at Miami University helped to make my journey to the Hill a reality. Many individuals at University of Michigan Press have helped to shepherd our work to completion, including Scott Ham, Danielle Coty, Meredith Norwich, and the editors of the Legislative Politics and Policy Making series, Janet Box-Steffensmeier and David Canon. And of course, Bruce and I are very grateful to the reviewers who took time to offer us insight and direction that greatly improved the final product.

Oxford, Ohio
June 2017

## Bruce Wolpe

My contribution to *The Committee* began in March 2009, when I joined the staff of Rep. Henry Waxman (D-CA), chair of the Committee on Energy and Commerce (always described by others as "powerful"). My title was senior adviser. I was motivated to make the transition from professional life in Australia to Washington and to rejoin Henry's staff after almost twenty years away (I served as his first legislative assistant when he was elected in 1974) because of the election of Barack Obama as president. I firmly believed that this was a pivotal moment in American history and that the chance to play a small but very meaningful part in it simply could not be missed.

I was certain that Henry and the committee would make legislation of unique and enduring importance, and I decided from the outset to record the events—to capture a part of the Obama legacy as it was created. And so I began my "Washington Journal," which ultimately totaled 240,000 words over more than two years.

\*   \*   \*

Friday, March 27, 2009. I always wanted to work in the White House. But this is not where this journal starts. The day began in Sydney with a long run through Balmain, trying to commit to eternal memory the streets and Harbour and sights and morning light I know so well. And it ends tonight in Washington, where I begin work Monday as a senior adviser to Henry Waxman, chair of the House Energy and Commerce Committee, through which much of what can be termed President Obama's legacy legislation— energy security, climate change, and universal access to health care—will be decided.

The day after the election last November, when Obama won and the Democrats had gained seats in Congress, further cementing their majority, Henry had announced a challenge for the post of committee chair against John Dingell of Michigan. Henry beat Dingell decisively in key votes among the House leadership and in the full caucus. It was a dramatic victory for change, fresh leadership, and strong action on the Obama agenda. In January, when we met the week before the inauguration, I said, "Henry, this is the moment you were elected for in 1974—this is the time, with this president, to finally get the legislation you have sought on health and the environment since you were elected in the reform wave after Watergate and Nixon in 1974. You could not do it with Carter or Clinton, but you can now." And he agreed.

My job is to help Henry with strategic relationships and support his presence—and hence his clout, which are already considerable. And also to help Henry marshal and manage the majorities necessary to pass the big legislation by working to keep the lobbyists for the vested interests from killing the Obama legislative program. It is a great and welcome challenge.

But I originally sought to work in the White House following Obama's election; it was something I had talked about from time to time with Phil Schiliro, Henry's chief of staff, who became Obama's liaison to Capitol Hill during the campaign. He was appointed assistant to the president for legislative affairs and is Obama's point man with the Congress. Phil and I talked after the election; he encouraged me to seek a White House position, and we talked through a couple options. Then, in late November, the conversation took a decisive turn:

> Henry has become chairman of the committee—fulfilling my fondest hopes for him. And I'm not there to help him as chairman at this greatest of times for him, and it's killing me. But you have some of the skills that I brought to him. And he needs those. And we need Henry to be as strong as possible to get Obama's program through. So would you consider coming back to work with Henry?

It was not the White House, but it had immense appeal. I was Henry's first legislative assistant in 1975 and left with his blessing and goodwill seven years later, and we stayed close through the ensuing years. And so to work for Henry again and to be in the center of the legislative action on the Hill— this was one hell of a prospect. I announced my departure to colleagues in Sydney at Fairfax Media, a major publisher in Australia, on the first business day of the year, January 5, and said in my note to senior executives there, "President Obama's election is, for me, the political calling of our time, and I want to be part of it." The reaction to my news was enormously supportive. I think everyone in Sydney wanted to quit their job and go work in Obama's Washington; I was about to live out their dreams. What could be more fun?

I spent a week in January and another week in March 2009 visiting with the committee and getting oriented. I left Fairfax yesterday, am flying today, and begin Monday morning. Henry has said he wants a climate change bill, with a cap-and-trade system, passed by the committee by the end of May. And a health care bill by August. It's prime time in Barack Obama's Washington.

\* \* \*

After leaving the committee staff in 2011, I wanted to have the journal published in hopes of telling the story of the committee's enormous influence on the legislation that would mark Obama's presidency. The journal was never intended to be the authoritative history of key legislation in President Obama's first term. But it is a story of how Congress—and especially one of its prime committees—did its work from the view of a senior staffer. So I recorded what I saw from my unique perch to help readers discern how legislation and oversight were developed and executed—to let readers see how the legislative process really worked at an historic juncture.

What I recorded is and remains my view of these events; like *Rashomon*, it is simply my take. In politics there are many truths, and *The Committee* conveys mine. I am sure that other participants in these events will not agree with many passages, but they reflect my best efforts to record what happened. I wrote in real time, since it would be impossible to reconstruct each day's developments months or years later.

My journey to publication began with a series of false starts. My journal, on its own, was too narrow, too "inside baseball" for publication, despite the best efforts of my friend Eddie Frits—the feedback on my forays into the publishing world was clear. But Michael Kerns, formerly of Routledge, saw a way to wrap the journal in political science to produce a book that was truly meaningful—a novel study of Congress. In 2014, Michael put me in touch with Bryan Marshall, now chair of the political science department at Miami University, and we instantly began an enthusiastic collaboration. Bryan brought academic discipline, rigor, and expertise to my account of the committee's work. And we found a publisher, the University of Michigan Press, that wanted to back us.

My partnership with Bryan has been a joy, as efficient a writing and editing collaboration as possible given that we are separated by ten thousand miles. I am so grateful that we could proceed together: he has brought *The Committee* to life.

For students of American politics and the Congress, we have produced an important work on how a congressional committee can function and what that functioning can mean for a president's policy agenda and political fortunes.

I also thank Danielle Coty, Scott Ham, and several of their predecessors at the University of Michigan Press. The team went to bat for us and gave our book great care and attention.

I thank Phil Schiliro and Phil Barnett for their review of the manuscript and guidance as the book was finalized. Any flaws in the account of these events and our analysis of them are wholly mine and Bryan's.

I am forever grateful to Henry Waxman, who gave me the chance to work with him more than four decades ago and then to rejoin his staff. I believe that Henry is the most principled, cunning, and effective lawmaker in modern times. A grandmaster of politics and legislation. An ethical and moral man. He is deeply shaped by his views of politics and how it should be practiced. And he is a truly great human being.

I am indebted to Phil B., Phil S., and Henry for their trust in me as *The Committee* developed. They did not know that I was keeping a journal, and when I told them about it and discussed the possibility of publication, they gave their blessing. John F. Kennedy often remarked, "History depends on who writes it." That took a lot on their part, and I am so very thankful to each of them.

And my deepest appreciation always to my wife, Lesley Russell, who continues to make all things possible.

Sydney
June 2017

# Preface

## *Outline of* The Committee

*The Committee* is distinct from most other texts in this area in that it offers the unique perspective of a senior congressional staffer. The story that unfolds in *The Committee* provides both a window on legislative history and a fascinating perspective on the practice of politics and how policy is made on the Hill: what really happens from day to day and why. The reader occupies a front-row seat that enables an understanding of the trade-offs necessary in making public policy, the intra- and interparty struggles of coalition building, and the challenge of no-holds-barred partisanship in the modern Congress. The text thus offers a more granular view of the role(s) of Congress, the president, and interest groups and lobbying forces. Throughout, the text reinforces key analytical ideas from the congressional literature, such as committee power, coalition building, and the president's role in shaping legislation.

Chapter 1 outlines an analytical framework from the political science literature to serve as a lens to view congressional politics. It illustrates a few of the literature's key perspectives for understanding the factors shaping congressional policymaking and politics, including committee power, partisanship, and coalition building. The chapter draws out the three major theories of legislative organization and their respective explanations for committee power. From these theoretical underpinnings, the chapter then outlines the growing power of the political parties and party leaders in Congress. Since the 1980s, the increase in ideological homogeneity within the parties and heterogeneity between the parties has raised partisan conflict to historic heights. As a result, decision-making processes, especially in the House, have become largely characterized by a party-driven model, as opposed to the committee-dominated model associated with the prereform era of the 1950s and 1960s. The majority party and power of party leaders have come to dominate decision making, mostly at the expense of committee autonomy and influence.

In addition, chapter 1 brings the House Energy and Commerce Committee into focus by discussing how changes in critical factors such as the political environment and the national agenda over the past several decades have affected the committee's role and power. The committee's status as a preeminent and effective policy committee reached its height with the progressive national agenda (environment, energy, civil rights, and so forth) of the 1960s and 1970s. But the committee's ability to promote policy change receded significantly during the 1980s, with the onset of severe budget constraints and a more conservative agenda shaped by the Reagan administration. Finally, the chapter sets the context of the 111th Congress and unified Democratic control on the heels of Barack Obama's historic 2008 election. GOP majorities had controlled Congress for most of the Clinton and George W. Bush years. Even though majority party power shifted after the 2006 elections, President Bush remained a critical player, with veto power to block the new Democratic majority's policy initiatives. Thus, there was pent-up desire to pursue policy change among the party rank and file. And now, with the Obama victory and the Democrats adding significant numbers to their majorities in both houses, the Energy and Commerce Committee would take center stage—the tip of the spear for the progressive agenda.

Chapters 2, 3, and 4 discuss the passage of cap-and-trade, health care reform, and tobacco legislation, respectively. These legislative case studies highlight several critical factors in understanding successful policymaking, including the role of the committee, party leaders, and the president in shepherding legislation; internal and external coalition building; the exercise of influence by lobbying and organized political interests; and the tactics of policymaking. Partisan dynamics are a central feature of the policy process across these issues, as is readily apparent from the beginning, with Henry Waxman's (D-CA) selection as the new chair of Energy and Commerce. In this role, Rep. Waxman would help carry the Democratic Party's progressive agenda, hunting for the votes necessary to win. These chapters reflect how each policy offered some unique challenges for coalition building in the committee and the House. For example, the nature of cap-and trade legislation allowed for a more transactional process, while health care reform resurrected deeply moral issues such as abortion and exposed underlying fissures in the Democratic coalition, especially between its liberal and Blue Dog wings. All of the chapters integrate the broader related political science literature where appropriate as well as reflect back on the elements of committee power and the themes of legislative organization introduced in chapter 1.

Chapter 5 illustrates the committee's central role in oversight and responding to the BP oil spill disaster. The chapter illuminates a number of key themes, including the committee's political power in oversight, as well as jurisdictional battles between committees and how broader economic and political interests can shape Congress's legislative response to national disasters. Chapter 6 highlights the importance of divided government and the limits of power in the separation-of-powers system. The chapter explores the challenge of coalition building in the context of the momentous debt-ceiling agreement. Chapter 7 compares the 111th Congress with past Congresses in the modern era and assesses Congress's role in the Obama policy legacy along with the wider implications for policymaking. The 111th Congress witnessed the passage not only of the president's milestone domestic initiative, the Affordable Care Act, but also of other major policies, among them the economic stimulus package, Lily Ledbetter, sweeping tobacco regulations, credit card and Pentagon acquisition reforms, major financial reform, expansion of national service programs, and Obama's first budget resolution. The 111th was probably more productive than any other Congress in the modern era except for Lyndon Baines Johnson's years. The chapter circles back to the key literature and the theories as they relate to committee power and reflects on recent Congresses and policymaking under Republican majorities.

# ONE

# Hope and Change Meets the Hill

Barack Obama's successful 2008 campaign for the US presidency was premised on "hope and change"—the hope of an extraordinary new and vigorous leader who proclaimed on election night in 2008, "Change has come to America." Behind this dynamic theme was the promise that the president would transform Washington and be a unifying force to overcome partisan and ideological rivalries that had stifled progress on profound social and economic problems facing the American people. However, the Framers set a high bar for US presidents by combining their role as head of state with that of prime minister or head of government in a constitutionally established separate but equal legislative branch of government. Accordingly, presidents live in two contradictory political worlds and must be both "ecumenical and divisive," appealing to the best in Americans' shared values while navigating the ruthless politics needed to form winning congressional coalitions around policies that inevitably divide the nation (Greenstein 1994, 235). Obama's campaign message proved highly effective among voters hungry for change after eight tumultuous years under President George W. Bush and with the country on the brink of economic catastrophe. This yearning for profound, positive change, paired with a formidable candidate, gave Obama a significant popular and electoral vote victory (the largest in three decades). Yet real policy change would necessitate much more than goodwill at the ballot box.

Obama's historic election delivered unified party control of the federal government, with large and relatively cohesive majority party coalitions in Congress, an asset unmatched by any of his recent Democratic predecessors.[1] Delivering on his campaign policy promises would require the expertise and cooperation of Congress. According to some accounts, extraordinary care went into assembling a White House staff that would feature one of the most effective congressional relations teams in modern times (Friel and Young 2010).[2] Obama's team of senior advisers possessed levels of experience and connections with Congress that previous administrations would almost certainly envy.[3]

Even with these significant advantages, the making of public policy in the US separation-of-powers system is an incredibly difficult and sometimes impossible mission. By constitutional design, presidents, senators, and members of Congress answer to different constituencies, and they consequently are often at odds over policy prescriptions, especially under divided government. House and Senate members come to Washington with their own unique policy interests and political motivations—and with their own political machines and sources of financial support. The former vice chair of the GOP conference, Jack Kingston (R-GA) makes the point nicely: "Congress is 535 ants floating on a log down the Potomac and each one thinks he's the captain. Everyone sees it from their district, belief system or filter" (Dumain, Fuller, and Krawzak 2015, 2). Not surprisingly, presidents commonly learn sooner rather than later that getting legislative support tends to be highly uncertain, costly, and fleeting, even among members of the president's party.

Indeed, the prerequisites for legislative influence in Congress are quite high for presidents. Prior to signing legislation into law, presidents must at minimum get their policy initiatives on the congressional agenda, advance a viable and pliable policy vehicle supported by the relevant committee(s), and assemble sufficient floor majorities in both chambers. Yet this minimal view of what it takes to get a president's agenda passed hides much more than it reveals about the procedural, partisan, and policy conflicts that are mainstays in congressional politics today.

The pathways taken by legislation and the processes that shape policy outcomes have changed dramatically in the past four decades. "Unorthodox lawmaking" is the best characterization of the changing legislative process, which is strewn with veto points (Sinclair 2012). Since the creation and development of standing committees at the turn of the nineteenth century, the committee system has been at the heart of Congress's collective efforts in making legislation (Stewart 2001). But electoral and institutional changes have significantly sharpened partisan conflict within Congress (Smith 2007; Theriault 2008), not only transforming how committees go about their legislative business but also greatly enhancing party leaders' power and ability to shape legislative outcomes (Smith 1989). In the contemporary Congress, which is often characterized by unortho-dox lawmaking in a highly partisan environment, committees neverthe-less remain the key incubators of legislation by virtue of their expertise regarding issues under their jurisdiction, but their processes, powers, and products are increasingly likely to respond to partisan demands from the caucus, leaders, and the White House. Thus, the House Energy and Com-merce Committee, one of the most powerful panels in Congress, as well as party leaders consistently had profound effects on legislative outcomes during the first term of the Obama presidency.

This book examines congressional committees' power and policymak-ing and how the work of one exceptional panel, the Committee on Energy and Commerce, shaped legislation during the first Obama administration. *The Committee* illustrates the many factors that help explain how commit-tees as well as party leaders drive policymaking and congressional politics. For example, how do party leadership decisions and behavior support or detract from the committee's influence in policymaking? What strategies and powers did committee chair Henry Waxman (D-CA), one of the most effective and adept legislators in modern times, employ to build coalitions inside his panel, and how did such actions shape House politics? Moreover, our analysis shows how the House Energy and Commerce Committee was affected by an array of political forces (e.g., party leaders, the House and Senate, the president, and external political interests). And because the committee's jurisdiction includes nationally salient issues that invoke sharp partisan differences, we see the central role of party leadership at work in shaping President Obama's legislative agenda and its legacy.

An analytical framework from the political science literature serves as a lens for viewing congressional politics. In particular, we need to understand the role of committees and the factors that shape congressional policy-making and politics. In this light, it is then useful to consider the growing power of the political parties and party leaders in Congress (Rohde 1991; Sinclair 2006). Partisan conflict has risen over the past three decades, creat-ing a political ecosystem with historically unprecedented levels of toxicity. The majority party and its leaders have come to dominate decision making, primarily at the expense of committee autonomy and influence, creating a competition for power and influence that has many characteristics of a zero-sum relationship.

These tensions continued to play out in the twilight years of the Obama presidency. The GOP vote for House Speaker on the first day of the 114th Congress seemed at least in part to expose some of this tension between committee and leadership power. Meeting to organize for the new Congress, elements of the House Republican conference put Speaker John Boehner (R-OH), a veteran with more than two decades of service, on notice. Rep. Thomas Massie (R-KY) explained his anticipated revolt against the House Speaker the day prior to the vote: "The House of Representatives has devolved into a theatrical stage for congressmen to perform for their constituents, while most legislative power is vested within the office of the Speaker" (Massie 2015, A5). Massie went on to say that nearly every member of Congress resents this type of perceived abuse of the Speaker's power and legislative malpractice but that few would vote against the Speaker for fear of jeopardizing their political careers. Majority party defections in voting support for the election of Speaker have been quite rare in the contemporary Congress, and the 114th kicked off with the largest revolt of this kind in over more than one hundred years, with 25 House Republicans voting for someone other than Boehner. In the months that followed, Speaker Boehner failed to defuse conservative rancor in the GOP conference and resigned his post and seat in Congress. New Speaker Paul Ryan (R-WI) promised a more bottom-up, open process where committees would be free to work their will.[4] However, it is not at all clear if the recent conservative angst was more about process or policy outcomes. But the fact is, to the extent that process and policy outcomes are linked, Ryan will have a limited ability to balance the variety of demands within his conference. The continued existence of differences between the hard right and mainstream Republicans will mean that the Speaker will face tough choices in using his powers to keep the peace in his party on one hand and finding a sufficiently unified policy agenda on the other.

In addition to growing partisanship, changes in the political environment, the national issues agenda, and Congress as an institution have affected the role and power of committees in the House. To be sure, some of these developments reflect cyclical trends. The Energy and Commerce Committee's status waxed along with the rise of a progressive national agenda regarding such issues as the environment, energy, and consumer protection during the 1960s and 1970s and waned during the 1980s in accordance with the Reagan administration's more conservative agenda and budget cuts.

Congressional partisanship has subsequently continued its growth largely unabated. The committee's jurisdiction put it front and center in the landmark partisan battles of the Obama presidency: on issues such as health care, consumer protection, energy, and environmental regulation.

This chapter briefly examines the broader historical contours of electoral and institutional change that speak to the tension between committees and the party leadership, setting the stage for understanding committee power in Congress and why committees' policymaking roles have changed over time. We then outline a short theoretical framework for understanding committee power, how some of these specific forces affected the House Energy and Commerce Committee, and why its policymaking role has become critical to the political parties. This approach provides a more comprehensive context for the actions and role of the House Energy and Commerce Committee and the committee system more broadly.

## Historical Foundations: The Changing Role of Committees and Party Leaders in Congress

How have the role and power of committees and party leaders changed over time? What are the sources of committee power, and what roles do committees play in helping members achieve individual and collective goals? Developing this historical and theoretical framework for committees and parties provides a useful understanding of politics and policymaking in the contemporary Congress.

### The Impact of Electoral and Institutional Change in Congress

The committee system and political parties are the dual pillars underlying congressional organization. These structures, more than any other, determine who has power and how it is exercised in the US Congress. Committees and party leadership help members achieve both individual (e.g., reelection, policy influence, and institutional power) and collective goals such as policymaking and building an electorally advantageous party reputation (Fenno 1973, 1978; Cox and McCubbins 1993). As member goals shift in response to changes in the political environment, the roles of committees and party leaders also change, both within the institution and between the House and Senate (Sinclair 1989; Rohde 1991).

During the textbook or prereform Era (1920–65), Congress had largely delegated legislative authority to its committees (Shepsle 1989). Independent committees and their powerful chairs exercised great influence over policies under their jurisdiction, while party leaders remained relatively weak and less relevant. For decades, the electoral environment helped to maintain the system of dominant chairs. Interparty competition in the South was nearly nonexistent, and in the late 1940s, almost half of the

Democratic seats were controlled by southerners (Key 1949). The southern wing of the Democratic Party enjoyed electoral security that advantaged them in accruing seniority; because seniority determined who held the chair, southerners had a disproportionate amount of power (Rohde 1991; Black and Black 2003).

In contrast, House leaders had only limited power during this time because the committee system was the main vehicle through which members achieved their goals. Party leaders had little coercive power to unify their party around policies or to challenge autonomous committee fiefdoms, particularly in the House Rules Committee, one of the most powerful and independent panels (Shepsle 1989), which controlled the House floor agenda through its decisions to grant special rules to legislation.[5] Like most other committees, it was led by a lineage of conservative southern chairs such as Judge Howard W. Smith (D-VA, 1955–67). And together with a voting bloc of conservative members (southern Democrats and some Republicans), the Rules Committee chair maintained a tight grip over the flow of the House's legislative business (Maltzman 1997). In fact, the Rules Committee was the last resting place—a legislative graveyard—for major progressive labor policies in the 1930s–40s and civil rights in the 1950s–60s (Robinson 1963; Shepsle 1989; Rohde 1991).[6] But the electoral context that solidified southern conservatives atop a system of powerful committees began to give way to changing electoral forces (Black and Black 2003). Large liberal classes entered in the 86th Congress (1959–60) and in the 89th Congress (1965–66), causing what would become a strong leftward shift in the center of gravity of the overall membership of Congress and igniting pressure to change the conservative-dominated committee system (Shepsle 1986, 155).

One of these forces of change directly resulted from President Lyndon Johnson's strong civil rights agenda: Democratic electorates in the South became more like their northern counterparts, setting off a gradual realignment of the congressional parties. GOP candidates increasingly sought and won seats in the South, sharply diminishing the southern wing of the Democratic Party (Black and Black 2003).[7] A parallel electoral dynamic occurred within the Republican Party. Liberal-leaning Republican members from the Northeast were increasingly targeted and unseated by Democrats, shrinking the GOP's moderate wing. Throughout the 1970s, 1980s, and 1990s, these trends eroded the party coalitions' old regional bases (Polsby 2003). By the mid-1990s, southern seats, once the backbone of the Democratic Party's support, had become a source of immense strength for the GOP majority, and over the next two decades, the decimation of the old southern conservative Democrats and the northeastern moderate Republicans became nearly complete. For example, in 2008, more than four dozen Blue Dogs (conservative Democrats) remained in the House, but the Republican wave in the 2010 midterm elections wiped out more than half of them, particularly those from Georgia, Tennessee, North and South Carolina, and Texas. The number of southern Democrats in Congress continued to dwindle in 2012 and 2014. Today, those once-dominant southern Democrats are all but extinct, as are the northeastern Republicans. The overall effect of these electoral forces has been the large-scale trading of each party's regional area of strength to produce party memberships in Congress that are ideologically more internally cohesive and are increasingly different from the other party (Cooper and Brady 1981; Rohde 1991; Abramson, Aldrich, and Rohde 1995, 263–64; Sinclair 2006).

The growing ideological homogeneity of the political parties resulting from these patterns significantly restructured member incentives to overcome the costs associated with institutional change (Sinclair 1985, 1989; Smith 1989; Rohde 1991). In effect, these electoral changes provided the impetus for greater intraparty cooperation and the development of a reinvigorated agency relationship between the party leadership and the majority party. This translated into institutional reforms designed to foster the political and policy goals of Democratic (and later Republican) majorities. The early reforms targeting the House Rules Committee are noteworthy because of the panel's centrality at that time to the House's legislative agenda and the system of strong committees that the independent Rules Committee helped to foster (Robinson 1963; Pearson and Schickler 2009). After years of frustration and half measures, liberal Democrats struck hard at the Rules Committee.[8] In 1961, Speaker Sam Rayburn (D-TX) increased the number of seats on the House Rules Committee, thereby breaking conservatives' hold, which had effectively stopped President John F. Kennedy's liberal policy initiatives (Schickler, Pearson, and Feinstein 2010). Judge Smith's defeat in the 1966 primary also helped to loosen conservatives' grip on the committee. And in the early 1970s, another major step in bringing the Rules Committee more in line with sentiment in the Democratic caucus occurred when the Speaker was granted the power to appoint members of the majority party to the committee (Marshall 2005). The Rules Committee therefore evolved to become an arm of the party leadership, and it remains so to this day, providing the Speaker with a crucial mechanism to control the House's legislative agenda (Oppenheimer 1977; Marshall 2002; Schickler and Pearson 2009).

Many other important institutional reforms, among them the adoption of the Subcommittee Bill of Rights in 1973, codified the jurisdiction and rights of subcommittees, placed control of subcommittee budgets with the party caucus, and established the selection of subcommittee chairs by seniority, thus unwinding the chair's heavy-handed discretion over subcommittees (Rohde 1991). The strengthening of subcommittees was a decentralizing force on the policy process. It put in place a period of "subcommittee government," greatly enhancing the policy relevance especially of liberal rank-and-file members of the Democratic majority. Subcommittees flourished, exerting greater influence over committees' legislative business through the 1980s—that is, until the Republican majority of the 104th Congress (1994–95) reversed course and placed subcommittees back under the thumb of loyal party chairs.

The passage of the Congressional Budget and Impoundment and Control Act of 1974 also contributed to the shift in committee power (Davidson et al. 2016). Among other things, the Budget Act created the Congressional Budget Office (CBO) as well as the House and Senate Budget Committees, allowing party leaders to exercise greater top-down coordination and discipline among spending, revenue, and the authorization committees. The act put in place a leadership-driven budget process and forced the reconciliation of program spending with budgetary markers. This fostered greater interconnection between spending and federal programs that enhanced the party leadership's ability to manage the majority party's priorities and increased congressional parity with the Executive Branch on budget issues—the bread and butter of power in Washington (Krutz 2001; Sinclair 2012).

In addition, during the 1970s, the Democratic Party made a series of changes to its caucus rules that were designed to make committees and their chairs more responsive to the majority party and to strengthen mechanisms enabling party leaders to control policy. For example, in 1971 the caucus adopted a rule that made it possible for ten members to trigger a chair election by secret ballot, providing the potential to signal recalcitrant chairs that they needed to take into account the more liberal positions of the party caucus.[9] In 1974, the newly created Democratic Steering and Policy Committee became the party caucus's Committee on Committees, giving the Speaker, who became chair, significant influence over committee seat assignments and thus the capacity to hold members to account for cooperating with the party. These and other reforms considerably advanced the potential powers of the leadership, especially the House Speaker.[10] Speakers Tip O'Neill (D-MA), Jim Wright (D-TX), and even the more conge-

nial Tom Foley (D-WA) became more inclined to exercise their powers
to advance the party's priorities. Republicans found these changes important when they came to power in the mid-1990s: Speaker Newt Gingrich
(R-GA) was widely compared with the House's most notable leaders of
past eras—such as Speakers Thomas Reed (R-ME) and Joe Cannon (R-IL)
(Sinclair 2000b, 139).

### The Republican Revolution of the 104th Congress and Beyond

Indeed, the Republican majority in the Gingrich House made major
changes that enhanced leadership power and control, largely at the
expense of the committee system. In sharp contrast to the slower-moving
Democratic reforms of the 1970s–1980s, the Republican changes during
the 104th Congress (1995–96) occurred in just a few weeks (Aldrich and
Rohde 1997–98).[11] Subcommittees lost much of their legislative authority and were placed under tighter control by committee chairs. But the
independent power of committees was the real target of major change, and
their leaders found their influence sharply curtailed under the new structure. Three full committees were abolished, and their jurisdictions divided
up among other panels, the tenures of both committee and subcommittee chairs were limited to three terms, and committee staff were cut by
one-third. Special attention went to the key panels that would carry the
weight of the legislative proposals contained in the Contract with America,
Gingrich's 1994 campaign manifesto that brought Republican rule back
to the House after thirty-eight years. Gingrich and the leadership stacked
Energy and Commerce, Judiciary, and Appropriations with new activist
members and tossed seniority aside to install loyal partisans at the committees' helms.[12] The GOP made many other changes in the early days of the
104th, but these examples provide a sense of the magnitude of institutional
changes designed to centralize power and further the majority party's policy priorities (see, e.g., Aldrich and Rohde 1997–98; Sinclair 2000b).

Although chairs pushed back, attempting to exert their authority in
subsequent Congresses, the golden era of autonomous committees was
over.[13] The average number of committee and subcommittee meetings fell
from 5,372 in the 1960s–1970s to 4,793 in the 1980s–1990s: in 2002–3, just
2,135 meetings occurred (Ornstein 2011). At the same time, the legislative process was also affected by increased leadership involvement (Sinclair
2006). On issues where the majority party agreed on its priorities, chairs
were expected to deliver or "they won't be chairmen of their committees,"

as chief deputy whip Dennis Hastert (R-IL) bluntly put it (Deering and Smith 1997, 134). Committees and their chairs remain important and possess significant powers, but their authority is much more dependent on the party leadership and responsive to the policy and political demands of the majority party than was previously the case.

In 1999, when Hastert became Speaker, the House GOP's Republican Steering Committee (Committee on Committees) began an elaborate interview process for committee chairs (Oleszek 2004). This process has continued under subsequent Republican Speakers. For Appropriations, Energy and Commerce, and some other committees, the interviews took on added significance because of the centrality of the committees' policy jurisdiction. For example, during chair candidate interviews for Energy and Commerce, Fred Upton (R-MI) took an aggressive stance against EPA regulations in a bid to get the backing of his far right colleagues (Goldfarb 2011). In the wake of Barack Obama's election and in anticipation of an aggressive progressive agenda, particularly on energy and environmental issues, Democrats also placed special emphasis on controlling the helm of the House Energy and Commerce Committee by supporting Waxman over John Dingell (D-MI), one of the most feared and powerful lawmakers of his time and one of the most senior members of the House, as committee chair. The committee's broad jurisdiction means that membership on the committee is valuable and that control is important to party leaders largely irrespective of the nature of the legislative agenda at any given time.

Overall, the modern Congress has seen the power of committees decline significantly relative to party leadership, especially in the House. In fact, the committees that were affected the most significantly by these institutional reforms were the major policy and prestige committees (Deering and Smith 1997). For the most part, these committees controlled nationally salient issues that were central to the party's electoral coalitions and so tended to be prime targets for the majority party to strengthen their control over these influential and powerful panels, which include Energy and Commerce. Moreover, members who want to shape major policies seek to serve on Energy and Commerce. For example, in [1992], representative-elect Gene Green (D-TX) described committees such as Appropriations, Energy and Commerce, Rules, and Ways and Means as "the moon and the stars" (Deering and Smith 1997, 61). Energy and Commerce is also a prime seat for raising campaign funds, and so service on the committee is one way that party leaders reward freshmen and boost their reelection prospects (Davidson et al. 2016).

## Theoretical Foundations of Committees: Powers and Roles

An oft-quoted aphorism of Washington is that on Capitol Hill, it is much easier to stop something than to start something. This emphasizes the idea of negative power—the ability to protect a status quo policy from being overturned by a rival policy. Committees enjoy such ability through their gatekeeping power in deciding whether to report legislation under their jurisdiction to the floor for consideration. The negative power of committees is enhanced through a variety of other procedures, among them the House germaneness rule and amendment depth structure. The former limits the content of amendments, while the latter constrains the amendments that can be applied to the committee's bill (Deering and Smith 1997).

At the same time, committees are also advantaged in policymaking through their positive power (Davidson et al. 2016). Positive power reflects the committee's ability to persuade a floor majority to adopt the committee's policy over some status quo or rival policy that would have otherwise been preferred. A committee's positive power can derive from many different sources. For example, committees have policy information and expertise that they can selectively use to persuade members and build floor coalitions. Committee staffs also work to anticipate and resolve members' policy and political concerns. These activities build trust and relationships that can help overcome opposition to committee legislation. Likewise, committee chairs work to build internal alliances with party leaders and utilize outside-in strategies that leverage the influence of interest groups, lobbyists, and other political actors (e.g., governors or the president) to create supportive external coalitions. Together, the mix of negative and positive powers has kept committees at the center of the policymaking process.

Not surprisingly, congressional scholars have paid especially close attention to the role and power of committees. Theories of legislative organization offer competing answers to the questions of what purpose(s) and masters committees serve. The theoretical demarcation between competing explanations of congressional committees comes from informational, distributive, and partisan rationales. These theories offer a variety of propositions about congressional policymaking, structure, and member behavior. Informational theory suggests that committees and the policies they produce reflect the chamber's collective majority.[14] From the informational perspective, congressional committees are agents of the chamber majority. The division of labor is intended to foster policy expertise among committees as well as to collect and communicate information about policies and outcomes. As such, a committee's structure, processes, and policy decisions should respond to the chamber median. From this perspective, committees are not autonomous or independent entities in how they wield their powers; rather, they are expected to fulfill their many policy and oversight roles as highly constrained agents of the chamber majority.

The distributive framework offers the handiest description of committees prior to the 1970s reforms (Weingast and Marshall 1988). According to this characterization, the committee system featured powerful chairs who oversaw largely autonomous and independent committees (Fenno 1966). The argument suggests that committees provided a gains-from-exchange mechanism by which members could obtain disproportionate influence over policies important to their constituencies. Members seek out and self-select onto committees with policy jurisdictions that are in high demand among constituents or critical to fulfill reelection goals—a more parochial self-interest. Such high-demanders are likely to have policy preferences within their committee's jurisdiction that differ substantively from the larger chamber. In this way, the committee system fosters logrolling and policy deference among high-demanders on a committee; in exchange, those committee members are expected to reciprocate policy deference on other issues under the control of different committees. In terms of committee power, this perspective suggests that committees would tend to operate independently in their policy space and exercise their powers free from constraints of the chamber or political parties.

Partisan theory emphasizes the importance of parties and leaders in congressional politics. The "parties matter" framework suggests that committees serve the interests of the majority party and should be representative of its median member (Cox and McCubbins 1993). Party leaders can strategically employ committees such as the Rules Committee to control the legislative agenda. Even more, the leadership can use committee memberships to induce rank-and-file members to pass legislative priorities on the majority party's agenda. The strength of the majority party's influence over congressional committees can vary depending on factors such as ideological homogeneity and the extent that particular issues separate the collective interests of one party from the other. For example, Rohde's (1991) theory of "conditional party government" focuses on how rank-and-file members of a homogeneous majority party will be inclined to empower leaders with powers to pass policies with widespread party support. However, the members of a more heterogeneous majority party will be less inclined to empower their leaders because of the increased likelihood that many party members will not accept legislation or have different political goals. Thus, with a more homogeneous majority party, committees tend to be more responsive to its policy and political interests. And under conditions of greater heterogeneity, committees are expected to be more autonomous and employ their powers more independently of the majority parties' interests.

Although each perspective offers a stylized role of committees and expectations for how they use power, the empirical reality of committee behavior is very complex and multifaceted, suggesting that all three theories offer lessons in understanding committees in Congress. In the case of the House Energy and Commerce Committee, Waxman was a powerful chair who worked somewhat autonomously in the committee's policy space who also operated within a party-dominated House and under the scrutiny of a very powerful party enforcer, Speaker Nancy Pelosi (D-CA), focused on advancing the party's majority status and its policy agenda. Waxman ultimately was part of the majority-party team and was expected to deliver on the party's policy priorities. But because the committee's jurisdiction is one of the broadest in all of the House, some issues became critical to the majority party (see chapters 2 and 3), imposing greater constraints on the committee's decision making, while other issue areas provided greater committee autonomy (see chapters 4 and 5). Thus, this characterization of the House Energy and Commerce Committee suggests that the partisan framework may offer important insight into this very powerful policy committee.

## Understanding the Committee-versus-Party Tension

These different theoretical perspectives on the role of committees in Congress make a variety of trade-offs. The emphasis on generalized explanations requires giving up some understanding of the nuances of how committees differ from one another. This simple revelation brings Richard Fenno's work on committees into sharp relief. Fenno's *Congressmen in Committees* (1973) begins the theoretical reconciliation of these perspectives by shifting the focus to how committees vary and why these differences are consequential for understanding congressional politics and policymaking. Fenno develops his explanation by examining how committees differ with respect to individual and collective goals as well as to environmental constraints.

Deering and Smith (1997) extend Fenno's groundbreaking analysis, offering a much larger and systematic empirical analysis of committees in Congress over time. Their work also highlights and examines the important differences among committees. Deering and Smith developed committee typologies that capture the predominant mix of individual-member motivations across all of Congress's standing committees. The prestige committees—House Rules, Ways and Means, Budget, and Appropriations—help members achieve greater institutional power. Constituency committees—Agriculture, Armed Services, and Transportation— primarily serve members' reelection interests. Major policy committees— Energy and Commerce, Judiciary, and Education and Labor—provide the means for members to shape national issues.

Deering and Smith (1997) provide a theoretical framework for understanding when we might expect committees to be more (or less) autonomous and when committees should be more (or less) responsive to the political parties. Their work takes into account not only the changing mix of member goals and policy preferences but also the importance of the policy agenda and the political and institutional environments. Specifically, Deering and Smith argue that when committees have a greater mix of salient and interconnected issues within their jurisdiction and when these issues are characterized by party cohesion, committees can be expected to be more responsive to the majority party and should foster greater levels of leadership involvement. In contrast, committees with less salient and more separable issues should see less party cohesion and consequently would be expected to be more autonomous and to have less leadership involvement. Deering and Smith argue not only that committee jurisdictions and policy issues they supervise shape the desirability of a committee in terms of helping members achieve their goals but also that policy jurisdiction determines the mix of groups in the committee's political environment.[15] A committee's political environment reflects the variety of political interests inside and outside of Congress that seek to influence committee actions. The committee environment is a function of interbranch interests (e.g., bureaucracy, the White House, or the courts), institutional interests (e.g., party leaders and the House and Senate chambers), and public interests (interest groups and external organizations). All of these elements play a role in constituting the politically relevant audience that may want to shape a committee's decisions.

Committee environments, like committees themselves, vary significantly from one another and can be conceptualized on a continuum from simpler (with small, narrow, and relatively uniform audiences) to more complex (with large numbers of competing political interests). The variations in environment impose different levels of constraints on committees' policy options and activities. Similarly, committee environments impact the opportunities or ways that individual members pursue political goals (see R. L. Hall 1996). So on one hand, members of the Agriculture Committee may be constrained in the politics or policies they can pursue by the groups competing for farm subsidies. How do members position themselves to make the best case for the important programs in their district—for example, taking the side of dairy subsidies over sugarcane? On the other hand, members serving on the Judiciary Committee considering civil rights issues or on Ways and Means considering tax reform (or Energy and Commerce considering health care) would face a much more complex, broad-based, and conflict-ridden set of political interests. These more complex committee environments have greater potential for partisan conflict and are more likely to attract members whose political circumstances mean that they are motivated more by ideology and/or goals of influencing the national contours of public policy (Deering and Smith 1997).

This argument has implications for the business before the House Energy and Commerce Committee during President Obama's first term. In particular, why would the committee be central to party interests and subject to leadership influence that places significant limits/constraints on its autonomy within the House of Representatives? Energy and Commerce has one of the House's most complex committee environments. Indeed, Deering and Smith (1997) show that Energy and Commerce, Judiciary, and Appropriations are the only House standing committees that are high in jurisdictional fragmentation, salience, and conflict. Moreover, the breadth of Energy and Commerce's jurisdiction is second only to that of Appropriations. Consequently, the Energy and Commerce Committee receives an extraordinary amount of attention from a wide array of interbranch, institutional, and public interests. The committee's weight with federal agencies was cemented in the mid-1970s, when it received oversight responsibility for a broad swath of federal agencies and activities.

The complexity of Energy and Commerce's political environment is a function of its highly fragmented jurisdiction, which covers many highly salient issues, among them energy, environmental regulation, consumer safety, and health care, all of which feature numerous competing interests. The parties have taken divergent stances on these issues, which tend to invoke significant partisan and ideological conflict. In fact, because of the centrality of the committee's jurisdiction, the Republicans treat Energy and Commerce as an exclusive committee (along with Appropriations, Ways and Means, Rules) and limit each member to service on only one such committee (Deering and Smith 1997, 103). The issues within the jurisdiction of Energy and Commerce continue to carry great weight with voters and electoral coalitions. These types of issues are particularly likely to move the needle in elections—they are important to broad constituencies of voters and to the parties' policy reputations.[16]

The Energy and Commerce Committee undoubtedly will play a pivotal role in determining whether President Donald Trump and Speaker Ryan can keep their promise to voters that unified GOP control of Washington will lead to effective governance. The core Republican promise in the 2016 election was the repeal of Obamacare. This and other highly salient domestic policy priorities of the GOP majority fall within the Energy and Commerce Committee's jurisdiction, making it a key player in the GOP's quest to give voters reason to keep the party's majorities in Congress in 2018 and beyond.

In November 2008, before the start of the 111th Congress, the Democratic caucus, backed by its leaders, voted 137–122 to make Waxman the chair of Energy and Commerce. Behind closed doors, the caucus showdown took on the aura of a dramatic clash between two titans. According to Rep. George Miller (CA), a longtime and powerful ally of Waxman and Speaker Pelosi, "It was like Zeus and Thor in there, hurling lightning bolts at each other. You just wanted to duck and get out of the way" (Davenport 2008a, 3149). Since 1981, Dingell had chaired the panel, aggressively expanding its jurisdiction to touch nearly every facet of domestic policy and building a base of substantial power.[17] But Dingell's reputation and his pitch to protect the seniority principle likely carried less weight with the caucus's younger members. Instead, Waxman's behind-the-scenes campaign for change and more progressive policy stances resonated with younger members, many of whom he had assisted with fund-raising (Davenport 2008b). Moreover, Dingell had a history of political clashes with Pelosi. During the 110th Congress, the newly elected Speaker had created a new Energy and Commerce subcommittee to handle the issue of global warming and appointed Edward Markey (D-MA) as its chair over Dingell's protests. Dingell had proven himself out of step with a majority of the Democratic caucus on environmental issues—he was viewed as too friendly with the automotive industry.[18] And several years earlier, in 2001, Dingell had backed Pelosi's opponent, Steny Hoyer (D-MD), for the post of Democratic whip, which she nevertheless won.

Waxman wrested control at least in part because he convinced the Democratic caucus (and enough of the leadership) that he would work more closely with Pelosi and Obama.[19] In other words, the caucus and the leadership valued policy agreement and responsiveness over pure seniority in their collective choice to chair Energy and Commerce (A. B. Hall and

Shepsle 2014). This seems to support the partisan argument for legislative organization and to be consistent with conditional party government in that the greater homogeneity of the majority party provided the caucus with the incentive to exert greater control over the committee and its legislative powers (Aldrich and Rohde 2001).

Even though the Democrats had regained control of Congress after the 2006 elections, President George W. Bush had blocked the party's policy initiatives. Thus, Obama's 2008 victory put the party in a position to act on its long-suppressed desire for deep and meaningful policy change. And the House Energy and Commerce Committee would play a central role in promoting that progressive agenda.

# TWO

# Cap-and-Trade Bill

## *American Clean Energy and Security Act of 2009*

The American Clean Energy and Security Act of 2009, known as the "cap-and-trade" bill,[1] filled a rather complex policy space intersecting with both domestic and international political interests. The key elements of the bill were designed to foster energy innovation and competition in energy production and thus make the United States a leader in the new clean-energy industry. Cap-and-trade was designed to transform the energy economy and bring new jobs to American workers. At the same time, the legislation would set in place significant carbon-reduction targets and spur an international commitment to the reduction of greenhouse gases and mitigate its consequences for global warming. The legislation was important to give credibility to the newly inaugurated president, Barack Obama, when he met with world leaders in Copenhagen to discuss the need for action on global warming. Environmental policy and global warming were not priorities during the Bush years, so for the liberal wing of the Democratic majority, this legislation represented an opportunity to deliver on a policy cause critical to their political base.

When the members of the Democratic caucus elected Rep. Henry Waxman (D-CA) to chair the House Committee on Energy and Commerce, they expected him to not only pass cap-and-trade but to carry other key policies of the majority party's agenda—and the president's agenda—for the 111th Congress. Waxman's longtime ally, Speaker Nancy Pelosi, also wanted landmark energy legislation, but she, like her recent predecessors, had a much broader role and interests in terms of advancing the size, status, and agenda of the majority party (Sinclair 1995; Aldrich and Rohde 1997–98; Cox and McCubbins 2005). During the first few months of Obama's presidency, the Speaker was a very successful "legislative ramrod" for the president's agenda (Lerer and O'Connor 2009, 1), routinely reminding the rank and file that their political prospects would rise or fall with those of the president. Indeed, heightened partisanship in Congress has meant that the political fates of presidents and their copartisans have become increasingly intertwined over time (Aldrich 1995; Edwards and Barrett 2000; Lebo and O'Geen 2011; Sinclair 2011). The cap-and-trade legislation was not only a test of that proposition but also an early marker for Pelosi's leadership and ability to deliver legislative initiatives to the new Democratic president. Once the bill left the committee, she and the rest of the leaders would play a key role in persuading just enough senior Blue Dogs and members from rural areas to support the bill so that newly elected Democrats from more conservative districts would not have to do so (Lerer and O'Connor 2009).

The cap-and-trade bill ultimately passed the House by a razor-thin margin that included a crucial handful of Republican votes but did not become law because of the stifling opposition it received in the Senate, opposition that included several Democrats from energy-producing states. Moreover, passage in the House cost the Democrats considerable political capital (Brady, Fiorina, and Wilkins 2011). Hoping to swing wavering members against the bill, minority leader John Boehner (R-OH) warned, "Mark my words: The American people will remember this vote" (Davenport and Palmer 2009, 14). And on the day the bill passed the House floor, Boehner went well beyond the traditional ten-minute window at the end of debate reserved for the opposition to speak against the bill, pillorying the legislation and reading selected questionable-sounding provisions out of context for maximum effect as the majority party leadership staff scrambled on the floor to shut him down. The C-Span video of his floor filibuster was widely circulated, becoming known in conservative circles as the Boehner-buster. It was just one early volley in a much larger and well-coordinated attack that included targeted issue advertising against vulnerable House Democrats (R. L. Hall and Reynolds 2012). The GOP attempted to make cap-and-trade an electoral issue, framing the legislation as a heavy-handed energy tax on the middle class.[2] Some House Democrats were concerned about how this issue would play in their districts (Samuelsohn and Bravender 2010), and some more vulnerable House Democrats resented being forced to walk the plank—taking a difficult vote on cap-and-trade while the Senate just sat on the bill. Some House Democrats justified their resistance to party leaders' plea for support on health care in the coming months because of their earlier support on the politically costly cap-and-trade bill. In general, both parties knew that their electoral fates would depend on voter perceptions of the economy. For the Democratic rank and file, this meant members were more concerned with helping their constituencies recover from the biggest economic downturn since the Great Depression. But the manipulation of political pressure on cap-and-trade, President Obama's landmark health reform legislation, and the economy formed part of the larger mix of issues that affected the 2010 midterm elections.

Prior to taking up cap-and-trade, the House Energy and Commerce Committee had already passed and Congress had enacted the $860 billion stimulus package in response to the Great Recession, an enormously important response to a free-falling economy. And now the full Obama agenda was front and center on Capitol Hill, starting with legislation designed to reduce America's dependence on imported oil and move the country toward a clean energy economy. Waxman decided to work from a blueprint proposed by industry leaders—including several energy companies—to build a strong base of support against relentless opposition from Republicans and conservative interests. At the same time, other crucial legislation was moving—including a bill to place tobacco under the control of the Food and Drug Administration, a major public health initiative that had been fifteen years in the making.

Tuesday March 31, 2009

There was noise post Obama's first budget that things were too complex, that it was too hard to do it all: economic recovery, energy security, climate change, universal access to health care, education. And particularly climate change—that what it would be perceived as politically would be just a "carbon tax": punitive pain by the liberal greenies on working Americans who could hardly afford the luxury of paying more for electricity and other energy essentials for the nobler cause of winning Al Gore's war on melting ice caps. You could smell the commercials on cable TV before the ink was dry—as it was today on the most massive energy bill in a generation, HR 2454, the American Clean Energy and Security Act (ACES) of 2009, authored by Henry and Ed Markey (D-MA), chair of the subcommittee that will have the first crack at the bill. Waxman and Markey have held extraordinary private briefing sessions with the Democrats on the committee to outline the legislation and its logic. But clean air did not materialize out of thin air. The first hearing of the year was with an unprecedented coalition of business, energy, and environmental groups—including GE, Chevron, and the Environmental Defense Fund, who call themselves US Climate Action Partnership (US CAP)—and what they told the committee before Obama was inaugurated was, *There is a real problem with global warming. We can step up to it. We want certainty, sanity, and responsibility in policy. Let's work together and crack it.* And the legislation is based on the US CAP blueprint, so it has ready-made support across the mainstream spectrum of interests, and it's grounded in the real world. And what is so interesting about Waxman and Markey is that they have gone from member to member over the past several weeks, soliciting views, listening to what those members must have, and then crafting solutions that are responsive—at least to a degree. For instance, coal is still king in this country, a huge energy source. Well, coal isn't banned—it is developed more safely, with a huge investment in clean coal technology. This helps lock in members from the Coal Belt and the Midwest, providing key votes to cement a majority.

So the sensibility in the committee room from the Democrats present is that they appreciate the outreach and they know there is no radical play at work here. There is an old saying in Washington that the best ideas mean nothing without the votes—I don't care if you have invented safe and cheap nuclear power; if you cannot convince 218 members of the House of the merit of your proposal, it is not going anywhere. The Commerce Committee, with 59 members from districts of all demographics, economies, and geographies—more than half the membership of the entire US Senate—is truly a proxy for the House as a whole. The jurisdiction of the Energy and Commerce Committee has been characterized historically by issues high in both salience and fragmentation. Nationally visible issues like the environment, energy, and health care have long attracted the interests of a wide variety of members (liberal to conservative) from different regions of the country. The committee's high level of diversification meant that a relatively large number of divergent issues fell within the committee's jurisdiction, so it tended to attract different kinds of outside groups with unrelated interests. Thus, it represented one of the few panels that could serve the policy and political interests of a wide variety of members—a cross-section of the House.

So if this bill can clear the committee, it can pass the House—even without any Republican votes. From what I've seen, the Republicans have not been interested in working with us to pass policy. They want all manner of consultation, and they give back borscht. Not one vote in the House for the Obama economic recovery package, even after they were courted and snuggled. So it is not a two-way street. But it means many Democrats, particularly those from more conservative districts in the South and West, need to hold their nerve and support initiatives articulated by the president and managed by the congressional leadership—and then hope like hell, if enacted, they will indeed work and change the face of America for the better. That's what the Democrats did with Franklin Roosevelt in the First 100 Days and in the four years after that, and it created a paradigm for Democratic rule that effectively lasted for more than thirty years. So there is a lot at stake. We do not know if happy days are here again, but we sure as hell are going to try.

A two-week recess for Easter and Passover is coming up this Friday, and members will be at home: the "carbon tax" crowd will be pummeling them. Staff have armed members with fact sheets and briefing information, and I've suggested Henry do some major roundtables with the national newspapers to get the word out that this is a responsible bill. Americans know that the awful gas prices of last year can revisit them again—nothing has been done to date to prevent that; the country is extremely vulnerable. And when they see glaciers melting, blossoms in February, and drought and horrendous storms, they know that something is up with the planet. And business really does want certainty about what is expected, when, and what it will cost—just so they can get on with it. Waxman and Markey brief the Republicans on the energy and climate bill tomorrow morning. It will not be pretty.

### Wednesday, April 1

It was a remarkable morning. The energy and climate bill is going to need all the political lift it can get, and any Republican votes will be sweet. To be certain, there should be a large handful of Republicans from the East, Upper Midwest, and Florida that can back the bill, but the issue is how much pressure Republicans will come under from their leadership not to cooperate at all with Waxman and Markey. And the signs are not encouraging. From the outset under President Obama, the Republicans have said, *Consult, consult, consult.* And Obama did just that, from visiting their caucus to cocktails in the West Wing. But only three Senate Republicans voted for his stimulus bill—none in the House. Henry has done the same with the committee Republicans, from addressing their strategy retreat in January to what happened today—a private briefing on the bill with their members on the committee. It was tough. Their leader, Joe Barton (TX), who was chair of the committee until the Republicans lost the House in 2006, does not accept the science, and he really has problems with the cap-and-trade provisions—even as he said he understood the politics and what happens when political power is exercised. The bill will "de-industrialize America," he said, taking the country back to the carbon emissions of Nigeria today or what the entire country belched into the air in 1905. We will hear more of this as the bill progresses. "The country can't accept cap-and-trade right now," another Republican said. The issue for Waxman and Markey is how much to keep playing the Republicans out. Clearly, they need to hedge that this bill will become law, so they want amendments on their industries and districts and businesses and utilities. But if you give them amendments, will they vote for the bill or keep kicking you in the teeth? We need to get some Republican governors on board—Arnold Schwarzenegger in California and others—just as Obama did for his economic stimulus package. The governors are not ideological—they are practical and want to get the job done. If we have some Republican governors, it will make the House Republicans look zealous, out of touch, irrelevant, and so twentieth century.

There was a further briefing of the Democrats later in the day. Memories are still raw, some fifteen years later, after Bill Clinton and Al Gore forced Democrats to vote for a BTU tax (an early form of carbon tax) in 1993. Many veteran members believed that vote helped trigger the Republican seizure of Congress in 1994 and led to twelve years of wandering in the wilderness of the minority. What was worse was that the House voted for the BTU tax—it passed by one vote—but the Senate was so scared that it never took it up. So the House members on the record on that deeply unpopular vote were left twisting in the wind. Many were mauled in the election the following year. And so a Democrat today told Markey, "We are not going to get BTU-ed!"

I was walking with Henry and we saw Rahm Emanuel, Obama's chief of staff, in the hall. Strong impressions: direct, wiry, wired, intense, focused, powerful. You don't mess with Rahm. We will need him and the White House—politics in Congress is a team sport, and everybody will have to play their best game.

## Friday, April 17

Henry's voice is key in framing the policy argument, and he's working the PR angle hard today. A morning interview with Al Hunt of Bloomberg TV, an eight-minute segment to be broadcast a dozen times through the weekend. Cap-and-trade as a tax comes up front and center. Henry counters, "People look at the costs, but you've got to look at the benefits to the whole economy." And he expanded on the interrelated goals of the omnibus bill: increasing energy security by getting America off OPEC oil, combating global warming, and transforming the American economy by investment in renewable and green technologies that will drive job growth. Later, at a messaging meeting with the PR reps of business and environmental groups behind the bill, one of them observed that an Environmental Defense Fund principal crystallized the bill this way: "Carbon caps equals hard hats." Each of us wished we had coined it first. That's the message we want to sell.

The message became easier during the course of the day. The Environmental Protection Agency (EPA) announced, in response to a Supreme Court ruling, that it was required under the law to heavily regulate greenhouse gasses. For those opposing us, it's like giving them the choice to do this the easy way or the hard way—to work with us on a policy we can all live with, or there's always the gun behind the door. With Bloomberg, Henry framed it perfectly in expectation of the EPA announcement: it would be far preferable for Congress to write the rules—they can be better tailored, more sensible, and pragmatic, reflecting what industry and consumers need. The regulator in this instance would be the bluntest of blunt instruments. And business interests get the message. The big business groups this afternoon all said that they want Congress to write the bill. Please. And the only bill on the table is Waxman-Markey.

Monday, April 20

A very good messaging weekend capped by some help from our friends across the aisle. *This Week with George Stephanopoulos* is one of the Sunday talk shows that Washington uses to send tom-tom messages to itself about what is happening politically, where people are positioned, and issues the troops need to be thinking about. The House Republican leader, John Boehner, was closely questioned about energy and climate change, and particularly what his party's position was on global warming.

Question: What is the Republican plan to deal with carbon emissions, which every major scientific organization has said is contributing to climate change?

Answer: George, the idea that carbon dioxide is a carcinogen that is harmful to our environment is almost comical. Every time we exhale, we exhale carbon dioxide. Every cow in the world, you know, when they do what they do, you've got more carbon dioxide.

By early afternoon, staff emails were flying: *Hey, did you see Boehner.*

*Almost comical?* I couldn't believe it. So, together with Ed Markey's staff, we decided not to go the *New York Times* route and have a high-road critique of the distinguished leader. Rather, we went viral with the blogs. When the transcript was up, it was sent to the key political writers in the blogosphere, and by early evening there were dozens of pillorying references to Boehner. He had a tough day—death by a thousand keystrokes. But for us, it was an excellent way to start the week, giving Henry a strong hand going into pivotal sessions of the committee markup and amending the climate bill.

Wednesday, April 22

If there was ever any doubt about what it meant for policymaking to have a Democratic administration in power, those were settled today. Three cabinet secretaries came before the Energy and Environment Subcommittee, chaired by Markey, to give testimony in support of the American Clean Energy and Security Act of 2009. Henry exercised his prerogative as full committee chair to chair the session. In front of the subcommittee were Lisa Jackson, the administrator of the Environmental Protection Agency; Stephen Chu, secretary of energy; and Ray LaHood, secretary of transportation and one of Obama's Republican appointees to the cabinet. LaHood, who had served as a member of the House from Illinois, was vociferous in supporting the bill. He was a dear colleague with all the Republicans on the panel, and their discomfiture at Mr. Republican Secretary endorsing the work of Waxman and Markey was palpable. And there is nothing like strong ammo from the White House shelling the holdouts on Capitol Hill. "I believe this is a jobs bill," Jackson said, intoning the key message behind the legislation. "Clean energy technologies will be in the 2010s what Internet technologies were in the 1990s." Chu added to the barrage: "We need to bring these high-technology jobs back to the United States." Observing that a lot of green technology is made in Korea, China, and India, the energy secretary described the greenhouse targets as "aggressive but achievable."

If that was not bad enough for our friends across the aisle, next up was the panel from US CAP, the industry-environment group that wrote the blueprint for the cap-and-trade system in the bill. The CEO of DuPont Chemical started it off: "Voluntary efforts are not enough. . . . This will take legislation. . . . This is an opportunity for our industry to reinvent itself." A cascade of industry leaders followed. Alcoa Aluminum said that since 1990, they had reduced $CO_2$ by 36 percent, with production up and costs down. It must have been like fingernails on chalkboard for our Republican friends to listen to. Joe Barton looked stricken when they heard the CEO of Duke Power say that the company was the third-largest $CO_2$ emitter in the country and that they knew they were part of the problem and now wanted to be part of the solution. Henry pressed the panel to respond to the concern that his bill would tank the economy, that it would cause the price of energy to rise too much, would cost jobs, and would cut growth. "The success of the economy depends on this bill," Mr. Duke Power said. Barton, whose political base in Texas is the energy industry, just shook his head. "If we get this bill right, and we get the transition right, this bill will make our economy stronger over time," Duke told another Republican from Texas. He started shaking his head, too.

The political optics also were good outside the committee room, thanks to the president. Obama was in Iowa at the site of a closed washing machine factory that had been reborn as a windmill manufacturing plant, bringing with it new jobs and a future for its workers. It was a good day for the energy bill. There will be much harder days ahead. Our Republican friends are still shaking their heads tonight—and plotting.

Friday, May 1

It has been a week of meetings with lobbyists and interests as everyone seeks position and advantage on the energy and climate bill. Independent natural gas producers, renewable energy technology mavens, energy infrastructure exporters—they all troop through. Everyone is awaiting the crucial negotiations by Henry and Markey with the coal state Democrats to get a deal on global warming pollution targets and the workings of the cap-and-trade system. Henry and Ed met with Rep. Rick Boucher of Virginia, the key coal and electric utility Democrat, and agreement appears close. Boucher's support would cue like-positioned members and would mark a major advance for the bill.

Henry also had a private thirty-minute meeting with the president in the Oval Office. Henry endorsed Obama long before the primaries were completed and ensured that his stimulus program was expedited through the committee, with provisions for health, broadband, and green technologies. Obama's endorsement of more aggressive stem cell research was a long-standing Waxman priority. And the administration endorsed Henry's bill to put tobacco under the authority of the Food and Drug Administration. So they are in major sync in terms of policy, and the meeting helps them to know each other better. What has not yet become apparent is Obama's willingness to directly bring his power to bear on the outcome of the energy and climate bill. It's a fine line: you want to have his influence felt, but not too early. As a general rule, Congress resists direct pressure from the White House in the early to middle stages of legislation. But in a major crisis that has really hard issues, like the global financial crisis, Congress is happy to cede significant responsibility and oversight to the president. If the White House dictates a bill, it's an easier target to attack; the best result is to build a bill through consensus, creating buy-in from as many members as you can, and that is what we are doing. But it's time for some presidential suasion. Shortly after Henry returns to his office from the Oval Office meeting, an invitation comes from the president to all Democratic members of the committee to meet Tuesday in the White House. The president wants to weigh in—just before the committee markup of the bill. It's a good omen.

## Thursday, May 14

Henry met early this afternoon with the leadership of the Edison Electric Institute (EEI)—about a dozen CEOs whose companies constitute 90 percent of the electricity-generation capacity in the United States. They are not in full agreement with the bill—the discussions are not complete—but EEI supports the bill to continue the process of developing policy, and they will work for support from key Democrats on the committee. This is a major breakthrough. This bill is the biggest coal bill in American history, the biggest energy jobs bill in American history, and the formula for carbon trading provides good protections for utilities against price shocks for their consumers. And EEI knows it. Following that meeting, Henry and Markey and Boucher held a press conference where Boucher said firmly that he will vote *yes* on the bill. This will bring along other moderate coal-state Democrats. Late in the day, Henry and Markey successfully concluded the last major negotiation with oil-state Democrats on the treatment of that industry. And so with these deals—on trade-affected industries, autos, renewable energy, utilities and coal, and some other discrete issues—enough Democrats are locked in on enough deals to assure, as of tonight, passage of the bill in committee next week.

This morning, I convened a meeting of Democratic staff to hear the latest polling research on energy and climate issues. The poll clearly showed that except for climate-change deniers, the energy legislation, when packaged as a clean energy jobs bill, an energy security bill, and an investment and growth for the future bill, trumps by decisive margins the scare arguments that we cannot do this in a recession or that the bill is a tax on your light switch. The people are smarter than that. They know that nothing today stands between them and four-dollar gas. They know that the jobs that have been lost in the Great Recession are not coming back for a long, long time; that we need to create new jobs, in a new economy, in their place; and that new programs that give us a better energy future are part of the solution, along with the rest of President Obama's stimulus and recovery package. So it was important for members to be armed with this polling data as they prepare to vote next week.

The White House was in touch during the day about the president's weekly Internet address. It will be on this legislation. What could he say about organized labor? They have not endorsed the bill yet—they want to see the final language, and jobs are at stake—but they do support the principles behind the legislation. After a couple emails with staff, these words go over to 1600 Pennsylvania Avenue: *Labor strongly supports the priorities in this legislation: creating clean energy jobs, protecting good-paying manufacturing jobs, securing energy independence, and pragmatic, effective steps to combat global warming pollution.* I don't know if the president will use this formulation, but it is the truth.

## Saturday, May 16

We're corralling the votes and the interest groups. The past two days spent on the phone with the lobbyists to get them targeted on the nine Democratic members of the committee who are of concern, notwithstanding the substantive political deals struck on all major issues. With no Republican votes coming our way, Henry can afford to lose six of thirty-six Democrats and still prevail. We feel pretty good about the vote on the overall bill, but there will be cunningly crafted Republican amendments that will squeeze Democrats in coal states or facing close election races— such as a vote that will highlight the cost of the bill on electricity prices. We have two hard Democratic members against the bill, two others leaning against, and five others who are leaning for support but who are not locked up for various reasons. Others, mostly from coal and industrial states, wonder—even with the compromises that dial down the targets and caps and deadlines, and even with the strong support for electric utilities, oil, gas, and automobiles—whether it will hold down the road, and they worry that a more aggressive environmental bill will eventuate. So I am on the phone with superlobbyists who have clients on the bill and are working it and who have ties with these nine members we are tracking, and I'm talking with senior utility executives who have worked these guys for years and know them so well. They take temperatures daily and report words, nuance, mood—and what it might take to solidify a disposition to support the bill. A call from a senior member here, an amendment on a fuel issue there, a new provision ensuring tight regulatory authority over this vast new market in permits and allowances that will develop and start trading. (Echoes of Wall Street, greed and derivatives are a subtext.)

And you have to be opportunistic. The president today named Jon Huntsman, the governor of Utah, as the new ambassador to China, and a Democratic holdout on our committee is a Utah congressman, Jim Matheson, so I'm asking Phil Schiliro if the president can ask the governor to call our Utah friend and get him to support the bill. Some coal and oil interests want no bill at any price, and they have taken aggressive ads in swing districts, and some of the ads contain the names of companies in the business coalition supporting our bill, so there are damage-control calls to their Washington offices to ask them to get their names off those ads if they can't stop the ads altogether.

Ads are running on our side, too, in these same swing districts, led by a firm aligned with Al Gore's anti-global-warming movement. And we're targeting calls by Al to liberal members who think that too much may have been given away to the energy industries with not enough money left over for larger public purposes. There is one virtue of being attacked by the Left on this bill: we look like centrists—like practicing the "ruthless pragmatism," to quote President Obama, that is a real attribute in a troubled world where new answers are required for deep and complex problems. So, yes, make my day with the moderates by coming at me from the far left.

And I am trying to shore up a coalition of Evangelicals and Catholics who care about cushioning the costs of carbon mitigation for the most vulnerable in our society and who strongly support a generous commitment of dollars and technology to developing countries to get their greenhouse gases in order. We want these groups because of their stroke with conservatives, whose political base has a large Evangelical Christian component. This is a recent development, but stewardship of the Earth has growing appeal among religious conservatives—the idea that God's creation should be preserved. And this is what we believe, too. So there is a prospect of a significant cross-cultural political alliance being forged, and we want to explore it. Our bill has strong provisions to help the poor and leave them whole on energy prices—and more than ten billion dollars in aid abroad— but some Evangelical and Catholic groups have written to me saying it is not enough and that they may oppose the bill:

On behalf of the Evangelical Environmental Network and the Evangelical Climate Initiative we welcome the proposed legislation released today and the leadership and initiative, in particular the leadership of Chairmen Waxman and Markey, in moving forward climate legislation in the House. Addressing the causes of global climate change is both urgent and necessary and the legislation represents important progress in this area. However, the legislation must also address the consequences or impacts. It must be structured in ways that effectively address the disproportionate and unjust burdens that will fall on the poor and most vulnerable in our nation and around the world. Unfortunately, the resources committed to international adaptation still fall fundamentally short of what is needed for the US to be credible in meeting the needs of the most vulnerable developing nations and in meeting a key requirement to secure a global treaty—namely, a substantial down payment for adaptation funding. The current funding for helping the poor in poor countries adapt to the consequences is less than adequate. It must start higher and grow faster. Until that is achieved, the bill falls short of what is morally supportable.

And so today, on the Sabbath, I wrote them back privately:

I just wanted to reply privately to you on this. The good words and sentiments are very much appreciated. They mean a lot to me personally. But I sincerely hope you might rethink where you are and be able to conditionally endorse our legislation—and help with some Members whose votes we very much need.

To be brief:

If this bill goes down, there will be no program internationally and no help for the most vulnerable—here or elsewhere. Is nothing better than something?

If this bill goes down, there will be no US effort on climate change. Will the Earth be safer from a tipping point?

And if you know anything about Henry Waxman, it is that he always endeavors to achieve what can be achieved—the maximum attainable amount today—and revisit the problems and issues in the future, and take more steps to resolve them. Acid rain control legislation in 1990 was a 10 year effort. Putting tobacco under the FDA has been a 12 year effort. This bill is on the verge of passing the House just months after Obama's inauguration.

Yes, we have so much more to do.

This is a classic case, in my judgment, of where the best should not—must not—be the enemy of the good. So by all means exhort us to do better. But don't exhort us to defeat this bill—because that means you are really exhorting us to do nothing. Because there will be no other bill. We need your help urgently on this bill and we need it with some key Members we believe you can effectively reach.

Nothing will happen if nothing continues. Tell us by all means that you want the bill to be better—much better—but tell the Committee please to keep this legislation moving in order to have the opportunity to do better. Thanks for listening. I hope this is helpful to your thinking.

We will see if our prayers are answered. The president's weekly Internet and radio address was on this bill and health care, both under Henry's jurisdiction. With the weekend, you get a twenty-four-hour news bump out of the Obama webcast: during the day today as it is reported, and in the big Sunday newspapers tomorrow.

President Obama told the nation:

> Chairman Henry Waxman and members of the Energy and Commerce Committee brought together stakeholders from all corners of the country—and every sector of our economy—to reach an historic agreement on comprehensive energy legislation. It's another promising sign of progress, as longtime opponents are sitting together, at the same table, to help solve one of America's most serious challenges.
>
> For the first time, utility companies and corporate leaders are joining, not opposing, environmental advocates and labor leaders to create a new system of clean energy initiatives that will help unleash a new era of growth and prosperity.
>
> It's a plan that will finally reduce our dangerous dependence on foreign oil and cap the carbon pollution that threatens our health and our climate. Most important, it's a plan that will trigger the creation of millions of new jobs for Americans, who will produce the wind turbines and solar panels and develop the alternative fuels to power the future. Because this we know: the nation that leads in 21st century clean energy is the nation that will lead the 21st century global economy. America can and must be that nation—and this agreement is a major step toward this goal.

And yes, labor's support was mentioned, too. A great way to start the day.

## Monday, May 18

The Republicans blinked. We have only four days to mark up this bill before Congress breaks for Memorial Day, and every day counts. On the table is a 932-page bill from Waxman and Markey. For parliamentary purposes, also introduced is a substitute of equal length. The Republicans could have forced a reading of it all, taking many hours of well-mannered professionals reading in a monotone into a microphone to record for posterity that the bill was read. And undoubtedly better understood by the Republicans after such an insipid exercise. They saw we were prepared to do it, and they hesitated, knowing that the story would be, *Republicans have no alternative and so go into mindless delaying tactics on urgent energy and climate bill*. Would have taken them right back to the nineteenth century. They have threatened hundreds of amendments. What they should do is offer proposals that counter ours and make members vote a few times—just enough—to provide fodder for the political commercials a year from October decrying radical Democrats for passing the biggest energy tax in American history. But they may not be able to help themselves and may try to filibuster by amendment. However, under the rules, the bill is maneuvered into a parliamentary position where Henry can order, in effect, a final vote at a time of his choosing. I do not know for sure what is in his mind, but I expect it will be sometime after midnight early Friday morning—Friday of Memorial Day weekend, when the country officially begins its celebration of summer. There are barbecues to be had, and beer and beaches and sunburns and golf and the stuff of American relaxation. By midnight Thursday, the committee members will want airplanes, not amendments. Henry began the markup with these words:

> Our nation is at a crossroads. Our economy is suffering; we are squandering billions of dollars to feed our addiction on foreign oil; and our environment is overheating. We can continue to look the other way and leave these problems to our children. Or we can adopt a new energy policy for America.

Lobbying checks through the day indicate a continued strengthening of our position. Letters from across the spectrum—businesses, like GE and utilities in California, and environmental groups like the Environmental Defense Fund and Natural Resources Defense Council—flowing in to the committee urging members to report this bill.

Word came to me from the White House that Huntsman was indeed calling Matheson. We will know his vote when we vote.

## Tuesday, May 19

Over twelve hours of near-continuous sitting for the first day of markup; we broke just before midnight. Hundreds of amendments pending; a virtual factory for processing amendments sought by members has been established in my office. And a very good day. The Republicans endeavoring to filibuster by amendment (which is a common strategy in high-profile contentious legislation), with repeated attempts to force votes on politically charged propositions: amendments to suspend the operation of the bill if gas prices go up to five dollars a gallon, or if unemployment rises to 15 percent, or if China and India don't adopt pollution controls. And as soon as the votes are taken, the Republican political machine spits out email press releases in Democratic districts: *Congressman McNerny votes to protect jobs in China!* What was so heartening through the day is that our members held quite uniformly. There are nine members we have been concerned about, but only four broke away, and never in a concerted pack to possibly threaten the outcome; we lost no amendments. Our side was not intimidated. And in the end, the Republican amendments were so facile and transparent that they lost their punch in the translation. And we also got two Republican votes here and there—one potentially very significant. Mary Bono Mack (CA), quite modern and hip, widow of Sonny Bono of Sonny and Cher fame, killed skiing late one day on a mountain he loved. She is in a district with strong progressive sentiment and may have a green opponent next year, and her Republican governor, Arnold Schwarzenegger, supports our bill. It could be that she will break with her leadership on final passage in committee. If this can be maintained for another day, the inexorable logic will be evident and the push to passage will be quite distinct. But it is a long day, with hours of desultory debate spiked with humor and insult. The cavernous hearing room and its anterooms have the smell and feel of a locker room by the time evening settles in. So we are voting in the dank.

Before noon, I went to the UN Foundation, invited by former senator Tim Wirth, who became director of the institution set up by Ted Turner with a billion-dollar grant more than a decade ago. The UN Foundation had assembled a dozen former world leaders, including Mary Robinson of Ireland and Lionel Jospin of France, for a conference on climate issues. They were (pleasantly) surprised by my upbeat report on the energy and climate bill and for prospects for a strong American position going into Copenhagen.

## Wednesday, May 20

We are on the verge of victory tonight. The day was a series of skirmishes and test votes. There was an early scare—on a pro-nuclear-industry amendment—where the industry had really done its work, lining up three Democrats to support a Republican initiative to give nuclear a leg up in a carbon-controlled world. And our side was lazy, with one senior Democrat not voting, causing the margin to be uncomfortably close—only two votes. (I went up to the absent member's office immediately afterward and politely but firmly expressed our disappointment and that we expected it was not to happen again.) And sniffing the hint of a shift of fortune, the Republicans went on the attack—but it was uncoordinated and unstrategic, and they overreached. When a Republican invoked fear that under a provision to strengthen energy codes for the nation's building stock, regulators would swarm over properties and become the "Global Warming Gestapo"—well, that's when Waxman got into a discussion of the demerits of demonizing the integrity of government and regulation in the public interest. It cooled their jets—the congressman who made the crude remark was clearly chastened—and through the afternoon the mood shifted again, with amendment after Republican amendment being clearly defeated with no hope of a breakthrough and Democratic amendment after amendment being ratified healthily.

By the twenty-fifth hour of markup, not one Republican amendment had prevailed over the objections of the chair. Phil Schiliro, the president's legislative affairs director, was in the room, and he went back to meet with Henry and Joe Barton, and after a short discussion, the terms of truce were reached. The morning papers had quotes from Barton responding to questions about whether Henry would, as he had promised, report the bill from committee this week. "It ain't going to happen," Barton said, and he implied that Henry was dreaming. Just before midnight tonight, Barton announced a Republican caucus to discuss their plans for tomorrow, and Henry announced that the bill will be concluded shortly after the House finishes its business for the week and the month at 5:00 pm tomorrow (Thursday), in time for the long Memorial Day weekend. Barton had a nice quote in the morning paper. But it was not to be.

## Thursday, May 21

A complete victory in the committee. The final vote for the American Clean Energy and Security Act of 2009 was 33–26—we lost 4 Democrats (of 9 potential soft votes that we were working), and the Republicans lost 1, Mary Bono Mack. One of theirs was absent, so the real margin was 3 votes. But 3 votes in this business is a landslide—and the Republicans know it. The biggest development through the day was Barton's growing realization that he had been well and truly defeated, and it showed on his face and in his demeanor. And that was crystallized in the increasingly apparent regard in which he holds Henry. Previously, I think he viewed Henry as an effete liberal, tenacious but not especially capable. Tonight, Barton knows he has more than met his match, that he was outplayed in the chess that can be politics, that he is facing a grandmaster. The Republicans lost every single one of the more than one hundred amendments they offered, which meant that the deals Henry struck among the Democrats last week not only stuck but were glue. They could not be shaken. And the Republicans kept playing tactics, not strategy. They offered dozens of mind-numbing amendments; there was not a sound bite in any of them. What they should have done was pick a dozen killer issues—high electricity prices, bringing on nuclear, more old renewable energy sources (hydro, municipal solid waste)—to make the Democrats uncomfortable in a very public and understandable way. Obama proposed a greenhouse gas reduction target of only 14 percent (from 2005 levels) by 2020. The original Waxman-Markey bill was 20 percent; negotiations with the moderate Democrats lowered it to 17 percent. We were terrified the Republicans were going to offer 14 percent—How could we be against what Obama proposed? But they blew it; it never came up. And they are weaker tonight, after the deluge, than ever before. And they know it. At one point this morning, sensing some blood, Barton said, "The majority is at war with itself." To which Henry responded, "Let me say that this majority is going to win the war." And it did. On the night when Barton had said, "It ain't going to happen."

We got word early that Gov. Schwarzenegger had engineered a broad statement of principles on energy and climate issues—principles that were broadly aligned with our bill. Thirty governors—twenty-three Democrats and seven Republicans—signed on. We had a member from Florida announce it to the committee, with the statement distributed, and you could see the faces in the Republican ranks fall as they gesticulated among themselves about who had signed and what it meant.

Just before the vote, Henry addressed the committee to express thanks to the members he had worked with—Democrats on policy and Barton, who, to his credit, played straight in terms of debate and seeing the bill through on Henry's schedule. Everyone knew the outcome of the vote that would be taken in a few minutes. Henry said:

This bill, when enacted into law this year, will break our dependence on foreign oil, make our nation the world leader in clean energy jobs and technology, and cut global warming pollution. I am grateful to my colleagues who supported this legislation and to President Obama for his outstanding leadership on these critical issues.

We can build on the Republicans we won—there should be twenty at least on the floor when we get there. But we lost Matheson, who was indeed called by Gov. Huntsman. Politics is tough—even when you win.

## Wednesday, June 8

Preparing for the House floor fight. The war plan is straightforward. First, a whip operation of twenty strongly supportive committee members who will go after two hundred House members—to lock in, reinforce, and persuade their targets to vote for the bill. We have an excellent database of the members and intelligence on their likely vote. Second, Henry and the prominent Blue Dog members on the committee will meet with the Blue Dog caucus. We hear regularly that the Blue Dogs are nervous about the bill, wary that they will be tagged as taxers and punished at the midterm. The green movement so at home on the two coasts is at war with the heartland of America, where coal is an important energy source, a mining resource, and embedded deep in its political culture. With little Republican support for the bill, the Blue Dogs will mean the difference between winning or losing. Third, we will work with interest groups and allies to lobby members directly. This is a bread-and-butter operation, and the companies, unions, and environmental groups will just have at it. Fourth, we will extend outreach to open-minded Republicans; we think that between ten and twenty votes may be gettable on their side. Fifth, we will ensure the flow of materials and information to members. Sixth, we will ask allies from evangelical Christian groups to work on conservative members—those interested in protecting and defending God's creation. Seventh, we need to ensure disciplined and focused media outreach. Most important, we need to bring to bear the muscle of the Speaker and her staff, engaging the leadership and the president to carry this the last five yards over the finish line.

## Monday, June 22

Speaker Pelosi has told Henry this evening that we are a go for the House floor on Friday. Late today, we already began working on a hard and scrubbed whip list of the votes: the White House needs it because President Obama wants to make calls—and does not want to make wasted calls. By tomorrow midday, we will have the very best assessment of the votes and a pool of members for the president to tap with his special charms. Through the day, a diverse range of groups weighed in on our side: the Evangelicals, the Baptists, eminent scientists, and the UN Foundation, chaired by Ted Turner, and run by our good friend Tim Wirth. The letters go up on our website and we get echo chamber effects from other groups circulating the endorsements. It all shows momentum, which is what we must project.

All of this comes at the end of the day that the president held a Rose Garden signing ceremony for the tobacco regulation bill (see chapter 4). Henry was positioned just off the president's shoulder as he signed the bill; several times this week, Obama mentioned Henry's work for the past fifteen years, since that famous hearing where the tobacco execs swore that nicotine caused no harm.

## Tuesday, June 23

A huge boost tonight with the announcement that Henry and Collin Peterson (D-MN), chair of the Agriculture Committee, had reached agreement on big issues of concern to big agriculture. Emails were buzzing from K Street with congratulations; it gives us significant momentum going into the final few days before the vote. It is a signal to all moderate Democrats that this bill, which the president wants, and the Speaker wants, is OK to support. The deal followed some carefully articulated remarks by the president at his news conference a few hours earlier:

> This week, the House of Representatives is moving ahead on historic legislation that will transform the way we produce and use energy in America. This legislation will spark a clean energy transformation that will reduce our dependence on foreign oil and confront the carbon pollution that threatens our planet. This energy bill will create a set of incentives that will spur the development of new sources of energy, including wind, solar, and geothermal power. It will also spur new energy savings, like efficient windows and other materials that reduce heating costs in the winter and cooling costs in the summer. These incentives will finally make clean energy the profitable kind of energy. And that will lead to the development of new technologies that lead to new industries that could create millions of new jobs in America—jobs that can't be shipped overseas.

At a time of great fiscal challenges, this legislation is paid for by the polluters who currently emit the dangerous carbon emissions that contaminate the water we drink and pollute the air that we breathe. It also provides assistance to businesses and communities as they make the gradual transition to clean energy technologies.

So I believe that this legislation is extraordinarily important for our country; it's taken great effort on the part of many over the course of the past several months. And I want to thank the Chair of the Energy and Commerce Committee, Henry Waxman; his colleagues on that committee, including Congressmen Dingell, Ed Markey, and Rick Boucher.

What a tactical difference having a president on your side can make. There are all these assets to deploy, and it helps advance the strategic agenda. Because, indeed, what is at stake is nothing less than the whole fate of his first term with respect to his domestic agenda. The vote on this bill on Friday is the first big test of the Obama agenda—yes, he had to do economic recovery. That was a given. And of course Congress was going to move to spend money and invest in the stimulus package. It was just a question of the overall size. But this is different: the first vote on something Obama has said he wants—something that defines his presidency. And if he fails, it will be because Democrats have deserted him—which is exactly what we did to Jimmy Carter thirty years ago. We crippled that president and had more fun going after his lame domestic policy agenda and naive politics than we did in attacking the Republicans. And we reaped the reward: Ronald Reagan won a landslide in 1980. And it cost seats in Congress for the Democrats, including control of the Senate after forty-eight years. So if Democrats think they can snub the president and escape unharmed, they better think again. Now, the truth is, we won't call the vote if we are going to lose—but if we delay the vote, it is hard to see how we will win in two weeks' time or two months' time. This bill will not grow in popularity; interests will demand more concessions, and it will collapse of its own weight. And there will be nothing to resurrect. So we have to win. And everyone in the White House knows it.

Earlier this afternoon, we met with the leadership staff and White House staff in the Capitol to go over all the 280 votes in play and begin to put in place the political touches with each that will coalesce a majority. The deal on agriculture tonight helps enormously, because it looks like this bill is now inevitable and so those who want to be with a winner better get with the program.

## Wednesday, June 24

And there are plenty of critical priorities we are juggling in the air simultaneously, not the least of which is a visit by the Secretary of Health and Human Services, Kathleen Sebelius, to address the committee during a morning hearing on health reform.

The balance of the day: working like hell for cap-and-trade votes. Directing ally traffic on the thirty or forty undecideds we have identified. Some gavottes with moderate Republicans who suddenly have some issue they would like addressed: and if we do that, do we get their votes? And then late asks, as the amendments are being finalized, by business and industries for this or that fix. The bill has become a big casino, and it is very transactional, and the asking for favors is without even a patina of homage to the bedrock purposes of the bill: to make the country more energy independent, more energy efficient, and less polluting. Those are afterthoughts in the crude Washington rush for carve-outs, exceptions, delays, special breaks, formulas, and statements of intent designed to guide the hands of regulators years from now. Forget about Kennedy's dictum of nearly fifty years ago, *Ask not what your country can do for you—ask what you can do for your country.* You can feel soiled at the end of such a day, because the noble purposes are not paramount in the legislative bazaar, and you just hope like hell it does not all collapse of its own weight of special pleadings. *There, there*, someone might say to me, *this is Washington. The imperial city. Get with it, pal.* We are still twenty-five votes short. Another forty-eight hours of bargaining, haggling, hair pulling, and brute force to go.

## Thursday, June 25

The eve of the vote—maybe. We have gained ground during the day but are still short, probably by fifteen votes, which is a lot at this stage. This evening, at the White House picnic on the South Lawn for members of Congress, I had conversations with the president's staff on the state of play. Carol Browner, head of EPA under Clinton, has been tireless and persistent in hunting down members and smoothing over issues. All day, I have helped direct traffic to get those votes: faith groups going after Democrats in Kentucky; a deal with Republicans in Delaware and New Jersey; generating a call list for Al Gore, who has had a solid strike rate through the day in getting members on board; lining up a learned expert to argue with the *Washington Post* over their editorial in tomorrow's paper on the cap-and-trade regime in the bill; providing guidance to the enviros on a massive call bank they will launch in the morning in thirty-eight key seats. Midday, Henry attended a fund-raising lunch for the Democratic congressional campaign, and he updated the dozens present on the politics; I worked the nuclear guys to get some of their CEOs to weigh in the Midwest, a mega-lobbyist to get her to weigh in with a dozen key Democrats she knows well, and a solar upstart to try to catch a member in Idaho (a patina of trending green in Boise). Utilities fanned out in Illinois and California, New Mexico and Florida, where we have a chance at three Republican votes. Their top lobbyist was positioned all day outside the doors of the House buttonhol-ing members to get their temperature. Word filtered back that Obama and Rahm and cabinet secretaries were on the phones through the day. But we are still short, and this evening the White House staff was very guarded. It gave me pause. I sent a late suggestion to Henry, headed for a strategy meeting tonight with the leadership, that Obama should meet with the entire caucus in the morning and get our Democrats in shape. If we pull the bill, the deals in it will fray and disintegrate quickly; we will not be able to bring it back. So it will be a defeat on the first Obama legacy bill out of the box. That would weaken our hand for health care. So we must win. But if we take it to the floor and lose the vote, it is even worse, because then there will be real blood on the House floor—Obama's and the Speaker's and Henry's. But sometimes you have to take risks to make a difference. *Yes we can*, Obama said in his campaign. Well, we must. Tomorrow is a huge day, one way or the other.

### Friday, June 26

We win, 219–212. A margin of four votes. Eight Republicans voted for final passage, and I helped get five of them. Three in Delaware and New Jersey depended on a deal involving DuPont, the largest company in Delaware, and the extent to which it would get credit for previous carbon-reducing efforts. Our staff worked out a sensible provision and the company issued a statement of qualified support for the bill, but this morning the Republican staff could not find the language in the thirteen hundred pages of text, a key member said he was not voting for the bill, and a minicrisis erupted. The language was pointed out, I got DuPont on the line, they reaffirmed support for the bill, and the Republicans were happy: three votes. A Wash-ington State moderate was courted by the White House; Larry Summers, economic counselor to the president, was on the phone with him, and I got Microsoft, based in Washington State, to weigh in as well. And then Upstate New York's John McHugh, whom President Obama has nominated to serve as secretary of the army but who is still sitting in the House and eligible to vote, wanted some assurances on the acid rain program affecting his forests, and I got the White House to make appropriate commitments in that regard. Mary Bono Mack, who instigated the letter on the bill from Republican moderates, stuck with her vote in favor, and they ultimately provided the margin of victory. Through the day, reports were trickling in of votes that would break our way, getting us to an absolute majority. Gore in particular made extensive phone calls and brought several wavering Democrats into line. One member from Texas spoke out against the bill this morning but then talked with Gore and endorsed and voted for the bill this evening. Early this morning, we gave the environmentalists a list of eighteen key House members, and phone banks went to work in those districts through the day.

The debate lasted virtually all day on the House floor, and the Republicans were rather listless, which indicated that they knew they did not have the votes and would lose; indeed, even with that close margin, the Speaker said afterward that she had a few other votes available for our majority if needed. The press conference after the vote, held in the beautiful Rayburn Room right off the House floor, was quite exuberant, with the Speaker, the majority leader, the whip, Henry, Markey, other senior members. Pelosi occupied center stage and said that this was a vote about the future, not the past, and about jobs and that on the eve of America's celebration of independence, this was a vote for energy independence and national security. And really, when you think about the odds of passing a thirteen-hundred-page bill with dense and numbingly banal paradigms for how to regulate a postcarbon economy, you would have to say there was no way in hell. But Henry Waxman did it. And that means he wields greater power and is perhaps the most intrepid legislator in Congress today. The president's authority is also stronger, since he has won his first major legacy issue when put to a vote. Our ability to drive through health care reform has suddenly acquired a stronger air of inevitability. And that, in politics, is a very good thing.

### Implications and Conclusion

The political dynamics of cap-and-trade were very different in the Senate, where GOP opposition and a handful of politically vulnerable Democrats prevented an agreement on the legislation. Political parties in the upper chamber have become nearly as polarized as they are in the House

(Fleisher and Bond 2004; Theriault 2008; F. E. Lee 2009; Theriault and Rohde 2011). With the growing levels of partisanship, the contemporary Senate has earned a reputation as a legislative graveyard, as was the case for cap-and-trade (Sinclair 2006). The Senate's smaller size, procedural prerogatives, and growing individualism, have meant that the chamber's committees have had less power and have been less critical for achieving members' individual goals than their House counterparts (Fenno 1973; Sinclair 1989; Smith 1989). The Senate had no counterpart to Henry Waxman—no legislative giant willing to own the cause. Moreover, the energy industry wielded much more influence with individual senators than with representatives, resulting in a considerable political hurdle that some Senate Democrats were unwilling to jump. Majority leader Harry Reid (NV) could not get his entire caucus to support the bill, meaning that he could not muster the sixty votes necessary to overcome a GOP filibuster. Not all policies on the presidential agenda are equal. Despite the significance of cap-and-trade, it took a backseat in the Obama White House to tackling health care reform and reviving the plunging US economy.

Although the cap-and-trade bill died in the Senate, its passage in the House Energy and Commerce Committee and then on the House floor points toward some important themes. The cap-and-trade bill's passage in the House reflects the traditional roots of committee power and theories of legislative organization. The committee's positive power rests on its ability to change the policy status quo by convincing members of the opposition party or who are resistant to change to support the committee's position (Deering and Smith 1997). The committee exercised formidable positive power in a variety of ways to shape the bill and produce significant support for passage. First, the committee—and especially Reps. Waxman and Markey—crafted a policy amenable to a coalition of powerful outside interests, including business, energy, and environmental groups. Business support was absolutely critical in that it showed that this legislation was not radical; in political terms, many of the business interests backing the bill had traditionally supported Republicans. The committee was able to devise such a measure as a consequence of the strong political relationships between leaders and external political interests (Deering and Smith 1997), and this strategy limited many sources of potential opposition to the bill. A committee's positive power thus extends well beyond garnering votes in the chamber, and the committee leadership plays an important role in managing external political interests to influence congressional policymaking. Similarly, by mobilizing support among GOP governors, the committee not only pressured the GOP House but also blunted some of the partisan arguments against the bill. And committee leaders' strong ties with environmental groups facilitated pressure from those outside political interests on individual members as the leadership coordinated environmental interests to lobby pivotal voters to support the legislation on the House floor (Rothenberg 1992; Wright 1996; R. L. Hall and Reynolds 2012).

The committee's institutional advantages also played an important role. For example, the committee's control and use of legislative hearings added to its ability to exercise influence over policymaking. Cabinet secretaries and White House allies testified in support of the cap-and-trade legislation. Harnessing and coordinating White House mobilization efforts to build coalition support was also a key task (Rudalevidge 2002; Beckmann 2010; Lebo and O'Geen 2011). In addition, Rep. Waxman used his post as chair of Energy and Commerce to obtain significant access to the media, which he used to promote the bill's policy message. Waxman strategically sought to highlight the bill's many benefits, expanding the frame of policy debate in a way designed to garner support and advantage its passage (Riker 1986). These strategies relate to a committee's positive power and result from political relationships, policy information, and institutional advantages a committee typically enjoys on issues within its jurisdiction over those who would oppose the legislation.

Beyond some of these classic elements of committee power, the case of cap-and-trade shows how partisan issues provide powerful environmental constraints on congressional committees, and party leaders wield tremendous power in legislative decision making (Fenno 1973; Maltzman 2000).[3] Cap-and-trade was a classic issue typical of many subjects that fall under the committee's jurisdiction: it was nationally salient and invoked a host of different external political interests. On one hand, it had the potential to appeal to a wide spectrum of members because it touched such a large mix of political interests. It was a bill to promote energy independence and security, a bill to promote innovation in an energy market and domestic growth in green jobs/renewable industry, and a bill for conservationists and environmentalists that promised to reduce the US and global carbon footprint. In this sense, it was a highly transactional piece of legislation where members of Congress could promote and trade discrete benefits to one industry or another to build a winning coalition and distribute the costs widely to dilute political opposition.[4]

On the other hand, cap-and-trade represented an opportune target for the Republican minority. Despite a concerted effort at outreach, only one Republican supported passage in committee, and just a handful supported the bill on the House floor. For most Republicans, the benefits of partisan opposition trumped any potential policy benefits from passage.[5] Cap-and-trade was a highly complex piece of legislation with only gradual economic impact; it would not immediately relieve voters' growing economic anxiety. The legislation could not overcome the threat it posed to the coal industry and its constituencies, a cause that the minority party opposition had nurtured (Clark 2015; Green 2015). Even though this was early in the president's first year in office, it was a key agenda item, and issues promoted by the White House have increasingly provoked partisan opposition in Congress (F. E. Lee 2009). It was also an opportunity to slow the Democratic majority's policy momentum and create public uncertainty about the new president and his party's ability to govern. Maintaining GOP unity against the Democratic agenda made for an effective political message and offered the minority party a strategy consistent with its quest to regain control of the House (Rohde 2013). The policy success (or defeat) of the president can carry electoral consequences for the political parties in Congress. A presidential defeat, especially for a new and unproven White House, may translate into seat gains for the opposition party in the next election (Lebo and O'Geen 2011).

Wolpe's account illustrates still other lessons about congressional politics and the important role committees play in shaping policy. For example, the Democratic majority in the House and the party's control over the committee's agenda prior to winning the White House provided President Obama with a considerable legislative head start. The committee's role in building a floor coalition in the House was crucial to uniting the party's diverse factions. Further, cap-and-trade illustrates that party loyalty is not automatic and that majority coalitions must be built member by member, often with the help of opinion leaders. The highly charged partisan environment can both make outreach to moderate opposition members more difficult and give ideologically extreme members more leverage to narrow the prospects for policy change (as in the incentives for nuclear power added to the cap-and-trade bill). Selective historical memory also can complicate lawmakers' calculations, as in the case of the 1993 BTU tax and more broadly in committing the FDR fallacy—thinking that unified government in a time of crisis necessarily allows the passage of major policies.[6]

Finally, party leaders play a decisive role in passing legislation in the House of Representatives. The cap-and-trade bill was important to a majority of House Democrats and a critical issue for Speaker Pelosi. Partisan theory leads to the expectation that party leaders will use their institutional powers to advance such legislation, as was the case with cap-and-trade.

Rep. Waxman was one of a handful of committee chairs who were particularly loyal to Pelosi and enjoyed her confidence.[7] Democratic leaders
would rely on the expertise and substantial experience of these chairs to
move much of the party's agenda. Cap-and-trade was one of the Speaker's most important issues: as one leadership aide said, "This was the big
one for us. Pelosi staked her prestige on this one. This was her flagship
issue, and this was a flagship vote for us" (O'Connor and Thrush 2009, 15).
Moreover, presidents have increasingly played a critical role in fostering
legislative support (or opposition) in Congress (F. E. Lee 2009; Beckmann
2010). Party leaders directed White House influence and the president's
personal touch to lobby reluctant Democratic House members to support the legislation. These efforts included a White House luau for House
members that set the stage for an all-out press by the party leadership, with
majority whip Jim Clyburn and his team working the crowd on the White
House lawn to shore up support.

A legislative veteran, Speaker Pelosi was uniquely capable at the bargaining table with other House members, combining charm with political
savvy, tenacity, and a mastery of the legislative details. She knew exactly
what had been traded or bartered, to whom, and at what political cost (or
benefit). The majority party leadership accrues informational advantages
about the distribution of political costs and benefits of legislation across
party factions and even individual members. This information is critical
for negotiations, putting together successful coalitions, and managing the
electoral risk for majority party members (Fortunato 2013; Rohde 2013).

The Speaker used her influence to force members to delay their travel
plans to increase support for the critical floor vote, even promising one
member an airport escort to make an early flight (O'Connor and Thrush
2009). Pelosi personally twisted arms, convincing Rep. Rush Holt (D-NJ)
that his vote against would bring down the bill and kill any chance of carv-
ing out a better deal with the Senate. Meeting one-on-one with members,
she emphasized the importance of comparing the bill not to the ideal (and
thus focusing on what it lacked) but to the status quo (and thus focusing on
its benefits). The leadership's ability to shift the dimension of policy choice
in favor of the party's position is a very real albeit difficult-to-measure
weapon in the leadership arsenal (Riker 1986; Hixon and Marshall 2007).

Passing cap-and-trade was very important to the Speaker and for a
majority of the House Democratic caucus, and the party rationale leads
to the expectation that those at the helm will use their power on policy
priorities like this one (Rohde 1991; Aldrich and Rohde 2001; Cox and
McCubbins 2005; Sinclair 2011). And in the end (at least in the House),

the leadership made the decisive difference in the outcome. Congressional decision making on cap-and-trade offers compelling evidence for the "party matters" framework of legislative organization. Party leaders held together most of the majority party and delivered a winning coalition on the House floor.

# THREE

# Confronting Waterloo?
# The Historic Moment
# for Health Care Reform

*The politics of health care were completely different from the energy bill, where regional issues such as coal and the price of electricity in old energy states are paramount, so we worry about the degree of support from moderate Democrats. On health care, the board is resized completely: every Member hears complaints about the scope of coverage, costs and insurance premiums, and quality. We have been working to put a winnable health care reform package together for an historic vote on the floor of the House and the last sticking point was something that was virtually immovable and so hard to negotiate out: abortion and how it would be funded under health insurance plans. But in the end, we delivered a major victory, with the House approving the Affordable Care Act, 220–215. (from the Wolpe Journal)*

The passage of national health insurance legislation had eluded Congress since the administration of Harry S. Truman. Barack Obama's landmark health care legislation, the Affordable Care Act (ACA) was the largest of its kind and was designed to significantly broaden health care coverage to more than thirty-two million uninsured Americans. Not only was health care unaffordable for so many, including members of the middle class, but health care spending as a percentage of GDP was the highest in the developed world and out of control. The American people were paying more and getting less. The new law sought to confront the problem of rising health care costs and make health care coverage affordable for the many Americans diagnosed with preexisting conditions. The ACA placed the states at the heart of reform efforts by weaving together a system of state exchanges providing subsidized insurance and supporting the expansion of Medicaid (Reichard 2010). Under the ACA, by 2014, the exchanges would serve individuals and small businesses and the expanded Medicaid programs would cover households with incomes up to 138 percent of the federal poverty level, making health insurance available to millions of Americans for the first time. The US Supreme Court eventually upheld one of the law's more controversial provisions—the individual mandate, which required all citizens and legal residents to have health care insurance. The law also carried politically popular provisions that would take effect more immediately: insurance companies could not deny coverage to children because of preexisting conditions, parents could keep children on their policies until age twenty-six, and the "doughnut hole," where Medicare beneficiaries had to pay high prescription drug costs, was phased out.

The expected price tag for the national health care overhaul was just under one trillion dollars over ten years. And unlike recent health-related legislation such as the 2003 Medicare Prescription Drug law, the ACA included significant and difficult provisions designed to pay for the policy's costs through such mechanisms as a tax on high-cost "Cadillac" insurance plans, which proved unpopular with labor unions, whose wage increases had slowed dramatically during the Great Recession. In addition, the measure reduced federal payments to Medicare Advantage plans, increased Medicare payroll taxes for high-income earners, and imposed fees on the pharmaceutical and health insurance industries as well as a tax on medical device makers (Jarlenski and Rubin 2010). Indeed, the law spread the pain of paying for the overhaul across a swath of health-related constituencies and was just as significant a piece of the political puzzle as any other.

Although few bills in the modern Congress follow the neat journey outlined in *Schoolhouse Rock*, the legislative path of health care overhaul was one of the rockiest and most difficult ones seen in recent times (Sinclair 2012). Three primary legislative vehicles carried health care reform, and each was filled with uncertainty until the last moments, when victory was obtained by the narrowest of margins. The House initially passed a version of health care reform (HR 3962) by a 220–215 vote in November 2009.[1] This was the legislation favored most by liberals. The Senate passed its own health care bill (HR 3590) in a historic and dramatic pure-party-line 60–39 vote on Christmas Eve (Jarlenski and Rubin 2010). The Senate bill differed from the House version in that the upper chamber weakened the language walling off federal funds from abortion and was less generous with subsidies and other provisions that appealed to liberals. But one of those sixty votes had come from Paul Kirk, the interim replacement for the Senate's liberal lion and staunchest warrior for health care reform, Edward M. Kennedy (D-MA), who died in August 2009. In January 2010, Republican Scott Brown was elected to serve out the remainder of Kennedy's term, depriving the Democrats of the key sixtieth vote needed to make the Senate filibuster-proof. Leaders persuaded Democratic members of the House to shift their strategy by taking up the Senate's health care bill, thereby preventing opponents of filibustering the measure in the Senate at the conference stage. And on March 21, during a rare Sunday evening session, the House passed the much more conservative Senate bill by a 219–212 vote— that is, without a single Republican in support (Wayne and Epstein 2010b).

The passage of the Senate bill was particularly painful for the Democratic rank and file in the House for policy and political reasons. For example, in addition to the differences noted earlier, the Senate bill was far less generous in its individual subsidies for health insurance and had numerous sweetener provisions providing differential Medicaid payments to certain states to win support from particular senators (Wayne and Epstein 2010b). House Democrats had to swallow these sweetheart deals (e.g., the "Cornhusker Kickback," the "Louisiana Purchase," and "Gator Aid"), which the media savaged as pandering to special interests.[2] The Democratic leaders in the House and Senate settled on an unconventional strategy, using budget reconciliation procedures to clean up these and other problematic provisions in the Senate bill. Passage of the reconciliation legislation would require only a simple majority of fifty-one senators, protecting against the possibility of a Republican filibuster and limiting the number of amendments.

House party leaders initially considered shielding the rank-and-file Democrats from voting directly on the Senate bill by using a self-executing provision in the special rule that would govern consideration of the reconciliation bill on the House floor—the "Slaughterhouse Rule," which took its name from the chair of the House Rules Committee, Louise Slaughter (D-NY). In effect, the procedural vote on the special rule would set terms of debate for reconciliation on the House floor and contained a self-executing trigger that would "deem the Senate bill passed" when the reconciliation vote passage occurred. By doing so, House Democrats would in effect vote on the reconciliation bill containing the fixes but would not vote directly on the less palatable Senate bill. However, the Senate parliamentarian ruled that the House had to vote on the Senate bill prior to the reconciliation bill because reconciliation only affects existing law (Adams and Wayne 2010).

To get support from House Democrats, the reconciliation bill (HR 4872) made "corrections" to the newly passed law, increasing subsidies to help the uninsured buy insurance, raising some fees and taxes to help pay for expanded coverage, and excising many of the Senate sweeteners. The House passed the reconciliation bill on March 21 by a 220–211 vote. Four days later, the Senate slightly amended HR 4872 and then passed it, 56–43; a few hours later, the House cleared the amended legislation, 220–207.[3] President Obama signed HR 4872 on March 30, ending the tumultuous nine-month roller-coaster ride for the health care reform legislation. But this colossal achievement only constituted the first hurdle on the ACA's arduous journey, which carried on into the Trump presidency as the Republicans maintained their bedrock commitment to repealing Obamacare.[4]

The ACA represents the broadest expansion of health care since the creation of Medicare in 1965 and was arguably the most important social reform since the enactment of Social Security under President Franklin Roosevelt in 1935. The ACA was a relatively rare policy achievement not just because of the sheer magnitude of the legislative effort but also because it touches so many constituencies and tackles a truly national problem. But the ACA was also distinctive because of the nearly intractable and deeply entwined political dilemmas it faced in passage. Indeed, health care reform was characterized by unique political challenges that explain why previous reform efforts from Presidents Truman to Clinton had failed (Johnson and Broder 1997). What was the nature of the political conflicts that made passage so difficult? First and foremost, it exacerbated a long-standing ideological schism that had been present in the Democratic Party since the 1970s (Rohde 1991). The liberal faction of the caucus favored aggressive government programs like the public option—a government-run single-payer system—while probusiness conservatives favored market solutions and fiscal discipline (Dallek 2009). So health care reform would test both ends of the caucus. If either the Blue Dogs or the liberals allowed their positions to become immutable or demand too much, the reform effort would die (Ornstein 2009). Moreover, because the ACA reflected must-pass legislation for Obama's legacy, Democrats of all stripes had greater opportunity if not an incentive to challenge the White House and party leaders to force concessions (O'Connor 2009b). President Obama had said he was willing to trade his reelection for passage of health care reform.

In addition, members of the Democratic Party had numerous conflicting political needs and policy goals. Groups such as freshman Democrats and Blue Dogs often found themselves at opposite ends of the balloon, and pushing on one side caused havoc on the other. Committee and party leaders had to walk a tightrope to balance competing caucus demands. Many freshmen, for instance, sought protection on votes raising taxes on the wealthy and medical industry, while Blue Dogs were in their constituents' crosshairs over the price tag. In addition, many substantive policy differences made coalition building painfully difficult. Some resulted from significant variation in health care infrastructure across regions and in urban and rural areas, differential Medicaid reimbursement rates and program expansion criteria, and divisive immigration issues. Then, there was the ever-present issue of abortion: more than seventy Democrats numbered among the two hundred members of the Congressional Pro-Life Caucus (Ota 2010c). Abortion caused a rift within the Democratic caucus that was immune to horse-trading and in some cases was not overcome until the very end, when President Obama issued an executive order designed to add extra assurances for wavering members worried about the exclusion of federal funds for abortions.

All of these developments unfolded in the context of profound partisan conflicts. From the outset, the Obama agenda had great difficulty finding support across the aisle. The loyal opposition's "go along to get along" strategy, which was designed to maintain the minority party's influence in shaping legislation, had for decades been receding, replaced by partisanship and strategies centered on blocking, taking positions , and messaging (J. H. Clark 2015; Green 2015; F. E. Lee 2016). Although the modern Congress had long featured intense partisan battles, they increased dramatically in the 1980s (Sinclair 1982, 2006). But with Speaker Newt Gingrich (R-GA) sparking the revolutionary House of the 104th Congress, partisan guerrilla warfare had become the dominant strategy for the minority (Aldrich and Rohde 1997–98). The Senate, too, had witnessed growing partisan rancor and tactics (Fleisher and Bond 2004; Theriault 2008, 2013).[5] The chair of the Senate Finance Committee, Max Baucus (D-MT), led a small group of Democratic and Republican senators who hoped to forge a bipartisan deal on Obamacare, but the intense political pressures from the Left and Far Right snuffed out any efforts at bipartisanship on health care.[6] This fruitless search for compromise in the Senate also delayed ultimate enactment for many weeks—in itself a political price that undercut momentum for reform.

The partisan politics on this bill were extremely intense. Party leaders on both sides had made clear that party loyalty was paramount and viewed the outcome from the perspective of its consequences for their parties (Lebo and O'Geen 2011; F. E. Lee 2016). In the committee room, on the floor, or across the airwaves, Republicans would yield no ground in the health care battle. Sen. Jim DeMint (R-SC) declared, "If we're able to stop Obama on [health care reform], it will be his Waterloo. It will break him and we will show that we can, along with the American people, begin to push those freedom solutions that work in every area of our society."[7] The health care reform debate stretched coalition building and vote whipping in both chambers to the limit. Votes were incredibly tight, and the range of policy options that could garner sufficient support in both chambers was extraordinarily narrow. The House Energy and Commerce Committee played a critical role in advancing the reform effort and crafting a strategic template to carry a winning coalition.

## Wednesday, May 13, 2009

The bare bones of the health blueprint were presented to the committee's Democrats in a midmorning briefing that went for more than two hours. As soon as the discussion opened, the enormity and complexity of the system and what needs to be done to expand it and reform it were immediately evident, from the relatively mundane to the profound. Where do forty-seven million uninsured Americans go to get their new health insurance? Where's the physical infrastructure in each state to handle that? This would not be a one-sided affair but would test both ends of the caucus. A push in any direction can simultaneously add and lose support. It will be a game of inches, every one of them hard-earned. And then there is the elephant in the room: the public option. The blueprint clearly provides for a government health insurance program that people can take advantage of. This idea is very troubling to moderate and conservative Democrats, who believe the arena will be tilted toward the government solution and against the private health insurance industry. Progressives believe the government health insurance option will provide discipline on the private sector to make sure that quality care is provided, costs are reined in, and access assured. To which the doubters reply: Who can compete against the federal government? This will be one of the defining debates on the issue and will tend to obscure the vicious infighting between providers, hospitals, pharmaceutical companies, aged-care services, specialists, and device makers over the rules that will govern what they can do, how much they will be paid, and the standards they have to meet. Any one of these, just by itself, could be big enough to rip a deal to shreds, and we will have to find a way to balance each and every one against the others.

Henry, along with the Speaker and the other two chairs of the committees with jurisdiction had just come from a meeting with the president at the White House. The time is now, Obama said; this historic policy must get done this year: "The stars are aligned." They certainly are in the sky, and everyone is trying to discern the constellation and how to navigate by it.

### Tuesday, June 23

Today begins four days of intensive hearings on health care and the new initiatives to cover all Americans with health insurance. There is a staff briefing this afternoon, and a sleeping issue suddenly rears its head: Will abortion services be permitted, encouraged, or banned by the panels of experts that the legislation says will determine the services insurance companies are to provide? Abortion services are classified under outpatient care, and the bill will require all major insurers to cover that generic type of care. Staff for pro-life members are now very alert on this, and when we get to committee, there will undoubtedly be amendments to ban abortion services under the insurance policies. Abortion has been a lightning rod in American politics since long before the Supreme Court's pivotal 1973 decision in *Roe v. Wade*. It's an issue that has resisted the normal rhythm and reason characteristic of most coalition building and promises to further complicate the extraordinary task at hand.

### Wednesday, June 24

Kathleen Sebelius, secretary of health, came before the committee this morning in its hearings on health reform legislation—our agenda item for July. She is very impressive: slight but forceful and very measured and articulate. Henry opened the hearing with a sense of history and mission:

> We continue today a journey that began over 100 years ago to provide health insurance coverage for all Americans.
>
> Some of our greatest Presidents of the 20th Century—Teddy Roosevelt, Franklin Roosevelt, and Harry Truman—were advocates for universal health insurance.
>
> President Clinton fought courageously for his Administration's proposal.
>
> Those initiatives may have failed, but the hope that inspired them was never defeated. The time has finally come to redeem that hope, and to deliver true health reform.

With President Obama in the White House, we now have the best opportunity ever to enact health reform. I am determined that we not let this opportunity slip from our grasp.

The partisanship is back big-time on the Republican side. A brown bag lunch to discuss health legislation was scheduled last Friday for all the members from both sides, but the press of energy and health developments forced it to be canceled. An hour after the lunch was supposed to take place, Henry and the other chairs unveiled their draft health bill. This went down very poorly on the Republican side, to say the least. Joe Barton (R-TX) said that he was very disappointed and that it was like a man had asked a woman for a date and she accepted, only to have the date turned down because the guy was getting married. "There, there," Henry said as he patted Barton's shoulder. It does not matter that what was unveiled was a draft; the final bill is yet to come. The Republicans feel dissed, and it will be even harder to work with them.

### Wednesday, July 8

Today we had a morning meeting with a key Republican on the committee who knows the medical system very well and who has a lot of constructive suggestions on health care reform. Henry says that he wants to put the Republican's best ideas in the bill, to which he replies, "I have had more meetings on my ideas as of this morning with Democrats than I have had with my Republicans"—which means he is not sure how much his side will want to work with his suggestions to forge consensus on the legislation. Indeed, it is still not clear that even if we move to adjust the public health insurance plan option that is to be included, the Republicans interested in working with us can vault party leaders' theological objections to this entire package and vote with us. We talk about this after the meeting breaks, and we will keep talking. Our staff knows they should go as far as they can to tweak the bill without doing violence to where we must be. We will see: it could prove pivotal.

This evening, Henry convenes all the committee's Democrats to discuss the next steps, which will be a full markup next week. "Everybody has to have access to health insurance," Henry said. "We have to help people pay for their insurance. And we have to hold down costs through the system." But as the legislation gets closer, more and more doubts and tensions set in, particularly on the issue of access to doctors, which involves reimbursement rates and is tied to real reform of the cost drivers through the system. Without Republican support, any unresolved deep divisions among the Democrats will mean the bill will fail in committee—an almost unthinkable prospect that is palpable tonight as we listen to members complaining about this or that shortcoming in the draft. "We have to keep talking to each other and work those things out because we won't have help from the Republicans on this bill," Henry said. The next several days are one-on-one meetings with the members to find the keys to their locks and seal the deals to make the Democratic votes stick. But no one on the committee—or in the House as a whole, for that matter—knows the issues better than Henry; he has been immersed in them for four decades. He speaks with authority and has a proven track record of immense legislative success, so he can induce a strong sense of trust that what he writes will deliver the goods. Yet the path is treacherous, and it looks darker at the precipice. The trick is for it not to go totally black.

## Tuesday, July 14

The week in Washington really begins on Sunday, with the emblematic network talk shows, which marry the key issues with the big kahuna players and a mob of elite journalists for a stew of hot topics. It is how Washington sends tom-tom messages to itself and how the city figures out what is happening, why, and what's next. At the end of Sunday morning, a distilled conventional wisdom emerges, and last Sunday it was that health care was in big trouble—too fast, too ambitious, too controversial, too expensive, and too unpopular. It will cost about $1 trillion over ten years (not much when you consider health care costs to the country of $2.5 trillion a year). Under the current budget rules, everything has to be paid for—it will require not only cost cuts but also revenues. Charlie Rangel (D-NY), chair of the Ways and Means Committee, announced those revenues last Friday: a tax surcharge on the superrich. Tax increases have been wildly unpopular since Ronald Reagan's revolution, but this is Barack Obama's revolution, and he broke the Reagan paradigm. Obama campaigned on keeping taxes where they were for Americans making less than $250,000 per year—which is 99 percent of the people. And so what we have in this proposal to pay for Obama's hallmark legacy reform—health care insurance for all Americans—is an assault on Reagan's legacy tax policy: no new taxes. That, along with any legislation that has the temerity to mess with a system that constitutes 16 percent of US GDP, is making the Washington chattering classes very, very nervous. Their message on Sunday to Henry and Speaker Nancy Pelosi (D-CA) and especially to Obama is, *Slow down and rethink this. Let's cool it, and maybe a smaller reform is the best way forward.*

I shot an email to Phil Schiliro later that afternoon: "For this week—which I think is the most pivotal of the presidency to date, and which will determine whether he will have a successful first term—my watchword of advice simply is: We did not come here to temporize. We came here to bring fundamental change to America—and this city—and get things done. To all those wise men and women who say, 'Take your time . . . not so fast . . . no we shouldn't . . . ,' the response has to be, 'Yes, we can.' Let's forge consensus and bring this baby home safe and sound." Clearly, I was preaching to the choir, because this has all kicked in—but not before some very hard yards are being ground out in Henry's office as he continues to meet with all manner of Democrats with concerns, objections, and doubts. The Blue Dog conservative Democrats want all the cost cuts, very little new spending, and huge improvements in service and quality. It's clear to Henry and all of us on the staff that health care reform is harder—much harder—to put together than energy. Every member of Congress is a health policy expert—they all have immense involvement and familiarity with the health care system through the benefits they get as members of Congress, and their personal experience guides their views of proposed reforms. Moreover, every day they deal with constituents on Medicare and Medicaid, and they know the ins and outs of those programs. And as a result, they each have to be worked. So pressures from the moderates ultimately force cuts to be made, sometimes driving the staff to near tears as precious initiatives for Medicaid, which serves the poorest, are cut back, compromised, or shelved. Once they are gone, there is no way they will be put back. It is extremely hard going.

But the overarching goals and objectives remain intact, and the president went on the offensive on his first full day back from Russia, Italy, and Ghana. He's not spooked. "We are going to get this done," he said in the Rose Garden to all the cable networks in the summer sunshine. "Inaction is not an option. And for those naysayers and cynics who think this is not going to happen, don't bet against us. We are going to make this happen because the American people desperately need it."

After those words, the president called senators and House members into the Oval Office and pressed them hard. After working through the night to put language together, the bill was duly introduced by the Speaker and the three chairs and their allies, with a huge press conference in the gilded Rayburn Room off the House chamber in the Capitol. "This is landmark legislation and a defining moment for the country," Henry said, and the leadership pledged to get this bill passed the House before August— intact and on track. Just a few minutes later, the White House echo chamber kicked in: "For decades, Washington failed to act as health care costs continued to rise, crushing businesses and families and placing an unsustainable burden on governments. But today, key committees in the House of Representatives have engaged in unprecedented cooperation to produce a health care reform proposal that will lower costs, provide better care for patients, and ensure treatment of consumers by the insurance industry," Obama said.

This is it. The success of Obama's first term depends on this work, because if we fail here, he will have no political capital to get energy through, and with the collapse of two top domestic policy priorities, Democrats in Congress will grow rebellious and look weak—we will all suffer in November 2010, leaving the president effectively checkmated on major issues at home. The seeds are there, in terms of frustration and doubt about whether the economy will recover, whether the president's package of stimulus programs will indeed work. Tonight, he was in St. Louis throwing out the first ball at Major League Baseball's All-Star Game, and there were boos in the crowd—a first for Obama at a major public event. He heard them, and so did the press.

## Wednesday, July 15

It was a good day in the Senate but a turbulent day in the House. Sen. Kennedy's Labor Committee passed the health reform bill on a 13–10 party-line vote, with Kennedy still absent being treated for brain cancer. In the House committee, a very lengthy briefing for the staff was capped by a plea from one of our most senior professionals: he choked up as he said, "I have been with these issues for twenty years, and there are people being trashed today by a system that denies them health insurance. . . . This bill solves this problem. . . . It is not the best bill . . . but it is our chance to make these fundamental changes." It was a stirring and memorable moment.

The Congressional Budget Office (CBO) discussed the impact on the budget and the health sector economy for more than two hours this afternoon in a closed session that afforded an opportunity to preview Republican attacks that will be coming tomorrow when the formal markup begins: *This bill is a job killer, it does not control costs, it will cut GDP, employers will find it cheaper to dump their coverage and throw millions onto the public system, regional and rural America is disserved, this strangles small business.* And then there are the Blue Dogs, who are really focused on the rural reimbursement issue over how doctors are paid and what the bill will do. They still have grave reservations about the public insurance option, and we are moving way too fast. This evening, Henry and I discussed the votes in committee. We can only lose six Democrats and still win: we count at least four *Nos* and two others likely *Nos*. It's too tight, too close. Obama has got to lean on these guys harder. But we're still early; the vote is a week away. There is an old aphorism in this city: *A week is a lifetime in politics*. We'll die a few times on this before we live.

## Thursday, July 16

The first day of committee markup was devoted simply to opening statements by the members, and all but one of the fifty-nine members of the committee spoke. It's like watching paint dry, but for those with patience, what these politicians say is as revealing as the sun, and it builds the political calculus you need to get legislation passed. What was clear is that we are behind. Today, nine Democrats made strong statements in opposition to the bill, six of them en bloc—the Blue Dogs declaiming in identically worded statements—and three others highly sympathetic to the Dogs. They wanted to send a clear message with a blunt instrument, and they did. Henry must reach a deal with them if he is to win. And it is larger than the committee: if we don't solve it here, we would face it on the floor. We are under no illusions: we won't have any Republican votes for this bill because of the tax increases to pay for health reform.

There is a pernicious back current, a riptide suddenly evident. Late today, in setting the ground rules for debate and markup, Barton, the senior Republican, asked if the markup might run through the end of next week "if bipartisanship broke out and we needed to accommodate that." Most people in the room listening thought that Barton was expressing a hope that he and Henry might work something out in the interests of the country on such a momentous bill. But on further reflection, it is clear that Barton is no fool and that he can count, too. He knows we don't have the votes, and maybe he wants to strike a deal with the Blue Dogs and decapitate the chair and roll the committee with a landmark Republican–Blue Dog health reform bill. So we discuss this internally and make plans to counter it. The logic is the same: strike a deal with the moderates and win the day. Notwithstanding all this, we still face an ugly vote on an amendment prohibiting insurance plans under the bill from covering abortions—we can't avoid it, and we may lose that vote, too. Then, this afternoon the CBO, which officially scores all legislation and makes pronouncements about its effects on the budget, said in testimony before the Senate that our bill did nothing to curb long-term health care costs and was therefore, in general, a fiscal disaster (see also Brown 2009, 15). This hands more red meat to our opponents. We have a long way to go, and there are countless improvised explosive devices (IEDs) all around us.

## Friday, July 17

The IED went off today. Committee markup was proceeding fitfully when the Republicans offered an amendment requiring the secretary of health and human services to conduct a study of all the new programs established in the health reform bill and eliminate any duplication she found. It sounds innocuous but nothing on the Hill is as simple as that. It is a poison pill. By permitting the secretary to terminate programs established by the Congress, she would be unilaterally overriding the will of the legislative branch since Congress would have enacted those programs. The amendment was presented as a good-government budget-reduction measure, and in the wake of the firestorm that resulted when the CBO director said yesterday that we were way off track in controlling health care costs, this was more red meat for the Blue Dogs. As the vote began, I shook my head at Henry— one of my jobs was to help keep track of each vote as it was under way to determine if we were going to win or lose, and we were going to lose. He persuaded one Blue Dog to leave the room and tried but failed to get another to switch his vote. We lost 29–27, and the Republicans cheered the result; we were bloodied (see also O'Connor 2009a). My fears of yesterday had come to pass. The only silver lining is that it was early yet and not on the cusp of completion, when an unholy Blue Dog–Republican alliance could truly tank the bill. So this afternoon, Henry convened a meeting with the Blue Dogs; Peter Orszag, the president's budget director; and the head of the CBO to talk more cost controls. At the end of the meeting, Henry said he could see the outlines of the deal that would need to be done. The substantive folks are to work over the weekend and come up with the fixes.

Late this afternoon the president spoke to the TV cameras. His message was essentially mine to Phil Schiliro on Sunday: this is not a time to hesitate or to delay; this is a time to finish the race and get the job done. This won't be pretty; it's much harder than anticipated, and there's treachery. Because the energy and climate vote was so tough and close, and after casting that vote, Democratic members went home for the July 4 holiday to get beaten up by Republican ads and the grassroots. Naturally, they are asking, *Why the hell do we have to cast another tough vote before the August recess, without the Senate doing the same, just like the global warming bill, and face the music all over again?* It's a good question, but the answer is, *Change has to come, and it won't come easily and will take courage. This is the time to step up; if you take this president down with health care reform—the heart and soul of the Obama presidency—you will take yourself down too. So we are going to do this.* And that's the way it is, as Walter Cronkite, the legendary CBS anchor and in his time the most trusted man in America, would have said. Cronkite died earlier tonight.

## Tuesday, July 21

Markup ended at 12:30 am after an eight-hour session in which we lost nothing and got our committee Democrats working together again. This was credited to two developments: a meeting with Henry and the Blue Dogs to follow up on Friday's session and then a premarkup session with all the committee Democrats to review the bidding. The session with the Blue Dogs was difficult, hampered by their lack of unity on substantive proposals that would translate their rhetoric into reality—they all want cost controls and cuts but don't have hard proposals to get there. At the same time, the meeting showed that they do want a health bill and want to work it out with Henry and the leadership. This was augmented by the session just before going into the full committee where upcoming Republican amendments were canvassed, including several that could cause us real trouble. But by briefing the entire team, all the members were enlisted in the tactical plays ahead, and during the markup they all voted, with an exception here or there, with the chair and against mischievous Republican proposals. By the time we broke past midnight, the disunity had been buried, and the Republicans had scored no victories.

President Obama put the pressure on again, for the third time in four days, with remarks at the Children's National Medical Center here in Washington:

> Just the other day, one Republican Senator said, "If we're able to stop Obama on this, it will be his Waterloo. It will break him." Think about that. This isn't about me. This isn't about politics. This is about a health care system that is breaking America's families, breaking America's businesses, and breaking America's economy. And we can't afford the politics of delay and defeat when it comes to health care. Not this time. Not now.

This morning, we had a preliminary meeting between Henry and the Blue Dogs in preparation for the White House session. It is clear that more costs of this bill have to be reined in. The good news is that the president's staff was able to affirm that much had been done in the bill to bend the cost curve in future health spending to more sustainable outcomes. Clearly though, for political as well as substantive reasons, with the deficit over a trillion dollars and a bump in health costs coming from insuring more than thirty-five million new people, other things have to be done. The president said he wanted more economies, and Henry responded that if this is what the president wants and if this is what we need to get a bill, he would go along with such Draconian savings. Frank Pallone (D-NJ), the chair of the health subcommittee, expressed his opposition—something that many find hard to do directly to any president. But the consensus was clear to move on this even though the Blue Dogs still did not commit despite the new savings provisions added in the bill. That is a discussion for tomorrow, back on the Hill, without the president, when Henry will try to corral this thing into a workable agreement that we can take to the committee and complete action. Then it will serve as a template for the full House floor.

With each marker of progress, opposition continues to build. The Republican Party has launched a ferocious advertising assault on the Obama health plan as a "risky experiment" with our health care. More House Democrats are asking why they have to vote on new taxes—and if the House votes first, members in vulnerable seats see the attack ads coming. The campaign waged on the airwaves is against him, his plan, his presidency (see also Bogardus 2009). There's a sense tonight that things are slipping. I think we can clear the committee in the coming days. But the hope of passing the House floor before August break is in doubt.

## Thursday, July 23

The last two days have been filled with frustration. Henry has been locked in negotiations with the Blue Dogs, and it appears that whatever he is signaling he can give them to satisfy their demands—principally over cost controls—they do not want to take *Yes* for an answer and lock in the deal. They have a sufficient number of votes with Republicans to block passage in the committee, and for the moment they are holding us, the Speaker, and the president hostage. But people are too nice to say that right now. The Blue Dogs are the ultimate custodians of the mantle of the Reagan Democrats—the conservative wing of the party that enabled Ronald Reagan to prevail with Democratic Congresses in the 1980s. Mainstream

Democrats can't pull the reverse today with the liberal wing of the Republican Party because that wing no longer exists.

So health care reform is threatened not by the Republicans but by a lack of unity within the Democratic Party. The Blue Dogs are scared and fall back on the one thing politicians know best: survival. They think they can survive in their center-right districts with Republicans in control of Congress and the White House. It is a cynical game because the things they rail against, like rocketing health care costs and a broken system, will not get fixed if they defeat reform with their own cost controls in it. If we fail on this initiative now, we might as well hang it up, because any other victories will be smaller and the legacy will be diminished. And it will all be because Democrats were not ready for what the election truly wrought. And it is why the voters will punish Democrats if we do not deliver because of cynical political calculations in Washington.

In end-game negotiations, tactics are everything. I reached the conclusion that it is better if we do not have the bill pass the House next week, as originally intended. It is controversial and has tax elements that are difficult. So why have it sitting out there for a month, inviting vicious attacks on our members who voted for the energy bill? Why offer up our good members to take the hit? The prevailing thinking is, *Why not get momentum from victory in the House committee and have the bill ready for the floor when we return in September, allowing our members to play offense instead of defense in August?* I suggested that there were two ways to get the Blue Dogs unstuck: meetings with the Speaker and a meeting with the president in which he locks everybody in the Roosevelt Room and nobody comes out until there's a deal. The Speaker did meet with them this afternoon, offering to incorporate their top three issues centering on costs into the bill in exchange for a pledge to vote for the bill and against all Republican amendments. They said *No*. And so this means one of two things: either they do not want a bill at all, or they are scared and want to know what the Senate bill will look like before they have to vote in the House. They want to know what their full exposure is before they decide whether to vote for it.

### Friday, July 24

Everything fell apart this morning, and several Blue Dogs went to the media, blaming Henry for not negotiating in good faith, suggesting that the chair had lied to them and that he had taken key issues off the table. The press reports were all about the intraparty carnage from a meeting of Democrats late yesterday where members of the Congressional Black

Caucus accused the "nondiverse" Blue Dogs of blocking action on the most important issue pending. So this was spiraling beyond issues to the racial context, too, and in the Democratic caucus, with an African American president, this was serious business. Henry knew this could unravel everything in a short time if it hadn't already done so. He called a meeting of all the committee's Democrats for midafternoon. We needed everyone at the table: the deal, if it was to be done, was bigger than any subset of the committee. Henry said this was the most important caucus he could recall ever convening, and not only issues but also the future of the committee were at stake. He took them to the cliff so they could see the abyss. He said that if we don't deal with this legislation, we will be bypassed. We would be seen as incompetent and unable to manage the president's No. 1 domestic priority, and the chaos would hand Republicans the reins—with the blessing of some Democrats—and allow them to divide the committee at will. There would be no recovery. To the members' credit, the mood did not get angry: there was no finger-pointing but rather an earnest discussion of the two key issues, which are how to keep the public option (the government program) in the bill and how to control Medicare costs. There are others, but they are not as big. The obvious deal is to make extensive cuts on costs (which the Blue Dogs want) in exchange for the public option (which the liberals and Obama want). Staff were kicked out of the room. By the end of the afternoon, all issues were back on the table, and members pledged to have staff work through the weekend and reconvene Monday morning. It was now clear that we had to move—now. If our committee does not approve the bill by the end of next week (August recess), the Republicans will have had a major tactical victory, and they can then use the recess to turn it into a strategic victory (see also Soraghan and Allen 2009). With that, the Obama dream would die, just six months after taking office. It comes down to next week, life or death.

## Monday, July 27

Henry's morning meeting with Blue Dogs centered around a meaty proposal for them that responded to nine of their ten concerns, with another issue held over for discussion. After over three hours of hard discussions, the chair of the Blue Dogs' health care task force, Mike Ross (D-AR), said that their side wanted to sleep on it and come back the next morning. Ross is the Blue Dogs' alpha dog, spearheading the conservatives' battle against the leadership's health plan. It was clear that they are afraid to agree with us without knowing what the Senate is going to do. If the Senate plan has greater savings and fewer taxes, the House Blue Dogs will feel exposed; they want to know what the final hand looks like before they place their bet. After tonight's talks, Henry said, "I've given them a very generous offer; they should take it. If they come back and want more, I'll probably give it to them." We're willing to do almost anything to get this done, send health reform on its way—to give Obama a big win that keeps the political momentum going and shows members there are rewards for supporting the Obama change agenda. There was a common thread to this argument—the perception that the party's reputation and the president's were lashed together. But then a dark thought crept in as we talked this through: the reform will take too long (it doesn't begin until 2013), and voters will wonder where the hell it is. Health care costs will continue to rise (before leveling off), and Republicans will take Democrats to the electoral woodshed for "socializing" health care and raising taxes. Even if tomorrow goes well, we still don't know whether by pushing in on the balloon from the Blue Dog side, we lose votes from the liberals. The votes are so tight. The calculation depends on everyone seeing things as clearly and calculating as Henry and the Speaker do.

## Wednesday, July 29

The past two days were extraordinarily rocky. Yesterday's discussion with the Blue Dogs quickly morphed into an all-day session with the Speaker; the president's chief of staff, Rahm Emanuel; majority leader Steny Hoyer (D-MD); the subcommittee chair, Frank Pallone; and the seven Dogs. The Dogs' ten points became twelve: they bobbed and backtracked, ultimately refusing to commit. Speaker Pelosi went hoarse with all the discussions, and the meeting broke with no resolution. We offer them something; they take it and ask for more. They know they own the controlling votes. Finally at about noon today, a deal was done. We would accept several of their provisions and they would give us four votes—enough to defeat all Republican amendments and approve the bill in committee. It was very pragmatic, as all hard-nosed political deals are. It was not pretty, though it did have a certain raw political elegance. We advanced the process so the president could claim victory, and the Dogs' made a real difference in lowering the bill's costs.

Henry made two big concessions to the Blue Dogs to get their support for reporting the bill. First, the government-sponsored public insurance option was tempered. The public option was designed to provide competitive tension with the private sector, but conservatives felt it would drive private insurers out of the market, creating a government monopoly. Second, the deal cut one hundred billion dollars in costs, getting the bill under the symbolic threshold of one trillion dollars over ten years. But when word about the deal spread, the Left went into full revolt. Henry convened the caucus of all committee Democrats. It was intense. As a procedural matter, the other twenty-six Democrats who were not part of the discussions felt disenfranchised. They were in effect being presented with a take-it-or-leave-it deal, because there would be no Blue Dog votes to report the bill unless the deal held. On the substance, many felt that the public option—the single-most-radical part of the structural reforms to health insurance—had been compromised to the point where it was no longer viable. The more searing criticism was what was done to pay for the one hundred billion dollars in savings: increasing the costs borne by working-class and middle-income households: *These are the people who sent us here. These are the people who elected Obama, and we are hurting them to help the Blue Dogs? Is this what we came here to do?* And then there was the concern that our bill can only get worse down the road when we come to a conference with the more conservative Senate. "How much more am I going to have to give to get a bill?" one member thundered.

John Dingell (D-MI), the former chair of Energy and Commerce, whose father served in Congress and who introduced a national health insurance bill every year for fifty years, said, "I am probably to the left of all of you" on these issues. "When this committee failed to pass a bill in 1994"—the failed Clinton health reform effort—"the reform failed. This committee has to act." There are other procedural opportunities to strengthen the bill again before we get to the Senate. Henry turned to the president's man, Phil Schiliro, who was at the table with the other members. Phil said that he had worked on the committee for twenty-seven years and was there in 1994: if this committee fails, it is all over. He said that every member present will have huge issues with the Senate legislation but that a bill had to pass the Senate, too, so we could get to conference and that President Obama would be involved in that conference every day, working for the best possible bill. Then, when the work is done, every member can look at the legislation and make their own judgment as to whether the reform is worth it. But, Phil said, the committee members would not get to that point of judgment unless they voted to advance this bill now. This is the best bill pending in Congress—better than the Kennedy bill in the Senate.

The logic, impeccable and compelling, brought everything together. The members resolved to find some other measures to cover the one hundred billion dollars so that the hit on working Americans will be smaller.

But there are still some unhappy lefties on our side, and they may yet decide to say *The hell with it. I'm not voting for these half measures that compromise our principles and hurt our base.* In the end, Henry brought the committee back from the precipice and delivered a good bill. "Somebody told me they thought I looked shorter after negotiations," Henry quipped to his colleagues. We'll see if we get this baby through by sundown on Friday.

## Friday, July 31

At 11:45 last night, after fourteen hours of markup, the committee recessed until 10:00 this morning. The deal with the Blue Dogs has held, with sufficient votes delivered—sometimes with no margin for error at all—to fend off Republican amendments. Our dissatisfied liberals held their fire. The other good news is that the abortion issue was skillfully navigated. The committee voted 30–28 to accept a pro-choice proposal that codifies existing law barring federal funds from being used to finance abortions but permits private funds in insurance pools to be used for those purposes. On the whole, the debate was civil and polite, but there was emotion on both sides. On ours, Lois Capps (D-CA), a very smart and determined legislator, observed that the abortion issue was introduced in much legislation as a pill to poison the well of the underlying legislative effort. Abortion opponents took umbrage at that. And a conservative from Michigan began quoting the Declaration of Independence, its self-evident truths that men are entitled to the fulfillment of "life, liberty and the pursuit of happiness"—one of the great crystallizations of human liberty ever written—and in those words, he discerned that life meant that the Framers had in mind the protection of unborn life. But we did not dwell there for long, and the outcome meant that our doomsday scenario of a successful antiabortion amendment driving liberals off the Obama health reform bill would not come to pass. Through the day, we never lost more than six votes, though on one amendment we did lose six votes, which meant it failed on a tie. We won the day.

Then we won the night. A little after 9:00 pm, after eleven hours of markup, the committee voted to report the bill to the House floor. It was a historic occasion: the first time this committee had reported a national health care reform bill to the House. The committee's action eclipsed the 1993–94 effort, when President Bill Clinton's health proposals, personally lobbied by Hillary Clinton on Capitol Hill, failed to clear any of the relevant committees. Indeed, this ignominious history with health care had informed President Obama's approach: letting the kings and queens of the

Hill craft their legislation and maintaining a ruthless pragmatism centered on the need to get something significant done—not allowing ideology to get in the way. Still, one of our own—a liberal from New York—threatened to offer an amendment to scrap our bill and replace it with a UK-style single-payer, government-run national health system. He knew he would lose badly but got a promise for a clean vote on the House floor. These are the minute calculations of politics at the coal face; this is how you advance the ball. And so now we have a template that can prevail on the House floor. The day was a seminar in Political Management 101.

Just prior to the committee vote on passage, committee Democrats broke briefly for a short caucus. It began with a spontaneous eruption of support for Henry—we were on the verge of delivering on this historic promise and commitment for the very first time. "Change is coming to America," as Obama intoned during his campaign, and we were about to deliver on it. A genuine moment; no TV cameras or journalists to record it. Henry received a standing ovation, but he immediately turned to John Dingell and thanked him for his leadership. Members erupted again. We returned to the full committee for the final vote. Henry again thanked the dean of the House, and once again members erupted, and even the Republicans stood in acknowledgment of this moment. Henry then yielded to Dingell to make the motion to report the bill to the House "with the usual instructions" and then Dingell so moved and the roll call vote began.

A little math: with fifty-nine on the committee, we needed thirty to win. There are thirty-six Democrats, seven of them Blue Dogs. The deal that was cut guaranteed four Dog votes, bringing us up to thirty-three and victory. However, we lost one antiabortion Democrat, narrowing our margin on final passage, and another Democrat from Virginia concluded he could not stomach government insurance and the cuts to Medicare, so we were down to thirty-one. The final passage tally was 31–28. We received no Republican votes, though I tried very hard with one Republican moderate who did get several amendments into the bill and who could have been a pivotal player for his party in the bargaining to come down the road. But his leadership made it clear: loyalty first, no treachery. He could not come with us. If Henry had not made the deal stick with both ends of the party—the Blue Dogs and the liberals—reform would have died in committee. Waxman's exceptional self-control makes him hard to ruffle. "He's uniformly even," said Rick Boucher (D-VA), a senior Democrat on the committee (see also O'Connor 2009a, 12). Simply put, Henry Waxman is a grand master of politics.

Saturday, August 29

We need Teddy, too, right now, but he is gone. The Lion of the Senate passed away late Tuesday night, and he will be buried next to his brothers in Arlington within the next couple of hours. Kennedy was the third-longest-serving senator and had a life of exquisite richness, tragedy, farce, massive scandal, complication, and in his last two decades great achievement. It is said that he finally became grounded with his second wife, Victoria, and his reconciliation to the fact that he would never be president and that to redeem any of the promise of his slain brothers, he needed to focus relentlessly on what he was innately and immensely good at: legislating. More than three hundred laws bear his name, and he was centrally involved in seven hundred more. He also had a special ability—perverse though it may have been—to negotiate and win the affection of some key Republicans and then cut the deals necessary to get some good laws in place. *Don't let the best be the enemy of the good*, he often intoned. And so, in the last months before his death, he worked with his proxy and best friend in the Senate, Chris Dodd (D-CT), to get a good health reform bill reported from his Senate committee (the parallel of ours) without any Republican votes. Republicans are piously mourning his passing and saying, *Oh, if only Teddy were here, we surely could negotiate the health bill*, but there is no reason in hell why they should let his death prevent them from doing the right thing by him and negotiating in good faith with the Senate Democrats to get a good bill. But that has not happened and almost surely won't. What Kennedy's death has done, however, is provide a circuit breaker on the frenzy of town hall citizen meetings and other eruptions against the health bill by conservatives—attacks that have so little basis in fact as to be laughable but for their political potency: provisions that would pull the plug on grandpa, finance abortions, or drive everything into one humungous government program. It is all lies, but the attacks have taken a toll. Kennedy's death, however, allows the president and the leadership to reset the debate at summer's end. The issue was unremarked in all the tributes and eulogies so as not to politicize the funeral, which was a wise move in tactical communications. Henry was at the funeral today, along with the Speaker and dozens of House and Senate members—many flew on a military plane together. And you just have to believe that after experiencing the lovely tributes, reflecting on his life and history, and knowing that this issue of health care for all Americans was the cause of his life, they will all come back to Washington freshly determined to get this done, to make Kennedy's dream a reality, and above all not to fail. Not now. God bless you, Teddy.

## Monday, September 7

To combat the Tea Party eruptions against health care reform at town hall meetings across the county, Obama has decided to reset the playing field with a speech to a joint session of Congress. Only a president can command a stage like that, and we need a stronger stage.

A *New York Times* headlines today: "Obama Faces a Critical Moment for His Presidency" and "The President's Team Fights New Setbacks." We will see what the headlines are a week from now, after the speech to the joint session of Congress on Wednesday. There is no doubt in my mind that the hard-core Republican opposition simply wants to stop Obama cold and end his presidency now. They see their opportunity to do it with health care. And they are stringing together all facets of the Obama program into a neatly packaged conservative narrative about socialism/big government spending/out-of-control deficits around which mainstream public opinion can be crystallized.

## Wednesday, September 9

A speech of power and eloquence and in the end real greatness. Obama made the case to the joint session of Congress and the American people with clear logic, simple explanations, real assurance, and sober sincerity. To Americans who thought this was all about the uninsured, they now know it is all about them—if they have insurance today, they can keep it tomorrow, unchanged. If they lose their jobs, they can get health insurance. If they get sick, the insurance companies cannot cancel them out. If they carry an illness, they cannot be denied coverage. *Security* and *stability* are the watchwords. Obama said he would take some Republican ideas and put them in the plan—a program from Sen. John McCain (R-AZ), whom Obama defeated last year, for those without insurance today who are facing catastrophic costs and former President George H. W. Bush's ideas for ways to prune the excesses of a malpractice system that is out of control, which can help bring down costs. Obama made it clear that he wanted the public option, and he steeled the party's left wing. But he couched this goal in almost minimalist terms to help assuage moderates and conservatives. (That needle will need more threading in the days ahead.) But the awful poison in the chamber tonight was the raw partisanship from the Republicans. To be sure, the president was not the least bit shy in explicitly pointing out the Republican lies against his plan—he showed his fangs and called them lies. This caused great unease in the ranks of the minority, and they squirmed in their seats and looked at the podium with venom. And when Obama said that nothing in his plan would provide coverage to illegal aliens, a Republican backbencher shouted out, "You lie!"—a very bad moment. For too many on their side, this fight is ultimately about whether they can take down the president, and he called them on it:

> This is the plan I'm proposing. It's a plan that incorporates ideas from many of the people in this room tonight—Democrats and Republicans. And I will continue to seek common ground in the weeks ahead. If you come to me with a serious set of proposals, I will be there to listen. My door is always open.
>
> But know this: I will not waste time with those who have made the calculation that it's better politics to kill this plan than improve it. I will not stand by while the special interests use the same old tactics to keep things exactly the way they are. If you misrepresent what's in the plan, we will call you out. And I will not accept the status quo as a solution. Not this time. Not now.

And then what was a very good speech veered into greatness. You knew it was coming because Victoria Reggie Kennedy, widow of Teddy, buried just ten days ago at Arlington next to Jack and Bobby, was in the gallery next to Michelle Obama. The president read from a letter Kennedy had sent to be opened only after his death. Health reform was the cause of his life:

> "What we face," Kennedy wrote, "is above all a moral issue; at stake are not just the details of policy, but fundamental principles of social justice and the character of our country."
>
> I've thought about that phrase quite a bit in recent days—the character of our country. . . .
>
> You see, our predecessors understood that government could not, and should not, solve every problem. They understood that there are instances when the gains in security from government action are not worth the added constraints on our freedom. But they also understood that the danger of too much government is matched by the perils of too little; that without the leavening hand of wise policy, markets can crash, monopolies can stifle competition, and the vulnerable can be exploited. And they knew that when any government measure, no matter how carefully crafted or beneficial, is subject to scorn; when any efforts to help people in need are attacked as un-American; when facts and reason are thrown overboard and only timidity passes for wisdom, and we can no longer even engage

in a civil conversation with each other over the things that truly matter—that at that point we don't merely lose our capacity to solve big challenges. We lose something essential about ourselves.

What was true then remains true today. I understand how difficult this health care debate has been. I know that many in this country are deeply skeptical that government is looking out for them. I understand that the politically safe move would be to kick the can further down the road—to defer reform one more year, or one more election, or one more term.

But that's not what the moment calls for. That's not what we came here to do. We did not come to fear the future. We came here to shape it. I still believe we can act even when it's hard. I still believe we can replace acrimony with civility, and gridlock with progress. I still believe we can do great things, and that here and now we will meet history's test.

Because that is who we are. That is our calling. That is our character. Thank you, God bless you, and may God bless the United States of America.

So this should go down as one of the more memorable addresses to a joint session by a president. But even these soaring words, as evocative of last year's campaign as any spoken since he became president, will not stanch the blood libels from the Republican leadership. We are better off tonight, but it is still a hard road. In the House, we have to carry the moderates without losing the liberals. In the Senate, the final product will be more centrist still, and the party will still have to hold together. One speech does not a majority cement, but it was bold and likely decisive for the cause. We lost August, but we are winning September.

### Friday, October 9

There are still key issues to be resolved in front of the whole House, such as Medicare reimbursement rates for providers and their budget impact. The Speaker is counting the votes. She wants provisions in the bill to get early benefits for voters, immediate deliverables.

### Saturday, October 17

A never-ending rush of lobbyists advocating for health-related interests of all stripes march in and out of the office. *Please stop cuts to oncologists. Please ensure home health care services are not penalized. Please promote our waste, fraud, and abuse detection software that will save the government billions. Can you tweak this or that provision on nursing homes?* On one level, many of the health issues are arcane and technical—a favorite expression is *in the weeds.* Even well-intentioned generalists grapple with the arcana.

### Thursday, October 22

Beyond the policy wonkiness of health care, there is another much more human and immediate face of health reform policy. There are two hearings today on the crisis in the health insurance industry and what it is not delivering to people. We wanted to have these hearings to shed light on the real issues behind health care reform and make the stakes understandable to the American people. Three witnesses tell their stories about having insurance and then getting sick. One had a child facing a liver transplant. All of them discovered that their policies were completely inadequate because benefits were capped or their policies were canceled. Bankruptcy or near bankruptcy is the common theme. Here are regular folk with good jobs and homes who play by the rules—and they lose. Their stories are heartbreaking. The point of the hearings was to help build further support in advance of the vote on the House floor.

In the afternoon, I joined Henry for a meeting with advocates for more Alzheimer's funding. Who could be against that? Except they are asking for two billion dollars and for Congress to tell the National Institutes of Health (NIH) how to spend the money. To bolster the case, they showed a huge cost curve from Alzheimer's that spirals to infinity. If we can find a cure through NIH, we can save the country billions. It is a tougher disease at this stage in its evolution than any other on the planet. After all, as they pointed out, there are cancer and heart attack survivors, but there are no Alzheimer's survivors. But Henry made no commitment to them—he dislikes the idea of directing an expert agency like NIH as to what to do in research, for what disease, and how fast. The meeting ended amicably but inconclusively.

### Friday, October 23

The Health reform bill is almost there, but it's stuck. We have no Republican votes; we need 218 Democratic votes. There are 52 Blue Dog conservatives. We can lose 39 and still carry the day. This is the relentless math. The Blue Dogs are fiscal conservatives, and they want a plan that costs less than nine hundred billion dollars over ten years. All to the good. But they also want money spent in their rural and poorer districts. All to the bad. So these fiscal conservatives, in assessing the options for a public health insurance plan, do not like proposals that pay doctors the Medicare reimbursement rates. In their areas, they argue, those prices are too low, doctors won't sign up, and health care will be denied. So these fiscal conservatives want higher, negotiated—not Medicare-fixed—payment rates for the doctors. But that means more money, putting pressure on the nine-hundred-billion-dollar cost threshold. So to get those savings, maybe we should put poorer Americans on Medicaid—the health insurance program for the poorest—which is cheaper than subsidizing their access to regular health insurance. So a huge money-politics balancing game is going on. The downside for the Left, which is a majority of the Democratic caucus, is that a public health insurance option tied to higher doctor fees means less coverage of the uninsured, so a key goal of protecting all Americans is at risk. This is a classic case of pushing one side of a balloon and the other side pops out. That's one issue frustrating completion of a House bill. The other is abortion. There may be twenty or thirty Democratic votes— some are Blue Dogs but many are not—who cannot abide by a government health insurance plan that covers abortion services. We finessed this in our committee, where the provision strictly segregates public money from private premium payments: no public money can go to abortion services. But antiabortion purists see this as a fiction—they want no public insurance involvement in abortion services. The Catholic archbishops, who desperately want a bill because it means health insurance coverage for all Americans, are negotiating with us on this, and it is very hard to thread the needle. They are demanding that the health insurance provided by the government be barred from providing abortions. If they succeed, we lose liberals and their votes. The bill could go down over this. I have to believe we will find the answer, but we don't have it yet.

Late this afternoon, a telephone conference call with a religious coalition out of Los Angeles. They want affordability for health insurance for the poor. We are with them all the way, and they appreciate Henry's leadership on this. I suggest they channel their political energy to Republicans—we have no Republicans voting for health insurance reform—and that they use their clout to try to pry ten Republicans loose. It would be a sea change. Henry and I had lunch today in between meetings with the Speaker. He is serene. He's working every issue, all the time, thinking through every angle. We are close. We have to close it out.

## Tuesday, October 27

Finally, the Senate is showing some signs of life. Yesterday, the Senate majority leader, Harry Reid, a moderate populist from Nevada, had a come-to-Jesus moment and announced that the Senate bill would contain a public option—that it was the fairest and most responsible thing to do, and he was getting a lot of pressure from the ranks of his caucus, which solidly support it. He put in a twist to make it more palatable to the center; an opt-out provision by the states. So the default is a public health insurance option for those without insurance or who are changing carriers, and states that do not want it can take it off the menu. This move has given tremendous momentum in the Senate to closing on a final bill, although Reid is still three or four votes short of cutting off a filibuster. But it is movement.

## Wednesday, October 28

The end of the beginning? Late this afternoon, in a caucus of the committee Democrats, discussion turned toward health care reform and where it is at. Henry announced that the Speaker was finalizing the bill, that there would be a caucus of all Democrats tomorrow morning to have a last look and say on it, that the Speaker would announce the Democratic bill later tomorrow morning, and that it would go into the legislative schedule. This means that the historic legislation would be on the floor toward the end of next week, with debate and votes likely on the ensuing weekend. It was quietly dramatic and compelling. Henry sounded certain and confident: the course was being set. On the substance, the last major issue was precisely what kind of public insurance option to provide, and it will be a little more expensive, which means it will cover slightly fewer people, given the spending caps governing the bill, with the underflow going into the Medicaid program. This approach is decidedly centrist, and I heard a very liberal member tell Henry later that he could not vote for the bill if we went that way because it was not the most aggressive public option. And two centrist members—one from Texas, one from Florida—told Henry that if the Senate plan prevailed, with states being able to opt out of the public option, they would oppose the bill because they knew what their conservative governors and legislatures would do: deny their citizens the benefit of a public option. So they also told Henry that their votes were at risk. And so it is. But we take this one step at a time, and at the end of the day, the vote has to be on whether they want health insurance reform—even imperfect—or not, and at that point, the right thing to do simply has to prevail. Well, that plus a hell of a lot of White House pressure, which is yet to manifest itself. But it will by this time next week. And we just have to press ahead. The fact is, as we start this, we are stronger now on this bill than we were at the start of the energy bill, where we were really in the hole. Indeed, a conservative member from Tennessee said during the caucus, when we were figuring out how long this bill would be on the floor (I think two days), that there has already been extensive debate on this, that it had been going on for months. So it is not like cramming a fifteen-hundred-page bill no one has seen down the throat of the House next week. It should be a very strong launch, a very proud moment for Speaker Pelosi, and the start of some "Big Mo" to carry the House.

## Thursday, October 29

I woke from sleep before 4:00 am and did not get back to it, for the same reason that Rep. Doris Matsui (D-CA) told me this afternoon, during a committee markup on the consumer banking reform bill: "I got up this morning so excited—we are going to pass the health reform bill!" And I felt the same way. Last night, the Speaker said it was on, and at 10:30 this morning, she convened a rally and press conference on the West Front of the Capitol. Norah Mail, Henry's personal assistant, and I watched the tableau from a balcony above the rally, facing the Mall, looking toward the Washington Monument and the Lincoln Memorial beyond it, with the trees lining the Mall burnt yellow in the autumn. The Speaker had assembled much of the congressional leadership and a good cross-section of the caucus, and the speeches from the leaders were interwoven with stories from real people facing real health insurance concerns. (The woman who cuts my hair emailed me this afternoon that she had found a swollen lymph node in her armpit, but when she went to get a scan and biopsy, the hospital would not accept her insurance carrier—one of the thousands of stories of quiet atrocity committed every day under the current system.)

Across from the rally was a pocket of protesters, carrying pictures of aborted fetuses (to protest health insurance that covers abortion if a woman requires it) and generic protest signs that read *Kill the Bill*. And that's fine: if legislative nihilism is the message of the opposition, we will win. From the rally we went to a staff briefing in committee, and the key take-away was something Henry and I had discussed in August and that was translated into the bill: some key benefits have been front-loaded and will be delivered beginning in 2010, before the midterm elections a year from now. Seniors, for example, will save five hundred dollars on prescription drugs, and brand-name drugs will be 50 percent cheaper. Any lifetime cap insurance companies impose on health care costs will be abolished. There are a dozen other such provisions designed to show real gains before the full reforms take effect in 2013 and 2014. All smart politics and policy.

The schedule as it stands today is for the legislation to be posted online for seventy-two hours and for a further package of amendments from our side to be posted for seventy-two hours, and then debate and votes on the bill—likely next Friday or Saturday. It should be an amazing week of build-up to the floor debate and vote, and although the votes are not all in hand today and the abortion issue continues to fester unresolved, the clear sense is that this is inevitable and that this historic opportunity will not—cannot—be squandered. And that is the other point: that this is history, that something special is occurring, and that we are here to see it through.

All of this happened on the day of an economic report of growth in the third quarter of 3.5 percent, the first growth in over a year and likely the official end of the Great Recession. The growth number was higher than anticipated: the Dow took off, close again to ten thousand. It is clear that the recovery is jagged and spotty, but perhaps this statistic will help jump-start further confidence, which will free up investments and spur job growth. That's the hope.

### Tuesday, November 3

The wait for the votes to be sealed on health reform among the Democratic caucus is rather agonizing. There is no final process of resolution and reconciliation. There is no currency to deal like we had on energy. (We got one Florida Democrat with a multimillion-dollar hurricane research center for his storm-ravaged state; we gave carbon allowances to utilities and industries that would be hit by imports; we had things to play with.) The issue is abortion, and while all these Democrats want the health reform bill, the forty or so who are stuck on abortion don't seem to let that desire for overarching policy progress to overcome the emotions governing abortion. So it drags on for another day, with the legislative clock becoming elongated, and what looked like votes on the floor Friday or Saturday I fear now will go to next Monday or Tuesday. In the Senate, it is worse. We are just working from a simple majority, but over there, a supermajority of sixty votes is required to stop the Republican filibusters. With not a single Republican member favoring health care reform over the status quo, the math is simple: all the votes must come from the Democratic Party. That means every Democratic senator has to support the bill, not just the eight out of ten that we need in the House. But which of the Democratic holdouts can we get? That's the puzzle the House leadership must figure out. And in the Senate, the issue is not abortion but the public option—and whether to have it, the overall cost, and the taxes to pay for the program. So we are at about 205–210 votes (and we need 218) and they are at about 57. So close but so far, as they say. So we will go into another day of uncertainty.

It is now evening on the Tuesday night a year ago, when Barack Obama won the presidency. Quite amazing. I was interviewed twice for Australian television, yesterday and today. I made three essential points. (1) Obama has had a good year, but there is much more to be done. (2) Progress has been hampered by the overhang of the economy, the viciously persistent unemployment, and the choppiness of the recovery, which are inhibiting people's confidence in the future and exaggerating their fear of change since they are reeling from two years of horrific economic circumstances. And (3) the jury is still out on foreign policy, especially the two wars we are fighting. All of which is to say that Obama is playing a long game, just as he did in the campaign. If the recovery program sticks, health care is done, energy is restructured, Afghanistan is executed smarter, we pull our combat troops from Iraq, and some foreign policy initiatives bite—well, in a year or two or three, this will really look like something. FDR came in, had his Hundred Days, and executed immense reforms but then suffered a second recession in 1937 and faced Hitler, Japan, and war. His greatness came initially at the beginning and then toward the end of his twelve years in office—and then forever after. Kennedy was assassinated with no major domestic political achievements; Lyndon Johnson seized the martyred president's legacy and in years 5, 6, and 7 moved the Great Society before those hopes were consumed by Vietnam. Ronald Reagan changed Washington for a generation—no question about it. His first economic program took until August 1981 to get passed—I was here, on Henry's staff, working to curb its most hard-edged excesses—but Obama got a larger package through in his first thirty days. Clinton lost health care and control of Congress in his first term. So yes, let's play the long game.

It's also an off-year election night. Two key governorships, in Virginia and New Jersey, and an open House seat in New York. We have lost Virginia—no surprise there, even though it was a year ago last night that Obama held his last campaign rally in that state and carried it into the Democratic fold. The Democratic candidate for governor is a weak campaigner and distanced himself from Obama—scared of his own progressive shadow, no doubt. The Democrat in New Jersey is a weathered incumbent with whiffs of scandal in his state, but he has wrapped himself in Obama and has a chance. The House seat has been in Republican hands for more than a century, but there is an opening to snatch it. If we lose all three, the Republicans will claim a grassroots revolution is brewing. Back to Reagan and his revolution: he faced recession in his first two years, and his approval ratings fell well into the 40s, but he won a landslide second term in 1984. Politics is dynamic. There are opportunities to seize—if only we are smart enough to do so.

### Wednesday, November 4

The morning after is the anniversary of Barack Hussein Obama's election to the presidency. The night before was not pretty. New Jersey lost; the incumbent governor had been there for eight years (and was a senator for six years before that), and his regime was tired. Time for a change. Virginia has a four-year, one-term limit, so there was no incumbent, and the election is always a year after the presidential. For more than twenty years, the governorship has gone the opposite of the president's party in the White House, and it happened again. But the pundits were in overdrive from last night, saying, *Democrats in big trouble! Obama took it on the nose! Too much change we cannot believe in!* The fact is that elections in this first off year never predict what happens a year from now and that the exit polling was fine for Obama. Voters were not citing him as an issue, and his approval rating was well into the 50s. In that peculiar House race in Upstate New York, the Democrat won. The Radical Right revolted at the Republican candidate—a woman who favored abortion and gay rights, because that's where her district is. The Conservative Party put up a candidate (who does not even live in the district), and he was endorsed as the true red-meat conservative by Sarah Palin, Rush Limbaugh, and Glenn Beck. The Republican was forced to get out of the race last Saturday; she endorsed the Democrat, and he won. So if this becomes the Republican playbook—a viscerally angry party, believing the country is in near revolt against Obama, seeks even more pure conservative candidates, pushing the party ever further to the right—then the center is open to us. And this is critical because the independent voters in the center in New Jersey and Virginia voted for the Republicans. Obama won these independents last year. So what is to be done? We need economic recovery and jobs. We need to pass health care and restructure energy. We need better programs on education. And Obama needs to make really intelligent choices on Afghanistan. The bottom line: end the economic uncertainty and lead smartly at home. Which is exactly what Obama is trying to do. There is no reason why the ship sinks next year. But you would never know it to listen to the bulk of the political analysts in this town.

We are forty-eight hours from being on the floor with the health bill or stuck over abortion. It feels like it is being worked out. The Rules Committee, which the Speaker controls, dictates the flow of bills to the floor and the procedures that govern their debate. It has set a meeting for 2:00 pm on Friday to hear from members seeking amendments to the bill and permission to offer them and to propound a rule for health care reform. This means a debate later Friday and on Saturday and a vote on Saturday night.

## Sunday, November 8

At a midnight press conference in the beautiful Rayburn Room, off the House floor in the Capitol, Speaker Nancy Pelosi gathered her generals—primarily Henry, along with John Dingell, whose father first introduced national health insurance legislation in Congress in 1943—to celebrate the victory won just a few minutes earlier. The vote was 220–215. It was a remarkable day, from the soft autumn sunshine to the president's visit with the Democratic caucus a few hours before the vote to the astonishing management and counting of the votes through the day that culminated in this pivotal moment. You see, it's all about the numbers: the best ideas in the world count for nothing on the floor of the House unless you have the numbers to prevail. And the political mathematics are relentless: 258 House Democrats, 218 needed for victory; we can lose 39 and still win. The final issue to be resolved was abortion coverage by health insurance plans. Antiabortion Democrats, led by the Catholic diocese and archbishops, demanded exacting fidelity to the Hyde Amendment (named after Henry Hyde, a conservative lawmaker from Illinois who was passionately pro-life), which came into effect more than thirty years ago. The amendment prevents any federal funding for abortion except in the cases of rape or incest or to save the mother's life. So the issue with respect to access to health insurance by all Americans is whether any federal dollars would be used to subsidize any insurance policies that provided abortion services. And to the antiabortion forces, this meant that poor people who received assistance to help buy health insurance could not buy policies that provide abortion coverage. They could buy supplemental policies out of their own pockets, but nothing with federal dollars. And the public option, so coveted by liberals, could also not provide abortion coverage because it, too, would use some federal currency. Why does this matter? Because these views are held by more than forty Democrats, and if their views were not honored, they would vote against the bill. And in the course of the week, they did not yield, bend, or budge. Their position was absolute, and the archbishops mounted a furious campaign, including pamphleteering their churches last Sunday to encourage parishioners to contact congressional offices. Through the week, Henry was locked in negotiations with the antiabortion members, led by Rep. Bart Stupak (MI), and they ended up in the Speaker's office last night, with the pro-choice legislators joining in discussions with Stupak and the archbishop of Washington. And it was an impasse. So Stupak demanded—and got—a commitment for a free vote on his amendment to apply Hyde *in toto* to the health insurance legislation. And the leaders acceded to Stupak's demand they calculated that if his amendment passed the House—as it surely would, with solid Republican support—then, on final passage of the bill, enough conservative Democrats would be satisfied on abortion that they could see their way clear to vote for our liberal health reform measure. And our liberals wanted health reform so much that their defections would be held to a minimum. So Stupak would win now, and we would win later. And that is exactly what happened. The Stupak amendment passed 240–194, with 64 Democrats voting in favor and 194 against. So a third of the Democratic caucus is pro-life. And of the Republicans, it was 176 to 0, with 1 voting *present*; there is not a single pro-choice Republican in the House. This is the extent to which the conservatives in the Republican Party have X-ed out the moderates in their ranks and how fundamentalism is prevailing on their side. Henry of course fought hard to get a big Democratic vote against Stupak and was prepared, if Stupak had been defeated, for the entire bill to fail. But he knew what the real-world result would be. And that victory is sweet indeed. Why? Here is what he said on the House floor as debate opened:

> Today, we have an historic opportunity. 65 years after Franklin Roosevelt and Social Security and 35 years after Medicare, we have an opportunity—under the leadership of President Obama and Speaker Nancy Pelosi—to reform our health care system and at last provide coverage to all Americans. We know that health insurance today is failing our families and our economy. If we do nothing, the system will go bankrupt, premiums will keep skyrocketing, benefits will be slashed, what you get will cost much more, and the deficit will increase by billions of dollars. Today, Americans with health insurance know that they are just one serious illness away from debt and bankruptcy. And millions of Americans have no insurance at all.

With this legislation, we can fix these problems. . . . Today, we have a chance of a lifetime to do something great and momentous for the American people. By passing this bill, we can reform health insurance in America and provide all Americans with the security of knowing that when they get sick, care will be available and affordable.

The floor debate followed President Obama's visit to the caucus and remarks to the media during the afternoon. This bill is Obama's legacy issue for now; this is his highest domestic priority. He was elected for a reason, and he means to make a difference. Here is what he said during the day:

I just came from the Hill where I talked to the members of Congress there, and I reminded them that opportunities like this come around maybe once in a generation. Most public servants pass through their entire careers without a chance to make as important a difference in the lives of their constituents and the life of this country. This is their moment, this is our moment, to live up to the trust that the American people have placed in us—even when it's hard; especially when it's hard. This is our moment to deliver. I urge members of Congress to rise to this moment. Answer the call of history, and vote yes for health insurance reform for America.

The abortion issue is not going away, because those sixty-four Democratic votes are not going away. When the bill comes back to us from the Senate, this will have to be managed all over again. It is a raw and ugly issue. And in thinking about it, the closest parallel in emotional terms is to slavery and the Civil War. And it calls to mind a letter Thomas Jefferson wrote in 1822, near the end of his life, in which he was reflecting on an 1820 compromise the Senate had reached on slavery. New states would be admitted to the Union in pairs, one "free" and the other "slave," to maintain the political balance in the Senate. Known as the Missouri Compromise, the deal felt good at the time. Calamity was averted. But only temporarily, as Jefferson recognized:

This momentous question, like a fire bell in the night, awakened and filled me with terror. I considered it at once as the knell of the Union. It is hushed indeed for the moment, but this is a reprieve only, not a final sentence.

Abortion is a fire bell in the night. The answer is not civil war but working to elect more pro-choice members—from both parties. When the math changes, the issue will go away. It is not an issue where you can win the debate and put the other side out of business. You can only do that if the other side is consistently outvoted. And the anti-abortion forces were not outvoted in the House yesterday evening.

Through the day, Ted Kennedy's name was invoked: national health insurance was the cause of his life. His son, Patrick, serves in the House, and at the midnight press conference, he said, "My dad was a senator, but tonight his spirit was in the House." This was the same week when the president's party lost the New Jersey and Virginia governorships and when unemployment hit 10.2 percent. Obama could take all that and still hold House Democrats to pass health reform. In politics, that is called resiliency.

## Monday, November 9

Phil Barnett—our committee's staff director brought the staff together in a late afternoon gathering to celebrate passage of the bill. Karen Nelson, deputy staff director and head of the health team, received a standing ovation that lasted for well over a minute. She has served with Henry for over three decades and knows as much about health policy as anyone. The health care policy expertise reflected in the bill is largely her work. There were stories from Saturday: the leadership did not have the votes in hand when President Obama came to address the Democratic caucus, notwithstanding the very public expressions of confidence earlier that morning when the Majority Leader, Hoyer, said unequivocally, "We have the votes." Later in the afternoon, as debate was proceeding, one of Speaker Pelosi's staff was asked, "So, how many votes do we have?" The answer, "218," meant that there was no margin for error. (I have to believe the leadership had commitments from 3–5 members that they would be there if they were needed; indeed, there was no delaying before we got to the vote on passage—no stunting or obvious arm-twisting or dramatics as the vote unfolded, which indicated that the leadership was indeed confident it had the votes.) And there was a concern that if this had been held over for another twenty-four hours, the pro-choice members would have become more aware of the magnitude of the realpolitik deal that had been done to their disadvantage and would have gagged and revolted, voting against the bill on the principle of abortion rights. The measure would have been doomed, and Obama would have been handed a horrible defeat. Such are the wisps and tea leaves of victory.

Friday, December 25

Christmas Eve was a corker, the Senate in session at 7:00 am, the first time a Christmas Eve session had occurred since 1963, in the weeks after President Kennedy's assassination, and the first votes on that day since 1895. The order of business was approval of the health reform legislation, which had cleared the third and final cloture vote, 60–39, the day before. The Democratic caucus held true. Ninety-two-year-old senator Robert Byrd (D-WV) was wheeled into the Senate for the fourth time this week and shouted "Aye! This is for my friend Ted Kennedy!" His widow, Victoria, was in the gallery alongside John Dingell. If everything goes well over the next few weeks as we put the House and Senate bills together in a final package, Dingell will not need to introduce a bill for national health care reform in January 2011—the first time since 1957 that he won't have to do that. The president will clearly be hands-on in this last great push, so he will come to own its provisions just as much as the congressional leaders. This will represent a tactical pivot for the president, but I think it will seal the last deals needed to hold all the Democratic votes on the final bill. Phil Schiliro was quite elated at the end of the vote. We are determined to move with utmost alacrity—this cannot sit or slip. We have an irreplaceable chance to do good, and we will.

Thursday, December 31

A year that began with so much hope is ending quietly, with a whimper. Obama deservedly got a solid lift from Senate approval of the health reform bill, and we are positioning internally to move promptly in January, do the deals and seal the bill for final approval. It will be the most significant piece of social legislation (aside from civil rights, of course) since Social Security and the most important health bill since Medicare in 1967. And we are on the verge of delivering on it. But on Christmas Day, a terrorist almost blew up a plane en route from Amsterdam to Detroit: three hundred would have been killed. Obama was on vacation in Hawaii (and he is still there today). On the talk shows over the weekend, Janet Napolitano, secretary of homeland security, said, "The system worked"—but it clearly did not. Part of this spin was echoed by Robert Gibbs, the press secretary. As details emerged about the bomber and about how many warning signs there had been, the scale of the failure to put him on a no-fly list and of airport screening systems to detect anything awry has left people dispirited and angry—especially since countless billions of dollars have been spent over the past nine years to prevent exactly this sort of thing. Republicans have been fully exploiting this failure, echoing the Bush-Cheney mantra that Democrats are soft on national security and terrorism and that only Republicans have the wisdom and perspective required to get ugly in a dirty war. Realism versus dewy-eyed naïveté. Reagan versus Jimmy Carter. Obama made a hesitant statement on Monday, three days after the incident, and then a more forceful one, directly acknowledging a "systems failure" and saying that it was unacceptable (which he should have said the first time, because it *is* simply unacceptable). But by then the critics had gotten control of the debate. So Obama is out there in Hawaii, on the defensive, and the mood as this year ends is glum and nervous. The failed bomber has ties to Yemen, so expect more military strikes against al-Qaida there. So on the last day of the year, the headlines are not trumpeting a dynamic new president who has successfully managed a horrible economy and engineered breakthrough social legislation. Incomplete is the highest grade that can be given. And Obama and the Democrats know it. And they are nervous.

Closer to home, the view is decidedly better. This has been a hell of a year for Henry and the Energy and Commerce Committee and for the House. We have accomplished a lot. For the House, this year has arguably been the most successful since the first session of the historic 73rd Congress in 1933—FDR's first year in office. Since January, the committee and the House have

- passed the president's economic recovery program—bigger and more sweeping than even Ronald Reagan's conservative reforms in 1981;
- passed health care reform;
- passed the massive energy and climate bill in the House, the most sweeping environmental legislation since the original Clean Air Act of 1977;
- enacted legislation placing tobacco under the full authority of the Food and Drug Administration;
- passed a renewed Children's Health Insurance Program;
- passed the biggest food-safety reforms in decades;
- renewed the Ryan White HIV/AIDS program to help treat children with HIV;
- managed the transition to digital TV (it may not sound like much, but you don't want 250 million televisions to go dark while you are in office!);

- enacted the Cash for Clunkers program, which jump-started auto sales in the midst of the downturn via incentives to trade in older cars for cleaner, more fuel efficient models, thus helping the environment as well as Detroit.

We will clear health. We have much more to do. And a fair shot at it. We will see where we are at the end of 2010. Most likely, at the end of events that are unexpected and that we cannot entirely control.

### Tuesday, January 19, 2010

A terrible election night. How cruel can irony be? That Sen. Ted Kennedy died and his successor in the most reliably Democratic state in the nation is a neophyte Republican who ran on the pledge to go to Washington and deny Democrats their sixtieth vote for the legacy Kennedy issue. And so this is a shock that will affirm the conventional wisdom that the Democratic majority in the House is in mortal danger, that Obama can be stopped, that his entire legislative program will be halted. Fear was palpable in the corridors on the Hill today.

### Wednesday, January 20

Strategy discussions centering on the necessity of the Senate bill. Complete the work with the Senate–White House conference. Pare the bill down. Put it all in budget reconciliation. By the end of the day, the logic is inescapable: the House should pass the Senate bill and get it into law—bank it and the benefits of reform. But it needs fundamental change, particularly regarding the taxes it raises and the limits on subsidies it pays to poorer Americans to expand coverage. Those fixes can be done in a parallel legislative process called budget reconciliation: the rules that apply to such special budget measures require only fifty-one votes in the Senate. It will take a while to get there, because there are really ugly provisions in the Senate bill, but ultimately it is the only way to go if health reform is to pass. And as Henry told NPR this afternoon, *If we do nothing, there will be hell to pay.* There will be a few more days of angst before the House caucus accepts what must be done. The members of the caucus will not get a free pass from the opposition attack machine by not making another vote for reform. They are already on the record, so they might as well complete the deal so the people can reap the benefits of reform.

## Thursday, March 18

At 2:07 pm, the Speaker posted the text of the health reconciliation legislation on her website, triggering a seventy-two-hour countdown to a vote. We will be in session all day on Saturday for debate and beginning at noon on Sunday for final debate and votes. Momentum appears to be building. The radioactive public option of a government health insurance policy is not in the bill. The cost controls are tighter, and support for the middle class is stronger. Several members who voted *No* in November are saying they can support this package. After four conversations with the president—including one on Air Force One earlier in the week on the way to a pro-bill rally in Ohio—Dennis Kucinich (D-OH) reconciled himself that the best should not be the enemy of the good. The only real drag on the final vote for us to win on Sunday is the abortion question. The Senate language is slightly more lenient than the House language, but it contains clear provisions that bar federal funding for abortion. And it has triggered the revelation that the anti-abortion views of the members so disposed are not monolithic. Several pro-life Democrats say they can live with the Senate language. The nuns have split from the bishops and written to members of Congress that the Senate bill not only protects life but also promotes life through its expanded coverage for today's uninsured. This all gives hope that we will pick up the votes needed to win on Sunday.

Late today, I finished a first draft of Henry's floor statement—clear, sharp, relentless, and focused on what reform means today for Americans with health insurance. You gotta carry the middle or you're dead.

## Friday, March 19

Every vector is pointing in the right direction. One by one, Democrats who voted against the health bill in November—principally because it cost too much, had too little in cost controls, or contained the public option—have come back to the fold. Democrats from Colorado, Ohio, and Pennsylvania are falling in line. Ohio's John Boccieri, who voted against the bill in November, said today he was voting for the bill even though he had been threatened with political defeat because it was the right thing to do. Members increasingly recognize that at this moment, after a century of presidents imploring the nation to do something about health care, they actually have the power to change America for the better. The Washington cynicism from November seems to be waning, and in its place is political courage. History is watching.

Our battle plan for the committee staff was laid out: tracking, caring for, and feeding the members was priority No. 1 to minimize strays. The president will come to the Hill tomorrow for a final conclave with his troops. He has had dozens of members into the Oval Office to get their support. (The reporting is that he doesn't break arms like Lyndon Johnson but listens to them to death until they agree with him.) Henry, along with the other chairs responsible for the bill, will speak in the Rules Committee, which will write the floor procedures for consideration of the bill on Sunday. The Rules Committee will craft the special rule governing floor debate, and in this case the House vote on the special rule will also deem passage of the Senate-passed health reform bill. Peggy Noonan has named the Rules parliamentary procedure *Demon Pass*, a play on "deem-and-pass." Lawsuits are being readied to attack this procedural sleight of hand as inconsistent with Article I, Section 7 of the Constitution. But we're gonna do it nonetheless.

## Saturday, March 20

The votes are very close to being in hand. The main game today was shoring up the troops. President Obama came to a meeting of the Democratic caucus in the Capitol. The caucus chair, John Larson (CT), said at the outset, "This is a fight about who we are as elected Democrats in the US Congress." And then the Senate majority leader, Harry Reid, delivered what everyone said was necessary given the distrust between the two Houses and House Democrats' skepticism that the Senate would do the right thing if they voted for the health bill: "We have the commitment of a significant majority of the Senate." The relief was palpable, and applause broke out. And then Obama spoke from his head and his heart for about thirty-five minutes. The basement room is a tough room to reach an audience, a big cavernous place, but he filled the space and weaved a blanket of unity over the members: "This is the single-most-important step we have taken on the health care system since Medicare. . . . I know this is a tough vote. If you think the system we have today is working, vote *No*. But if you agree the system is not working for average Americans, vote *Yes* for them. I believe good policy is good politics." And then he quoted Lincoln: "I'm not bound to win, but I'm bound to be true." He was imploring all Democrats to be true—to their values, to their consciences, to what the Democratic Party stands for—precisely in order to win. The feeling at the end of the president's remarks was clear: we were going to win; courage would trump cynicism, at least today.

The word this afternoon was that the House would in fact have an up-or-down vote on the Senate bill. No more charades. But the leadership proposed a cunning sequence of votes: first, a vote on the fixes to the Senate bill—the reconciliation package. Then if that passes, a vote on the Senate bill. So no enactment of a flawed Senate bill until the fixes are done. And then the fixes, we trust, will be passed by the Senate under the reconciliation rules—a simple majority vote. That's why Reid's pledge was so important to the caucus.

On abortion, however, there's no resolution yet. The scuttlebutt is that there are discussions about a presidential executive order regarding the expenditure of funding for health insurance to further ensure that no public funds are used for abortion services. We don't know if this will satisfy the remaining holdouts on the abortion question. But the overall scenario looks good tonight, though the votes are very, very close. We hope like hell it holds.

### Monday, March 22

It was a wonderful day, and a complete victory. The spirit of Saturday carried through Sunday morning, but it was still clear at midday that the hard-and-fast votes were not there yet: they awaited the silencing of that fire bell in the night—the siren of abortion. I still do not know who came up with the idea of an executive order from the president, but the strategem worked. An executive order, under the administrative statutes, has the full force of law, and what was agreed to with Rep. Stupak and his allies—and there were about eight of them—was full clarity that no public funds could be used for abortion or to subsidize access to abortion. The final tally on the bill was 219–212, so this deal was essential to enacting health insurance reform. Then something remarkable happened that showed the strength of the deal. The Republicans offered a motion to recommit the legislation to committee with an amendment that would put the anti-abortion language back in the bill itself—in place of the executive order. But that would mean the bill would go over to the Senate, where the budget rules governing the bill would mean that language be stripped out. The result would be paralysis, and the bill would be dead. Stupak, vilified for months by many for being so stubborn on abortion and extracting such a high price from the party on it, stood up and decried the Republican tactic. He said that he was for life and that it was pro-life to support insurance reform. It was a great contribution. And so the deal stuck, his members stayed with us, and the Republican motion was defeated.

The debate built through the day. At the end, it included references

to Teddy Roosevelt and all the subsequent presidents who had advocated
national health insurance. It included invocations of Social Security and
Medicare. And then Speaker Pelosi closed the circle by returning to Teddy
Kennedy, reminding everyone that his agenda was our unfinished business.
Access to health insurance, the Speaker said, was not a privilege but a right.
Henry spoke briefly early in the evening:

> Today is a historic moment. We will take decisive votes to provide
> quality, affordable health care to all Americans. This is a goal that
> Presidents of both parties have sought for a hundred years. We must
> act. The status quo is unsustainable. This bill provides all Americans
> the security of knowing they will always be able to afford health
> care for themselves and their families. The bedrock foundation of
> this legislation is that it builds on what works today, and reforms
> what doesn't. If you like your doctor and your current plan, you
> keep them. But we fundamentally reform the insurance company
> practices that are failing our families: Americans with pre-existing
> conditions can no longer be denied coverage. We abolish lifetime
> limits on coverage. And your health coverage can no longer be
> rescinded by your insurance company if you get sick. We strengthen
> Medicare. Seniors who hit the donut hole will get some immediate
> help: a $250 rebate this year, and a 50% discount on their brand-
> name drugs next year. And the donut hole will be completely elimi-
> nated within a decade. We provide coverage to 32 million uninsured
> Americans—not just those without insurance today but many who
> would otherwise be expected to lose their coverage in the coming
> years. We eliminate waste, fraud, and abuse and reduce the deficit
> by over a trillion dollars. The American people will see immediate
> benefits on enactment. Starting this year: Your children can stay on
> your policy through age 26. Preventive care under Medicare is free.
> And children with pre-existing conditions cannot be denied cover-
> age. Today we vote to make a profound difference for the better for
> the American people. Under the leadership of the President and our
> Speaker, we are poised to provide access to quality health insurance
> for all Americans.

There was tumult around the Capitol. The building was thronged by Tea
Party radicals and other opponents, and there was chanting and jeering.
It was uglier yesterday, when black and gay members of Congress were
subjected to slurs and one was spat on. So there is real anger. On one of the

talk shows, this morning, Karl Rove, President George W. Bush's political architect, was simply yelling at David Plouffe, Obama's campaign strategist, who has been brought back to save congressional Democrats from oblivion in November.

But after the vote occurred, and the news headlines filled cyberspace, it was clear that something quite dramatic had finally been completed after a year of talk and raging debate. All at once, to these biased eyes, the president looked more commanding, more positive, and more assertive. He seemed like more of a winner. And the Republicans, constantly crying that this is a "job-killing bill" and a "government takeover of one-sixth of our economy," that it would not work and should be scrapped so that we could "start all over again," just sounded tired, negative, and angry.

Another midnight press conference off the floor of the House chamber. The whip, Rep. Jim Clyburn (SC), said that he felt tonight we had contributed to the formation of a "more perfect union." Lovely. And Henry said, "Within two days, the president of the United States will sign national health insurance reform into law." Henry was quietly soaring tonight. A dream fulfilled, a career objective met. Decisive change for the better. A midnight thought: I hope it's sunny later this week for that ceremony in the Rose Garden.

At the end of this day, nearly twenty-four hours after passage on the floor, the rising Obama political tide could be felt. The media coverage was extremely favorable; the messages about what the new law will mean for everyday people are coming through loud and clear. The Republicans are on the defensive. Yes, the movement to repeal the legislation is already under way, but everyone understands it is going nowhere because Barack Obama will be president for another three—or seven—years, and he will veto any repeal. So the edifice of health reform is going to be constructed and opened for business. And some Republican strategists are wondering whether their scorched-earth policy to defeat the bill was wise. Sen. DeMint predicted that health care would be Obama's Waterloo. Well, a former speechwriter for President George W. Bush asked today whether passage of the bill was the Republicans' Waterloo. Around our offices, in calls and emails, there was a palpable sense that history was made, that something quite significant had been done. There is a real sense of achievement and accomplishment. And our side feels pretty damn good about it. The peculiar thing about politics and legislation in Washington is that you never quite know until the end when and how the bill will finally come together and where the votes will precisely fall. But then, when it is all done, you wonder why it was so hard to get here—it is so blindingly obvious that this is what we had to do. Why did we have to wait so long to take those votes last night? Amazing.

## Tuesday, March 23

A marvelous day. The president signed the health reform legislation into law in a rollicking, joyous ceremony in the East Room of the White House with a speech marked by solemnity and achievement and suffused with cognizance of this moment in history:

> Today, after almost a century of trying; today, after over a year of debate; today, after all the votes have been tallied—health insurance reform becomes law in the United States of America. Today. This year, we'll start offering tax credits to about 4 million small businessmen and women to help them cover the cost of insurance for their employees. That happens this year. This year, tens of thousands of uninsured Americans with preexisting conditions, the parents of children who have a preexisting condition, will finally be able to purchase the coverage they need. That happens this year. This year, insurance companies will no longer be able to drop people's coverage when they get sick. They won't be able to place lifetime limits or restrictive annual limits on the amount of care they can receive. This year, all new insurance plans will be required to offer free preventive care. And this year, young adults will be able to stay on their parents' policies until they're 26 years old. That happens this year. And this year, seniors who fall in the coverage gap known as the doughnut hole will start getting some help. They'll receive $250 to help pay for prescriptions, and that will, over time, fill in the doughnut hole. And I want seniors to know, despite what some have said, these reforms will not cut your guaranteed benefits. In fact, under this law, Americans on Medicare will receive free preventive care without co-payments or deductibles. That begins this year. I'm signing this bill for all the leaders who took up this cause through the generations—from Teddy Roosevelt to Franklin Roosevelt, from Harry Truman, to Lyndon Johnson, from Bill and Hillary Clinton, to one of the deans who's been fighting this so long, John Dingell. To Senator Ted Kennedy. And it's fitting that Teddy's widow, Vicki, is here; and his niece Caroline; his son Patrick, whose vote helped make this reform a reality. I remember seeing Ted walk through that door in a summit in this room a year ago—one of his

last public appearances. And it was hard for him to make it. But he was confident that we would do the right thing. Our presence here today is remarkable and improbable. With all the punditry, all of the lobbying, all of the game-playing that passes for governing in Washington, it's been easy at times to doubt our ability to do such a big thing, such a complicated thing; to wonder if there are limits to what we, as a people, can still achieve. It's easy to succumb to the sense of cynicism about what's possible in this country. But today, we are affirming that essential truth—a truth every generation is called to rediscover for itself—that we are not a nation that scales back its aspirations. We are not a nation that falls prey to doubt or mistrust. We don't fall prey to fear. We are not a nation that does what's easy. That's not who we are. That's not how we got here. We are a nation that faces its challenges and accepts its responsibilities. We are a nation that does what is hard. What is necessary. What is right. Here, in this country, we shape our destiny. That is what we do. That is who we are. That is what makes us the United States of America. And we have now just enshrined, as soon as I sign this bill, the core principle that everybody should have some basic security when it comes to their health care. And it is an extraordinary achievement that has happened because of all of you and all the advocates all across the country.

What was striking was the mood—not just that this extraordinary thing had been done, but that a bill that has been so pilloried, so vilified, so hated, so disparaged was seen today as the right thing to do. The Democrats—every member of Congress who voted for it was invited—reveled in it. And they reveled in their president. And for the first time in months, it seemed, members eagerly pressed to be close to Obama, to hug him, touch him, shake his hand, have a word—to be positively associated with Barack. For a party that less than a week ago was seen as on the brink of failure—or worse—this was quite a turnaround. And it has affected the media cycle quite dramatically. Since the weekend, with the buildup toward victory on the floor, to the afterglow of Monday, to today's ceremony, to what will happen Thursday, when the president flies to Iowa to tout the reform in the cornfields, this palpable shift in the mood has occurred, with Democrats seen as triumphant for the right reasons and the Republicans seen as abject losers and for the wrong reasons. Recriminations are setting in. How did they blow it? Why do they look so out of bounds? And the ugliness of the Tea Party crowd, with their epithets and narrow thinking, is sticking to the Republicans as well. And so for this moment—and maybe it will prove to be only a moment—the Democrats seem as if they are back. The president is strong and a winner. As a respected journalist for *US News and World Report* wrote on his blog today, the president "is making the tough choices—on the economy, on Afghanistan, on healthcare—and not wavering under fire." And fire there is. A day can be a lifetime in politics. We live again. If we can hold the House, we have the chance to do more.

## Thursday, March 25

It is over; we won. Harry Reid's pledge to the Democratic caucus held. The Senate Democrats were so secure that they gave back eight hours of debate they were entitled to. The Republicans used all their time and offered a couple dozen amendments including one from Sen. Tom Coburn (R-OK) to deny Viagra to inmates who are convicted rapists. Yes, really. But all their amendments went down, and Senate Democrats passed the reconciliation bill, 56–43. Republican senators did use points of order under arcane budget reconciliation rules to remove a couple provisions of the education part of the bill. And since what is presented to the president has to have passed both houses in identical form, the Senate reconciliation bill had to come back for one more final vote in the House. So when the Senate cleared the bill, around 2:00 pm, the House leadership went into overdrive. By 4:00 the House Rules Committee had convened to provide the terms of the last debate. It was anticlimactic because we already had the huge vote on Sunday and the president had signed the bill into law. This was the correction piece to that law—still incredibly important because it removed the rotten fish deals the senators had done to get it passed and it had pharmaceutical sweeteners for seniors and the subsidies for the middle class to buy insurance that are crucial to the program's success. And the vote came, our side held, and the tally was 220–207. It was done. Everyone was exhausted, but health reform is enacted. For the president, this has been a searing experience. But he has been transformed by it—tempered, tougher, more powerful. It augurs well for what we want to do before this year is out.

## Tuesday, March 30

Today, President Obama signed the reconciliation bill—the fixes to the Senate bill. There has been a significant debate over the past week on how important this was for the Obama presidency and what it means in the context of other major achievements by presidents. I think it sealed what history will ultimately say: *Barack Obama, the first African American president, enacted comprehensive access to health insurance for all Americans*. In historical terms, this reform comes closest to FDR's. FDR reformed capitalism to save it. Obama reformed private health insurance to save it. It really is conservative reform—nothing radical about it. In that sense, it is classically American, and Obama is squarely in that mold.

## Concluding Thoughts

The epochal political battles that delivered the ACA offers some important lessons. The 1994 defeat of health care reform informed the politics and strategies of the law's passage, especially the decision to give the relevant committees wide latitude in putting together an initial legislative vehicle that could win approval of a majority of lawmakers. In this regard, the committee's diversity served as an advantage in assembling a winning coalition in the House. The process illustrates how a pivotal faction or swing group such as the Blue Dogs can employ bargaining chips by getting hostile amendments approved and more generally how a faction's influence within the party can be partly determined by its representation on committees.[8] There is also evidence of spatial politics at work in how some of the principals talked about the policy status quo and strategized about which alternatives might get a majority (Krehbiel 1991; Shepsle and Weingast 1995). The majority-party staff play a critical role in piecing together the policy and political information that is needed in the back-and-forth negotiation between leaders and the rank and file that eventually leads to the assembly of a coalition (Fortunato 2013). In addition, the health care reform story shows not only the importance of bicameralism but also that behavior of members in one chamber can be affected by anticipating the action (or inaction) of the other chamber. Finally, the breadth and scope of the ACA also show the limits of distributive politics (Weingast and Marshall 1988). In the end, legislative success came at least in part because leaders appealed to members' desire to help the president of their party enact his policy goals and by extension their own goals (F. E. Lee 2009).

Did the passage of health care reform constitute "Obama's Waterloo"? We think not—even though enactment contributed to the Democrats losing their House majority in the 2010 elections. Obamacare has over time become a defining plank in Obama's legacy as president—and notwithstanding the reversal of fortune for Democrats in Congress in 2010, Obama won a second term in 2012, with fidelity to the Affordable Care Act a core element of his re-election campaign. Indeed, the recurring failures (up to now) by President Trump to repeal and replace Obamacare have highlighted the growing popularity of universal access to affordable, quality health insurance. After decades of failure to achieve this, from efforts undertaken by President Truman to President Clinton, Obama succeeded, placing the Affordable Care Act on a par with the initial enactment of Social Security by FDR and Medicare under LBJ, and earning growing popular approval.

# FOUR

# A Big Turn in Tobacco Road

The June 2009 passage of the Family Smoking Prevention and Tobacco Control Act (HR 1256) marked a momentous shift, as Congress chose to enact an aggressive regime of federal regulation and oversight of tobacco products, giving responsibility for their regulation to the US Food and Drug Administration (FDA). More symbolically, the legislation reflected Congress's decision to take a side and engage an epic struggle between the public health interest of citizens and private industry interests. For President Barack Obama, the tobacco-FDA legislation was an opportunity to deliver on a long-sought and hard-fought progressive reform and to strengthen his bond with Henry Waxman (D-CA) the powerful chair of the House Energy and Commerce Committee, a bond that would be tested in future legislative battles. In a Rose Garden ceremony to mark the signing of the tobacco-FDA legislation, the president showcased the victory for health care reform, the virtues of bipartisanship on health issues, and the fact that he was keeping his promise to govern without regard to special interests. Presidential signing statements offer unique and powerful rhetorical opportunities to allocate credit or frame policy arguments (Kelley and Marshall 2008; Conley 2011; K. Evans and Marshall 2016). Holding the bill up to cameras, Obama declared that it reflected "a step that will save lives and dollars" and delivered a powerful rhetorical line: "Today change has come to Washington." The president's remarks also reflected his personal struggle with smoking: "Each day, 1,000 young people under the age of 18 become new regular, daily smokers, and almost 90 percent of all smokers began at or before their 18th birthday. I know; I was one of these teenagers. And so I know how difficult it can be to break this habit when it's been with you for a long time" (C. E. Lee 2009).

The tobacco-FDA bill passed both houses with considerable bipartisan support.[1] The Senate passed HR 1256 by a 79–17 margin (Armstrong 2009).[2] Freshman senator Kay Hagan of North Carolina was the only Democrat to vote against the measure. The House followed suit, passing the Senate-amended legislation by a 307–97 margin and sending it to the president for signature. Both chambers had at times blocked the advancement of tobacco legislation, but in this round, the fight centered in the Senate (Armstrong 2009). The biggest threat to the bill came from opponents led by Sen. Richard Burr (R-NC). Burr, a longtime defender of tobacco, argued that granting FDA oversight authority would lead to a near freeze in the industry's ability to get new, safer tobacco products to market because of the agency's slow pace of approval for new products. In addition, he argued, the FDA was already overburdened (Cummings 2009). In the 110th Congress (2007–8), Sen. Burr had threatened to filibuster similar legislation and thus kill it before it even reached the Senate floor (Armstrong 2008a). But this time, Burr and the newly elected Kagan teamed up to support legislation that would place tobacco oversight in the hands of a newly created agency independent of the FDA (and within the Department of Health and Human Services).[3] The Senate spent two weeks of floor time debating tobacco regulation, and proponents ultimately fought the Burr proposal and others designed to weaken the legislation. When the bill passed, Sen. Michael Enzi (R-WY) suggested that it would decrease smoking and help millions by reducing those exposed to secondhand smoke: "This is just one step toward the goal I know we all share, which is to reduce the public health toll of tobacco use" (Armstrong 2009, 1378).[4] On the opposite side of the aisle, another champion against tobacco interests, Sen. Ted Kennedy (D-MA), who was absent from debate because he was battling brain cancer, released a statement: "Miracles still happen. The United States Senate has finally said 'no' to Big Tobacco" (Armstrong 2009, 1378).

The new legislation set in motion the most significant oversight and regulation of tobacco products ever. The FDA would have power to regulate nicotine levels, bar flavor additives, and require much tougher warning labels on cigarette packets. For example, the legislation forbade chocolate- or fruit-flavored additives to diminish underage smoking. The bill created a new arm within the FDA, the Center for Tobacco Products, and provided it with sweeping authority to regulate the production of, marketing, and sale of tobacco products. Funding for the new legislation's oversight activities would come from user fees on tobacco companies and importers, a provision expected to increase product costs and drive down demand (Armstrong 2009).

To hear Rep. Waxman's accounting, the fight against tobacco defined his accomplished career as much if not more than any other issue in his forty years in Congress (Waxman and Green 2009, 171). Policy interests motivate all members, although each member weighs policy and other goals differently, of course. Waxman saw tobacco use as representing the greatest health threat to US citizens, contributing to the deaths of hundreds of thousands of people each year and taking a staggering toll in health and economic opportunity costs. The Office of Management and Budget reported that tobacco use was a major driver of US health care costs, draining more than one hundred billion dollars each year from the economy (Cummings 2009). In Waxman's view, tobacco was the prime example of how private industry could circumvent scrutiny by controlling Congress from the inside.[5] No other industry had so skillfully gripped and manipulated congressional levers of power (Waxman and Green 2009, 172–73).

Tobacco is a classic distributive issue, illustrating how narrow, regionally based political interests can be protected and perpetuated through the institutional rules and beltway mores of Congress. Although a federal excise tax had been levied against tobacco products since the presidency of George Washington, remarkably little congressional scrutiny of tobacco occurred between that time until the middle of the twentieth century. Tobacco was a staple of the southern economy and a completely acceptable part of the social fabric, alongside the likes of baseball and socializing. Society's elite classes from Hollywood to sports stars made tobacco use hip and desirable. Detroit, with its unfailing watch over consumer tastes, took notice of tobacco too, as ashtrays and cigarette dash lighters were as much a part of car interiors in the 1960s as cup holders and Internet technology are today. Ashtrays sat next to every airline seat; smoking could occur in cinemas. And tobacco use was as common in the halls of Congress as it was in society at large. Smoking was permitted in the committee rooms on Capitol Hill, which featured handsome, weighty ashtrays that members and staff occasionally took home as souvenirs. Tobacco was a staple for the troops in World War II. It is therefore hardly a surprise that twentieth-century Congresses had mostly resisted tobacco regulation. One of Congress's most iconic and powerful figures, Joseph Cannon (R-IL), who served as Speaker of the House between 1903 and 1911, was typically seen in portraits or described as clenching a cigar.[6] As long as tobacco use remained an acceptable societal norm and its health consequences hidden or uncertain, keeping the policy status quo of little or no regulation was good politics and unquestioned policy for Congress. But as clarity regarding tobacco's hazards emerged, members of Congress faced a dilemma about what increasingly looked like bad and costly policy. The Energy and Commerce Committee played an important role in making health issues associated with tobacco use nationally salient, and regional politics eventually gave way to national public health concerns.

Tobacco interests had an incredibly tight grip on Congress that stretched back for decades (Glass 2009). The industry understood the regional politics its supporters faced, it knew the inner workings of congressional policymaking, and recognized how and where to apply influence. The industry had sewn itself into the fabric of members' Washington circles, providing tobacco interests with an enviable, unparalleled level of access to elected officials. The tobacco industry heaped its appreciation on Congress by shuttling members around on corporate jets.[7] The industry spent readily to fill campaign coffers and for decades was one of the largest soft-money contributors to both parties. Big Tobacco splurged on grand inaugural balls and underwrote members of Congress's favorite charitable events and foundations. The industry also had deep pockets to fund community and school programs in poor and minority areas both in cities and in rural America (Waxman and Green 2009, 174–75). And inside the walls of the Capitol and its hearing rooms, Big Tobacco used the committee system and well-positioned supporters as an institutional barrier against regulation or any policy change they saw as detrimental to tobacco's interests. (Other regional interests, too, dominated committees—for example, timber, mining, and other western industries wielded influence over the Interior and Insular Affairs Committee [Fenno 1973].) Legislators from tobacco regions accrued seniority and thus power to block unwanted policy change or to trade influence with members to protect tobacco interests. Big Tobacco encouraged representatives with district and regional ties to tobacco to seek seats on Energy and Commerce, which had oversight of the FDA. The industry even pressured the Steering and Policy Committee to place tobacco backers on Energy and Commerce (Waxman and Green 2009, 173), ensuring that the committee would continue to support tobacco interests and that a stream of senior members would continue to climb the committee's leadership ladder and maintain control of Congress's policymaking levers.

With congressional allies in place, Big Tobacco continued to protect its interests even as scientific evidence in the 1950s began to point to the harmful effects of tobacco use. Even after 1964, when the US surgeon general reported that smoking could cause cancer, Congress initially took only the relatively minor step of requiring cigarette packs to carry small and ambiguous warning labels declaring that smoking could harm one's health. Beginning in 1967, under the Fairness Doctrine, which required broadcasters to cover important issues in a "fair and balanced" manner and which was administered by the Federal Communications Commission (another agency under the jurisdiction of Energy and Commerce), TV stations were required to broadcast one antismoking public service announcement for every three tobacco industry advertisements aired (Glass 2009). The public service campaign seemed to have some impact on public awareness, and the number of domestic smokers subsequently began a slow decline. As opinion shifted about tobacco's potential harm, Congress made several attempts to ban tobacco ads, but tobacco interests blocked these efforts. However, with heightened public scrutiny, Big Tobacco relented. In the spring of 1970, Congress passed the Public Health Cigarette Smoking Act, which banned tobacco advertising on TV and radio (Glass 2009).[8] Big Tobacco devised even more effective ways to market its product, and the ban enabled the industry not only to forgo expensive TV ads but also to do away with the problematic public service announcements that had taken a chunk out of their market share. The 1970 legislation provided an early indicator of the difficulty of the tobacco fight in Congress, with the companies acquiescing only to policy that sustained their advantage yet allowed members of Congress to claim that they supported broader public interests (Mayhew 1973; Fiorina 1989).

Big Tobacco instituted a two-pronged strategy for maintaining the upper hand and remaining free from the pressure of congressional regulation (Waxman and Green 2009, 174–76). The industry mounted a systematic public relations campaign centered on associating tobacco use with an enviable and exciting lifestyle that appealed to both youth and adults (using such icons as Joe Camel and the Marlboro Man). In addition, to combat the mounting evidence related to health concerns, the industry sought to create significant uncertainty regarding the linkage between tobacco use and negative health outcomes. The tobacco industry hired doctors and scientists and funded such organizations as the Council for Tobacco Research to promote research that clouded the strong and ascendant scientific consensus about the linkage between tobacco use and negative health outcomes (Waxman and Green 2009, 182–83). For decades, this sophisticated dual strategy proved highly successful for Big Tobacco, as legislation targeting tobacco use remained very limited and moved at a glacial pace.

Changing the Political Landscape of Big Tobacco: Policy Salience,
Oversight, and the Health and Environment Subcommittee

Clearing a legislative path for tobacco regulation and thereby lessening the toll on public health would require a significant change in the politics of tobacco. Rep. Waxman saw an opportunity to change the public perception of tobacco use, first by tying it directly to the many tragic health consequences and later by illuminating the public regarding the industry's deliberate manipulation of information designed to increase market share at the expense of young smokers and public health generally (Waxman and Green 2009, 183). In 1979, Waxman became chair of the Health and Environment Subcommittee, one of six subcommittees organized under the Energy and Commerce Committee. Waxman's defeat of Richardson Preyer (D-NC) to chair the subcommittee with jurisdiction over the FDA and tobacco was one example of a broader push in Congress to allow the burgeoning numbers of liberal members to play a larger role in policymaking—that is, subcommittee government (see chapter 1). Waxman's ascendancy therefore marked an important change, since he would use his new post to bring public scrutiny to the tobacco industry.[9] Starting in the early 1980s, the subcommittee used its oversight to help expose the harmful health effects of tobacco use and make public health the No. 1 salient issue governing the politics of tobacco. Committee oversight thus enabled the reshaping of the political landscape in a way that increases the likelihood of legislation or regulation by Congress. The most vital step for Democratic reformers in this regard was building public support for legislative action. Once this change in the politics of tobacco regulation was achieved, Waxman would not necessarily have to persuade members of Congress on the merits of good policy; rather, he could simply present rational reelection-seeking members with a simple choice between good policy and politics (effectively regulating a public health menace) and the risk of vulnerability to pressure from activists and elites (e.g., doctors and the public health community) determined to change the status quo on tobacco (Cloud 1994).[10]

But exposing tobacco and changing public perceptions proved a very long and difficult battle. Two decades after the surgeon general's landmark report, signs indicated that politics and public opinion were finally shifting, leading to incremental policy change. In 1984, Congress enacted legislation requiring cigarette labels and advertising to carry warnings from the surgeon general that directly tied smoking to specific hazards like lung cancer and heart disease. Two years later, Congress extended similar legislation to smokeless tobacco products. That same year, surgeon general C. Everett Koop, a conservative appointed by President Ronald Reagan, issued a major report linking secondhand smoke to harmful health effects (Glover 1994b; Waxman and Green 2009, 179). Koop's conservatism and credentials gave his findings a big political as well as medical punch, although Big Tobacco and its allies continued to contend that the science was uncertain, that secondhand smoke did not cause harm, that the government therefore should stay out of the way of smoking as a personal choice. But the political landscape was shifting. In 1987, Congress, led by Rep. Richard Durbin (D-IL), passed the first legislation designed to combat the harmful effects of secondhand smoke, banning smoking on domestic airline flights less than two hours long.

In the early 1990s, Waxman's subcommittee continued to shine a bright public light on the tobacco industry, becoming a vital conduit for information and an outlet for industry insiders who wanted to make public their previously undisclosed findings about harm caused by tobacco use (Glover 1994b). FDA commissioner David Kessler, a Clinton appointee, was outspoken that his agency should have the authority to regulate cigarettes as a drug (Armstrong 2009).

In 1994, Waxman's subcommittee held a series of important hearings that dramatically altered public perceptions regarding Big Tobacco (Glover 1994a; Hilts 1994). Appearing on this public stage, Kessler declared that cigarettes were a high-tech nicotine delivery system and should be regulated by the FDA (Cloud 1994). Rep. Waxman invited the CEOs of the seven largest tobacco companies to counter Kessler's claims. In a subsequent subcommittee hearing that emerged as one of the most powerful moments of congressional oversight of an industry, the tobacco executives publicly testified under oath that smoking had no harmful effects and that they had no knowledge of any evidence that nicotine was addictive (Hilts 1994). These and other subcommittee hearings exposed the Big Tobacco executives as having presided over decades of cover-ups about the public health hazards of tobacco (Glover 1994a). Waxman put Philip Morris's CEO on the spot by asking him to allow one of the company's research scientists, Victor DeNoble, to testify about his research. The company had forbidden DeNoble from publishing his work, but the CEO had little choice but to permit him to testify. DeNoble then told the subcommittee that despite Philip Morris's contention that it had no evidence that nicotine was addictive, his research showed that nicotine was a highly addictive chemical commensurate with cocaine (Waxman and Green 2009, 182, 189).

While the 1994 hearings advanced the agenda on the public health front, the Newt Gingrich–led GOP was eagerly implementing a campaign to win back control of Congress. Republicans pointed at a congressional check-bouncing scandal and painted Democrats as the party of big government gone awry (C. L. Evans and Oleszek 1997; Rae 1998). The 1994 election saw GOP majorities in both houses for the first time in forty years, and the political winds appeared to shift again in favor of the tobacco industry. Rep. Tom Bliley (R-VA) took over as chair of the Energy and Commerce Committee. Bliley's district was home to Philip Morris's main plant, and the tobacco hearings came to an abrupt end (Waxman and Green 2009, 190).

But the tidal wave of scientific research conducted and supported by the industry in part to stoke uncertainty about tobacco's dangers, some of which had remained hidden, continued unabated (Waxman and Green 2009, 191). In 1995 and 1997, the subcommittee received evidence that tobacco companies were deliberately marketing their products to children to induce them to smoke. With the blessing of their respective party leaders, Bliley and Waxman worked secretly to put together regulatory legislation designed to decrease youth smoking and to limit smoking in public places (Glover 1994b). However, partisan warfare between Waxman and Gingrich over investigations into the Clinton administration ruined any chance for the bipartisan deal to make it to the House floor.

Thus, despite a growing bipartisan consensus that more effective regulation of tobacco use and marketing was in the public interest, the issue had increasingly become hostage to the larger political battles between the Republican Congress and the Democratic White House. In 2001, with the election of George W. Bush and unified Republican control of government, prospects for regulation had almost disappeared. Big Tobacco interests were being buoyed on other fronts, too. In 1998, the attorneys general from forty-six states who had launched a class-action lawsuit against Big Tobacco reached a settlement with the companies that had the potential to undercut legislative efforts at regulation (Gruenwald 1997; Jalonick 2005). Opponents argued that the financial settlement required only a pittance from Big Tobacco compared to the cost to public health.[11] Then, in 2000 the Supreme Court ruled that the FDA lacked authority to issue regulations prohibiting tobacco sales to individuals under age eighteen.[12] Many individual lawmakers supporting tobacco regulation argued the Court's decision was practically inviting a statutory fix but the collective political will in Congress was not there yet—sapped of its regulatory steam by the powerful tobacco lobby (Armstrong 2008b). In 2004, the Senate included language granting the FDA regulatory authority over tobacco in a corporate tax bill (Jalonick 2004). However, House Republicans and regional supporters of tobacco forced the excision of those regulatory provisions in conference committee, showing Big Tobacco's continued though weakening grip on Congress.

## Crossing the Last Legislative Hurdles: The Final Push toward Regulating Tobacco Use

The legislative effort during the 110th Congress showed that tobacco's control over Congress had grown more fragile. The change in party control—the Democrats took back both the House and Senate in 2006—placed advocates of tobacco regulation in a stronger position to pressure tobacco interests and increased the prospects for legislation. The House tobacco regulation bill (HR 1108) provided the FDA with sweeping powers to regulate tobacco products as well as tobacco companies' sales, packaging, and marketing activities, with the funding for this regulatory regime coming directly from fees paid by the tobacco companies (Armstrong 2008b). Nevertheless, the legislative effort eventually derailed. Multiple House committees engaged in turf battles over who had jurisdictional control over the legislation. The chair of the House Energy and Commerce Committee, John Dingell (D-MI), and Rep. Waxman settled jurisdictional disputes by negotiating a deal with the Natural Resources Committee on an Indian affairs issue and an agreement with the Ways and Means Committee regarding tax provisions (Armstrong 2008a).[13] This allowed the bill to move to the House floor, where it was considered under suspension of the rules and passed overwhelmingly, 326–102. But the vote margin belied the industry's continuing staunch opposition. Prior to the vote, minority leader John Boehner (R-OH) made a well-worn, fiery plea on the House floor: "Most people who smoke in America probably don't need the federal government to tell them that smoking isn't good for their health. This is a bone-headed idea! How much government do we need?" (Armstrong 2008b, 2123). Dingell retorted, "This legislation is on the floor because people are killing themselves smoking these evil cigarettes! And the distinguished gentleman, the minority leader, is going to be amongst the next to die! . . . I am trying to save him, as the rest of us are, because he is committing suicide every time he puffs on one of those."[14]

Just before the House began to debate the legislation, the Bush administration threatened to veto the bill on the grounds that it would undermine FDA's critical mission of protecting public health by misleading the public into believing that tobacco use was safe. The administration also objected that the bill's fees on cigarettes amounted to a new tax that would unfairly burden the poor. On the Senate side, Kennedy, chair of the Health, Education, Labor, and Pensions Committee, had built an impressive array of committee support for the bill (S 625), gaining the backing of conservatives such as Sen. John Cornyn (R-TX). Kennedy had also garnered fifty-six cosponsors, including the GOP's likely presidential nominee, John McCain (R-AZ). Despite this momentum, Democratic leaders never brought the tobacco legislation to the Senate floor during the 110th Congress, choosing to move other agenda priorities rather than provoking a showdown with opponents like Burr and the near certainty of a Bush veto.

As the 111th Congress began, some key changes finally opened the path to legislation. Democrats increased their margin in both chambers, and the regulatory coalition gained allies. Moreover, Obama's election as president removed the veto threat from the legislative picture, placing a strong supporter of the legislation in the White House.[15] And Waxman became the chair of Energy and Commerce. But beyond these institutional or structural changes resulting from the 2008 elections, the politics of tobacco had also changed dramatically. A systematic assessment of the impact of Waxman's subcommittee on the turn in public opinion is beyond the scope of this analysis (Glover 1994b). Nevertheless, it is quite clear that the subcommittee's actions had some effect on public attitudes regarding the costs of tobacco use, particularly the subcommittee's role in bringing to light the pernicious marketing campaigns by the industry to the country's youth. Waxman's subcommittee also played an important role as an information clearinghouse, removing the veil of uncertainty surrounding the consequences of tobacco use and forcing the industry to resort to its final fallback position—the argument that people should be able to make the personal choice to smoke. But even this argument was undermined by the overwhelming evidence showing that secondhand smoke had grave consequences for nonsmokers. These developments, along with the strengthening of public advocacy groups and tobacco reform movement, increased the costs associated with the politics of antiregulation.

Related to these changes, Big Tobacco's external political coalition had fractured into camps defined by marketing strategy in an increasingly hostile legislative and regulatory environment. Altria, the owner of Philip Morris and US Tobacco and the biggest player in the tobacco industry, concluded that regulation was unavoidable and consequently chose to embrace it—at least in principle—in hopes of shaping it rather than being trampled by it.[16] Altria saw an opportunity to gain market share since it could more easily absorb the costs of regulation than its smaller competitors. "Little Tobacco companies such as R. J. Reynolds and Lorillard continued the fight against regulation.[17] The rupture within the tobacco coalition also marked a significant shift in the balance of K Street lobbying influence. In a legislative fight a decade earlier, Big Tobacco had paid K Street lobbying firms more than sixty million dollars for one overarching purpose—to block legislation targeting tobacco. But Altria's strategic decision to embrace regulatory reform drained away millions in opposition lobbying dollars. In fact, tobacco spending on K Street lobbying fell by about half over the fifteen-month period leading up to the 2009 legislative effort (Zeller 2009). This fissure in the tobacco alliance also changed the political calculus for some members of Congress. For example, Altria's backing of the legislation provided political cover, reducing the risk of supporting the legislation for especially vulnerable tobacco-state legislators such as senators Mark Warner and Jim Webb (both D-VA) (Cummings 2009).

Thus, by 2008, the public perception of the tobacco industry had irrevocably changed, and the monolithic coalition that had formerly protected tobacco interests had begun to crumble. In addition, supporters of regulation now controlled both houses of Congress and the White House. But the legislative component comprises only part of the story behind tobacco regulation. Without the subcommittee's active role in connecting tobacco to its dire health consequences and in making that connection salient to the public, the historic political tilt in favor of tobacco interests might have been prolonged or might still persist.

The committee's exercise of policy influence did not end with the passage of tobacco regulation. A dramatic new law to protect public health was in place, but it faced legislative, regulatory, and legal challenges in the months following enactment. The committee came to play a paramount role in guiding and protecting implementation of the new law.

## Wednesday, April 1, 2009

Tonight, Henry's bill placing tobacco under the Food and Drug Administration for the first time is on the House floor. This has been a ten-year fight to get to this point. It was Henry's 1994 oversight hearing that brought the tobacco executives to Capitol Hill where they swore under oath that nicotine was not addictive. It was one of the most memorable moments in congressional oversight in modern times, and it was powerfully captured in the movie *The Insider*, starring Russell Crowe. Tonight Henry was on the

House floor saying that those executives lied and that this bill was going to place the most pervasive threat to the health of Americans under the most powerful public health laws we have. It isn't a ban on tobacco or nicotine, but it will severely curtail marketing of tobacco, especially to kids.

This bill will pass with significant Republican support—that's how broad and deep the political consensus is today on tobacco. So it is not all trench warfare all the time. But I tell you, listening to Stephen Buyer (R-IN) talk against the bill and try to shunt it into the Health and Human Services bureaucracy was painful. He would fail and he knew he would fail, but he was out there for tobacco. And this will get him political points at home and with the industry.

Some inside baseball: when the bill was marked up in committee in March, G. K. Butterfield (D-NC), a smart and amiable lawmaker, said that he had the biggest tobacco district in the country but that he was going to vote for this bill. It was amazing to hear. Thirty years earlier, Henry defeated a North Carolina Democrat, Richardson Preyer, to chair the Subcommittee on Health and the Environment, and he challenged Preyer over the tobacco issue. I was on Henry's staff at the time. How can we do public health if the public health subcommittee is chaired by a tobacco man? Henry beat Preyer in the Democratic caucus cleanly, and it was a precursor to his 2008 defeat of John Dingell, where the issue again was *How can we move Obama's agenda to remake energy and environmental policy if the key committee is chaired by Detroit's champion?* After Butterfield spoke, I went up to Henry and said, "Tell me how Richardson Preyer would have voted on this bill." "He would have voted *Aye.*" Now that is change we can believe in: clean air outside, clean air inside, all in one day. Not bad.

## Thursday April 2

There was a scare late last night on the House floor on the tobacco bill. The leadership had listed a vote earlier in the evening on a piece of banking legislation and suddenly the whipping system to garner support among the Democrats looked not up to snuff. Although Henry had done an excellent job in arguing the tobacco bill, the feeling was that the Republican amendment to gut the bill might be a little too close for comfort. So this morning, before the final votes, the leadership engaged the whip system.[18] In addition, the committee staff swung into action with letters to all House members from Henry and the other key supporters of the bill as well as from the public health interest groups, making the case in very stark terms that the Republican alternative would be a vote to kill the bill and leave our kids completely vulnerable to the predatory marketing practices of the tobacco companies. What was done worked, and 30 percent of the Republicans stuck with the Waxman bill—probably one of the biggest defections in the Republican Party on a major issue in this Congress. The overall bill passed on a crushing 298–112 vote.

"This is truly a historic day in the fight against tobacco," Waxman said after his victory, which was thirty years in the making and frustrated last year by President Bush's implicit threat to veto the bill should the Senate approve it. "Today we have moved to place the regulation of tobacco under the Food and Drug Administration in order to protect the public health, and now we can all breathe a little easier. I have every hope for firm and certain action by the Senate to pass this legislation so that we can at long last send it to the President and better protect the American people from tobacco with the full force of our public health laws."

It's possible that the team was just spooked last night, but the lesson is still valuable: take nothing—absolutely nothing—for granted in fighting these entrenched interests. They will not die or fade away. They will work to the last to peel off soft Democrats, southern Democrats, scared Democrats. And for sure, they will do it on energy and climate change and on universal access to health care. So the exercise in making the big push with members as a bill nears the floor has to be done a touch earlier, so that it sticks and the vote counts hold, and we can live through the night to win when the morning comes.

Friday, June 12

Victory over Tobacco Day. Passage of Henry's antitobacco bill, as cleared by the Senate, was the first order of business on the House floor. "It is hard to believe that we have finally reached this day," Henry told the chamber. After more than a decade of effort and with countless delays and defeats along the way, we are—at last—about to enact truly historic legislation to protect the public health and to end the tobacco epidemic. "The vote we take today is the final nail in the coffin of Big Tobacco and the grip it has held on the lives of so many Americans. . . . Today is the day when Americans can begin to truly kick the habit, with the full force of our laws marshalled to protect consumers, and especially our young people."

The vote was overwhelming, 307–97, even larger than when the bill first passed the House in April. And in the deepest split in Republican ranks this year, the party split 70–90 for the bill. Minutes before the vote, Henry spoke without notes, capturing the significance of this moment. "I remember the power of the tobacco industry that kept the Congress from acting. . . . We are today at the last gasp of the tobacco industry's profits at the expense of the health of the American people."

In a carefully orchestrated appearance in the Rose Garden moments after the vote, the ex-smoker-in-chief, President Obama, noted the passage of the bill. And he gave a shout out to Phil Schiliro, now the White House assistant for legislative affairs but previously Henry's chief of staff and the man who engineered the most famous congressional hearing since Watergate, the one where the tobacco executives denied any knowledge that tobacco and nicotine were addictive. Today, they know what they have wrought.

### Monday, June 22

In the Rose Garden, the president signed the tobacco regulation bill. Henry was positioned just off the president's shoulder as he signed the bill, and Obama mentioned Henry's work for the past fifteen years, since that famous hearing.

### Thursday, August 6

The House adjourned for the August recess last Friday; the Senate has been in session this week. And today once again proved the adage *The Republic is safe only when the Senate adjourns.* Since last night, we were on patrol against an amendment that might be offered by Sen. Mike Enzi (R-WY) on tobacco. Enzi wants to create a carve out an exception in our new tobacco legislation for clove cigarettes. Cloves are specifically banned as a tobacco additive under the bill. Indonesia, the major producer of clove cigarettes, believes that this provision is directed against them and is antithetical to our commitments under various free-trade agreements. And they have hired to carry their cloves—this is so Washington—Mickey Kantor, California Democratic political supremo who was President Clinton's chief trade negotiator. One thing about Mickey: he is indefatigable. One thing about Enzi: last week, he lovingly waded in to the controversy over health insurance legislation, and repeated the rallying cry that it was President Obama's Waterloo, and if it could be stopped, here and now, we could "kill" Obama's program. So this is what we are dealing with. And one other thing: in the Senate, there are almost no rules on what matter or amendment is germane to any bill at any time; almost any provision can be attached to any bill.[19]

So we had to worry about whether there would be something on the Senate floor with which Enzi could get to work. We were alerted to this earlier in the week and went on patrol beginning last night. Fortunately, the only legislation pending before the Senate adjourned was a must-pass bill—the Cash for Clunkers program, which provided incentives to trade in old gas guzzlers for new cars: the House had adjourned, the highly popular and successful program was running out of money, and to stay effective it had to be renewed immediately. Any amendment to the House bill would have killed the program, because the revised bill would then have to go through the House again, and that couldn't happen until it was back in session in September. We heard that Enzi might try to hot-wire the bill by seeking telephonic electronic consent from all Senate offices, and we had senators, such as Richard Durbin (D-IL), an antitobacco champion and deputy leader of the party, in place to object. So we stymied Enzi today. But the real issue is the administration's true position on this little number. The Department of Health and Human Services is vociferously against. But we sense that the office of the US trade representative, which Kantor headed under President Clinton, thinks there is a colorable case under international trade law in favor of the Indonesians. We simply have to tie this down. I can't believe that at the end of the day, President Obama would accept an egregious loophole in the new law. And I can't believe that the Senate would bend over backward for an amendment to support, of all things, Indonesian cigarettes or that a Republican senator with a mixed record on free-trade issues can take the floor with a straight face to protect imports of Indonesian clove cigarettes. Really? We have to be able to kill this thing. Tonight, the Senate adjourned until September. God save the United States of America. But who knows what other tricks they will conjure up?

## Wednesday, September 2

The tobacco companies have filed suit in—surprise—Kentucky (a prime home of tobacco) seeking to declare unconstitutional the marketing restrictions in the new tobacco control law. The new statute says their ads can't use color but have to be in stark black and white and requires graphic (color) warning labels showing the physical harm caused by smoking. They say that these restrictions violate free speech rights under the First Amendment. It will be a major test of whether commercial speech is on an equal par with political expression. We are considering whether Henry should file an amicus brief opposing the tobacco companies' suit.

We follow up with a call to a senior lawyer who is an expert on tobacco legislation to get advice about what to do. Our initial conclusion is that Henry should go ahead and file at the district court level to send a powerful message to the court that Congress stands by its decision to bring tobacco under a new regulatory regime. We are also keeping an eye on the Indonesians' pernicious effort to get clove cigarettes exempted from the new tobacco control legislation.

## Saturday, October 3

Our normal work proceeds. For me, it involves a major push against two renegade tobacco companies who are trying to evade the new tobacco law by transforming their flavored cigarettes into flavored cigars (arguably less regulated products). Waxman and the chair of our oversight and investigations subcommittee have sent sternly worded letters to the companies, demanding that they produce all documents and materials in their possession on the marketing of these products. We want to lean on them so that they desist. Henry will also join with Sen. Durbin in a stiff letter to the Secretary of Health and Human Services and the US trade representative rejecting entreaties made by the Indonesian government regarding clove cigarettes.

## Friday, October 9

Late this morning, I was in a meeting with the general counsel to the House of Representatives to discuss our interest in Henry's filing an amicus brief to defend the new tobacco regulation law in court in Kentucky. The counsel advises that Henry will have more standing and impact if he can file on behalf of his committee, which wrote the bill, and defend its findings, particularly on the constitutionality of the advertising and marketing restrictions, and the public health basis on which they were made. The counsel believes that the court would pay special attention to that official representation from a panel of another branch of government. But in pursuing this, we were also advised that the House counsel general intervenes in court cases if the executive branch is not defending what Congress has done, and that is not the case here, since the Justice Department is fully litigating the new law on behalf of our policy goals and objectives. It is not clear whether Henry should file in an individual capacity, which will carry less weight with the court. More work to do on this.

## Tuesday, October 14

Today, an executive from a Midwest tobacco company that does not produce flavored little cigars and other enticements for kids—products that are being regulated now and under threat of outright bans by the FDA under the authority of the new law—came in to tell all the secrets of what other manufacturers do to win market share among youth. That's why we are talking: his company wants to claw back some market share against competitors. We may be able to capitalize on some of his spilled beans. And there was a meeting with the Campaign for Tobacco-Free Kids to discuss the health reform bill. They love what Henry did in the final tobacco bill but are wary of a do-gooder provision in the Senate bill that they think could backfire. The Kennedy Committee essentially authorized 50 percent higher health insurance premiums for smokers. It sounds great on the surface, but when you dig into it, there are flaws: smokers are generally poorer. If health insurance becomes unaffordable for some, their families are uninsured, too, and those living with smokers get sick more often. This means that their health is at risk along with their insurance. We also want these groups to identify some pro bono legal resources to assist in the lawsuit the tobacco companies are waging in Kentucky against the new antitobacco bill.

## Monday, May 17, 2010

We will hold hearings on flavored cigars and expose the industry's ceaseless efforts to exploit every tiny opening under the new antitobacco law to market their products to children and hook new generations of smokers. (The law's treatment of cigars is slightly less restrictive than cigarettes, and tobacco companies are making flavored cigars and packaging them like cigarettes to get a little more visibility with young consumers.)

## Wednesday, July 28

We met with Human Rights Watch today. They uncovered the use of child labor in Kazakhstan by Philip Morris. Child labor was being used to harvest the crop, and Philip Morris has a monopoly license for Kazakhstan's tobacco. The Human Rights Watch findings were the subject of a major article a couple weeks ago in the *New York Times*, and we immediately asked Philip Morris for an explanation, along with all of the company's documents on the use of child labor and other labor practices in Kazakhstan. Philip Morris flew executives in to talk with our staff last week and pledged to end any child labor and improve their activities. We also asked whether other tobacco companies might be engaged in child labor in other countries, so we may have further leads.

Friday, December 10

Our monitoring of Philip Morris has had positive repercussions. They have hired labor auditors to assess the situation and recommend better practices. They have complied with our information request, sending thousands of documents. Their outside auditor will report to us with a briefing in the spring. We believe their responsiveness is genuine; they are trying to improve labor practices in Kazakhstan. They are being watched closely by human rights groups, and we want to keep a tension in the oversight relationship, just in case.

Monday, March 28, 2011

A quiet Monday is a good day to make a news splash in Washington. Not that there is not tons going on (just a war in Libya, a nuclear meltdown in Japan, and prospects for a government shutdown looming at the end of next week). But if the House is out, the first working day of the week is good space to get out a story. And so months of review of documents obtained by Kretek, the Indonesian tobacco company that uses cloves to flavor its tobacco, yielded a stinging letter from Henry to the FDA. Cloves and other flavorings were banned in the 2009 law that put tobacco under the FDA. We had monitored the emergence of flavored cigars in the market over the months following enactment, and it seemed that companies might deliberately be gaming the new law to transition products to less regulated cigars and keep hooking kids with the flavored weed. The Kretek documents, obtained last year, showed every likelihood that this is the case.

Henry's letter to the FDA today said:

> On September 22, 2009, the Food and Drug Administration banned the sale of flavored cigarettes, including those flavored with clove. FDA took this action under the authority of the Family Smoking Prevention and Tobacco Control Act. When you announced the

ban, you explained that "flavored cigarettes are a gateway for many children and young adults to become regular smokers." Dr. Howard Koh, the Assistant Secretary for Health, stated: Flavored cigarettes attract and allure kids into a lifetime of addiction. FDA's ban on these cigarettes will break that cycle.

The FDA ban applies only to cigarettes, which are defined as tobacco products wrapped in paper. The ban did not apply to cigars, which are tobacco products wrapped in tobacco leaves. The documents provided to the committee show that Kretek deliberately sought to exploit this loophole by creating a clove cigar with "exactly the same formula as our clove cigarette" and "launching a cigar replacement product that will continue our business." According to one internal Kretek document, "GOAL IS SEAMLESS CONVERSION TO CLOVE CIGARS." I urge you to protect youth from the dangers of Kretek's new product by extending the ban on flavored cigarettes to flavored cigars that have been designed and marketed to circumvent the FDA prohibition.

This will encourage the FDA to do its job. And Kretek had a very bad day.

## Monday, May 23

My day started with a midnight email from Dr. Lawrence "Bopper" Deyton, head of the FDA's tobacco control and public health programs. A threat is brewing in the Appropriations Committee to put limitations on funding for the next financial year, which begins October 1. The proposed language would prevent the FDA from acting to control tobacco and its marketing unless there was epidemiological evidence that it was justified. This is a far narrower basis than the Kennedy-Waxman tobacco law, enacted with such fanfare almost two years ago. So this would gut the law. And it would be an uphill fight in the committee for several reasons. First, the funding comes out of the Agriculture Appropriations subcommittee, which means that the interests of farmers and growers are paramount. They like to grow things, including tobacco. Second, a quick check of the 2009 vote on the House floor on the bill showed only one Republican on that subcommittee who voted for Kennedy-Waxman, and on the full committee, only eleven of twenty-nine Republicans supported it. We swung into a program of communications with the Democrats on the subcommittee, and by late in the day, the Republicans blinked: the feared language was not in the chair's proposed mark that would be debated and voted on tomorrow afternoon in subcommittee. But we remain on high alert. If it gets to it, I think we will just fight it out on the House floor. The vote for the bill two years ago was one of the strongest bipartisan votes in the last Congress, and we would present this as repeal of critical public health legislation. I think we would win that fight. And at least we ensure that the president would veto any funding bill with the offending language. So even if we lose, we should be able to win.

## Thursday, May 26

But it is far from over. The tobacco interests found a willing partner to carry the fight and take a shot at gutting the tobacco bill. This evening, word that the Appropriations Committee approved an amendment that ties the FDA's hands in regulating tobacco. A desperate move by the tobacco industry to strangle the new law just as new rules on the marketing of tobacco and additives are coming into force. The House Appropriations Committee approved the fiscal year 2012 agriculture appropriations bill with an amendment by Rep. Denny Rehberg (R-MT) that would undermine the FDA's authority to regulate tobacco and to protect the public from dangerous drugs and unsafe foods. Waxman responded,

> The Republicans have launched a pernicious assault on the Tobacco Control Act. This law barely two years old, is the most important health tool we have to reduce the ravages of smoking, which takes the lives of 400,000 Americans per year, and exacts a toll in health costs of $96 billion annually. There is no excuse for disarming FDA and giving the tobacco industry a blank check to continue to market tobacco to children and young adults. The House Appropriations Committee has imposed its judgment about the epidemiology and toxicology of tobacco over the expertise of scientists, doctors, researchers, educators, and public health officers. This is a shameful amendment, and it does not deserve to progress any further in legislation. I call on everyone who has worked so hard for so long to bring tobacco under the control of the Food and Drug Administration to join together to preserve the full authority of the expert agency to regulate this killer in order to protect the public health of the American people and to help keep children from taking up smoking.

We began setting strategy for a floor fight.

Tuesday, June 7

A day of meetings on the tobacco-FDA rider that the Republicans put into the agriculture appropriations bill. It seems that Henry's media statement last week unleashed a torrent of criticism on the author, Rep. Rehberg, and he is backtracking furiously. We're told he spoke with our committee chair, Fred Upton (R-MI), and asked him to assert a parliamentary rule that would knock the amendment out of the bill. Under the rules of the House, the Appropriations Committee cannot legislate (that is, add substantive changes to law under the jurisdiction of other committees) in a funding bill. The committee can cut funding or say that funding cannot be spent on a certain program, but they can't alter the underlying law. This appears to be what the Rehberg amendment does. So we spoke with the Democratic staff on Appropriations to line up their support for an amendment to strike if the parliamentary point of order fails. We met with a coalition of health groups to get them ready to swoop on the House members in support of an amendment to strike. We also asked their help to identify Republicans who would join us to make this a bipartisan effort. And we are checking the parliamentary point directly with the House parliamentarian. So this is moving in our direction.

Wednesday, June 8

This afternoon we advanced the ball on the tobacco-FDA rider on the agriculture appropriations bill. We have a clear advisory opinion from the parliamentarian that we can knock out the amendment on a point of order—that it is legislation on an appropriations bill, which is forbidden under the rules. So this afternoon, we began lining that strategy up: advising the Democrats on Appropriations that we want to move against the amendment through this parliamentary procedure; coordinating with the Democrats on the Rules Committee to ensure that they do not take action that would prevent us from lodging the point of order; reaching out to John Dingell's office to make sure he is on the floor to do the point of order if Upton, who says he will do it, fails to do so; and a conference call with the public health groups to let them know what is unfolding and to get their support. And just to be sure if this collapses, we've drafted the amendment to strike and we're writing a letter to all House members explaining why we need to strike. We also got statements ready for debate on what the bill does to food safety enforcement. So it was wired pretty well by the evening, and action should unfold tomorrow.

## Wednesday, June 15

Finally, a good day, the best day we've had since December 21, 2010, when we passed major legislation on the final day of the 111th Congress and the Democratic-controlled House adjourned sine die, to be replaced with the Republicans in power on January 3. Today, we won a fight with Republicans on the House floor. It came up very fast, and a quick tactical response led to the win. Rep. Cliff Stearns (R-FL) ambushed us with an amendment on the House floor at 3:00 pm. It would have cut nearly four hundred million dollars from the FDA's antismoking programs. This is all part of the agriculture appropriations bill. Stearns offered his amendment and pressed it in debate. At this stage of consideration of an appropriations bill, amendments come up and are debated under the five-minute rule and then followed by a vote on all the amendments pending in a bunched series of roll-call votes. We did not have time to get Henry to the floor to take on Stearns. The top Democrat on the Appropriations Committee did a good job but could only sustain an argument for a few minutes. Stearns thought he had won. We immediately drafted a letter to all members of the House, ran it by the top antismoking group for kids, and cleared it with the senior staff. It went to every Democratic and Republican office by 4:00:

> Today, Representative Cliff Stearns sought to amend the Agriculture Appropriations bill, H.R. 2112, by slashing $392 million for FDA's Center for Tobacco.
>
> This is a misguided amendment that will gut critical dollars for this newly established center. The Center for Tobacco Products is charged with the essential public health mission of protecting our children from the harms of tobacco. This Center was created as a result of the Family Smoking Prevention and Tobacco Control Act which passed the House on a strong bipartisan vote of 307–97 in 2009.
>
> The funding for the Center for Tobacco Products comes entirely from user fees paid for by the tobacco industry itself. Under the terms of the Family Smoking Prevention and Tobacco Control Act, these dollars must be collected and spent on tobacco activities at the FDA. Therefore, reducing the funding for the Center would serve only to give an undeserved windfall to the tobacco industry by reducing the amount they must pay in user fees.
>
> Further, the funding levels for 2009 through 2019 are specified

in the Tobacco Control Act itself. Representative Stearns complained that the President had asked for too much in his budget—but the President did nothing more than to request the amounts specified in the statute.

Tobacco industry fees are essential to combating one of our greatest public health threats. We all benefit when smoking—particularly by children—is curbed. I urge all members to vote against this dangerous amendment.

Sincerely,
Henry A. Waxman

The vote was 164–257, with more than 70 Republicans voting with us; we lost just 3 Democrats. It was just a great moment. And then, a few minutes later, they got to the section of the bill that had the anti-FDA, antitobacco regulatory language from Rep. Rehberg, and that was struck out on the point of order. The Republicans kept their word to move against the language, but we had people on the floor to press the point if they had faltered. That was all wired through direct email confirmation with the key staff on both sides of the aisle yesterday and today, with minute-by-minute tracking of the exact point in the bill is where the outcome rested—because if you do not lodge the point of order as soon as the section to be challenged is called up, you miss your shot. It was executed perfectly. And that made it a very good day.

Monday, November 7

Some quick work this afternoon: a federal district court judge ruled for the tobacco companies in one of their lawsuits against the graphic warnings on cigarette packages that are required under the 2009 tobacco law and are supposed to go into effect next year. The decision was reported by the media a little after 1:00 pm and by 3:00 pm we had a stiff statement from Henry:

The district court's decision is extremely regrettable. The evidence is clear: the current warning labels have run their course and are not as effective as they need to be to protect public health from tobacco's addictive and toxic qualities. The provisions on enhanced tobacco warnings were enacted in 2009 with broad, bipartisan majorities in the House and Senate. Congress carefully considered the First

Amendment issues involved and carefully tailored the legislation to ensure the FDA could act as it has proposed with graphic warning labels for tobacco products. I believe that, on further judicial review, these public health protections will be affirmed and permitted to go into effect next year.

The statement got strong coverage this evening. But even if we lose this—the court today said the prescriptive warnings were too much of a burden on First Amendment rights—it's not a killer for the new tobacco law. As I mentioned with Bopper Deyton, who heads up the tobacco program at FDA, a few weeks ago, in anticipation of what this judge might do in this case, "The important thing is what is in—and what is not in—the cigarette, not what the package says." And no court can stop what we have done to control what is in the cigarette. The court can't take that victory away. Finally, after all these years, the public interest won and tobacco's hold over Congress has been loosened.

### What We Learned from Tobacco's Big Turn

There are a number of takeaways from tobacco's road to regulatory reform. On one hand, special interests—in this case, the tobacco industry—can take hold of the institutional levers of power in Congress, and social and cultural acceptance can reinforce that hold. On the other hand, Congress as an institution plays an important role in shaping the debate over public versus private interests, and broader political forces affect Congress's policymaking regarding the line between the two. Congress was unable or unwilling to regulate tobacco until public attitudes shifted. In addition, partisanship played a more subdued role in tobacco politics than in cap-and-trade and health care. The negative public health consequences of tobacco were not inherently ideological or partisan issues that divided voters but rather were regional and economic issues. Reformers and the committee thus had the ability to operate somewhat more independently of party leadership.

An argument can be made on behalf of the old adage that good politics makes for good policy—or at least for policy change. Although the politics of tobacco changed before Congress could act as institution, individual legislators nonetheless made valuable contributions by braving the difficulties to do the right thing for the public interest. Indeed, leadership by reform-minded individuals from both parties was important in the fight against tobacco interests. That Waxman and Kennedy and Durbin and others worked for years—decades—shows what can happen when political power is applied over an extended period of time. Yet the making of public policy is a collective enterprise, less about the "profiles in courage" of individual members and more about understanding how political conditions affect Congress's ability or willingness to act.

The committee and the subcommittee played a critical role in hearings and oversight. Waxman's 1994 hearings not only made the public health consequences of tobacco use salient but also exposed the public to a side of the industry difficult to defend. By 2009, public opinion had changed, and the tobacco industry had growing difficulty credibly denying tobacco's harm to societal health. Lessening tobacco consumption would save lives, and even the industry's top CEOs admitted that they hoped their children would not use tobacco (Hilts 1994; Waxman and Green 2009, 186). Moving the politics of Big Tobacco made the political landscape more favorable to reformers and thus enabled regulatory legislation in Congress. The journey took decades, but major reform would not occur without a sufficiently broad external political consensus. A parallel process may now be unfolding in the committee's oversight of player concussions in the National Football League (NFL). The NFL's executive vice president for health and safety admitted in March 2016 testimony before the House Energy and Commerce Committee that a connection exists between concussions and degenerative brain disease (Chappell 2016). To some who serve or had served on the committee, this sounded like an echo from the tobacco industry.[20]

Similarly, once Congress adopts new policy—in this case, FDA regulation—there is no guarantee that policy is settled forever (although it is hard to see any return to the old pervasiveness of tobacco in American society). The tobacco industry may well continue to chip away at the new regulatory regime. We saw how the committee's work could have been undone if it had failed to protect the tobacco regulation policy. The fight for tobacco reform consequently brings to mind an important lesson about our separation-of-powers system—no issue is ever permanently settled (Waxman and Green 2009).[21] Thus, the committee's work did not end in the committee room. After the passage of tobacco reform, Waxman—as chair and later as the ranking minority member—and other pro-reform members of the committee continued the vital work of overseeing the policy's implementation.

With the change in party control, the new chair, Upton, could have worked to reverse the policy or stand aside while the regulatory scheme was weakened by starving it of resources through the appropriations process. But he did not. In this case, he chose to work with the minority members on the committee to defend Energy and Commerce's power against encroachment.[22] The example of the Appropriations Committee employing a policy rider in the agricultural funding bill reflects an increasingly common pattern in the contemporary Congress. Hitching a policy rider to the appropriations train to encourage (or discourage) agency spending or create new policy is the big business of lobbyists and lawmakers (Hallerman 2014). Policy riders by appropriators also represent a threat to the power of authorizing committees in that such riders are used to essentially make policy within the policy jurisdiction of the authorizers. Riders can take positive power out of the hands of the authorizing committee(s) and instead delegate such discretion to appropriators. Party leaders also have increasingly used appropriations riders to deliver on majority-party priorities (Aldrich and Rohde 1997–98). Riders have become an important source of partisan conflict on appropriations, a policy realm that because of its centrality to congressional power had been more resistant to the intense levels of partisanship that had become characteristic of other policy domains (Fenno 1966; Marshall, Prins, and Rohde 2000). And more generally, the tussle with appropriators reflects the fact that party leaders have viewed the appropriations train as a way to deliver on a range of majority-party priorities. The power of the purse remains Congress's most potent power, but it is not clear whether Congress may see the political benefit of allowing appropriators to run roughshod over or encroach on authorizing committees and their policy jurisdictions (Fischer 2000).

Finally, the regulatory fight over tobacco also illustrates the importance of the separation-of-powers system in shaping policy.[23] In 2000, the US Supreme Court struck down the Clinton administration's 1996 attempt to utilize executive discretion over the FDA to regulate tobacco.[24] Although supporters of reform saw the decision as the Court inviting Congress to act, prodding congressional legislation in the face of entrenched opposition was a very different and at that time very difficult matter.[25] Indeed, thirteen more years passed before tobacco control legislation was enacted. Whether by fostering congressional intransigence or counting on the prospect of a presidential veto, opponents of reform relied on the fact that the separation-of-powers system generally and in Congress in particular makes it easier to block policy change than to move the status quo. Yet the campaign against Big Tobacco was about much more than passing a new regulatory policy. This was a decades-long battle that hinged on Congress's ability to monitor the tobacco industry, shouldering the weighty constitutional obligation to protect the nation's common good and the public health by eventually bringing private interests to heel.

# FIVE

# From Presidential "Shakedown" to Congressional Apology

*The Politics of Committee Oversight of BP's Deepwater Horizon Crisis*

This chapter illustrates the House Energy and Commerce Committee's aggressive oversight of the BP oil spill crisis; how coalition fissures, especially in the Senate, thwarted the legislative response to the crisis; and how the politics of the spill affected the broader efforts at a grand bargain in climate policy. We begin by offering a brief sketch of the economic and political forces at play as the BP oil spill unfolded and how they shaped both the committee's and Congress's actions before we explore what this accounting says about the committee's oversight and legislative response in the context of congressional politics and partisanship. The chapter offers a vivid portrayal of the committee's investigative and legislative operations as well as the political strategies employed to confront the disaster. These events also highlight the formidable electoral and partisan constraints that hamstrung the committee's and Congress's legislative response, notwithstanding the very strong glare cast on the crisis by the committee's oversight hearings. The interplay of these powerful forces comes into sharper focus in light of the severity of the disaster. After all, the sheer magnitude of environmental degradation from the BP spill was unique. As the director of the Sierra Club noted, "We call it the biggest environmental disaster in history for a reason" (Magner and Dillon 2016, http://library.cqpress.com.proxy.lib.miamioh.edu/cqweekly/weeklyreport114-000004875441).

## The Context

Occurring about fifty miles off of the Louisiana coast, an area that was still suffering from Hurricanes Katrina and Rita in 2005, the BP oil spill was an environmental crisis on par with the 1979 nuclear meltdown at Three Mile Island; the 1984 industrial chemical accident at Bhopal, India, that exposed six hundred thousand people to a deadly gas cloud, and the damage caused by Hurricane Katrina in 2005, which affected the same area as the BP oil spill (Benkelman 2010). The spill caused unprecedented and incomprehensible damage to the Gulf Coast and constituted the largest environmental disaster in history (Magner and Dillon 2016).[1]

On April 20, 2010, an explosion on the Deepwater Horizon oil drilling platform in the Gulf of Mexico killed eleven people and injured seventeen others. The platform subsequently caught fire and sank five thousand feet into the depths, where the Macondo oil well was breached. The platform explosion resulted from a large amount of natural gas that had escaped into the drilling pipe and passed containment seals designed to control the oil flow for production. When the containment seals ruptured, a five-story valve assembly on the seafloor that was supposed to act as an emergency clamp on the pipe failed. After three months, the well was finally capped, but not before it poured about 4.9 million barrels of oil into the Gulf of Mexico—between fifteen and twenty times more oil than the amount spilled from the 1989 *Exxon Valdez* disaster in Prince William Sound, Alaska (Hobson 2011b; Harrison 2013).

The BP oil spill was in a class of disasters like no other "environmentally, economically, and politically" (Benkelman 2010, 1370). More than 150,000 people were directly exposed to oil and chemical dispersants during and immediately after the spill. Many still suffer from respiratory as well as psychological ailments, some of which resemble posttraumatic stress disorder (Magner 2016).[2] Nearly 90,000 square miles of state and federal fishing waters were temporarily closed. Oil soaked into about 650 miles of shoreline, beaches, bayous, and bays (Harrison 2013). A small delegation of committee members visited Louisiana to see firsthand the devastation from the BP spill. Tethered to a platform in the tail of a military transport plane, Rep. Edward Markey (D-MA) offered his birds-eye view: the oil slick extended "as far as the eye can see." (Ota 2010a, 1393). Six years later, some of the Gulf fishing industry had recovered, particularly with regard to such short-lived species as shrimp and crab, but troubling signs persist for larger marine life and the ecosystems needed to sustain barrier islands and coral reefs. In addition, a layer of oil and chemical dispersants covers an area "the size of the city Houston" on the ocean floor (Magner and Dillon 2016).[3]

Although many environmental costs remain unknown, the total price tag for damages has been set at about $55 billion based on the 2016 settlement between the US Justice Department and BP. Of that total, 48 percent (about $26 billion) is earmarked for economic damages to governments, businesses, and individuals. Another $15.8 billion (about 29 percent) is designated for initial cleanup costs and contributions toward a federal trust fund for future spills. The last—and smallest—piece of the compensation fund, $13.1 billion (about 23 percent), goes toward environmental repair.[4] And under the 2012 RESTORE Act, passed by the 112th Congress, the five most affected states can spend a significant amount of the "environmental repair" funds on economic improvement projects.[5]

The economics and politics of the spill were inextricably tied together and help provide clear insight into the underlying constraints on Congress's legislative response. Despite the uniquely significant cost of the oil spill, it ultimately did not result in drastic changes to national energy policy. To be sure, many environmental groups launched a concerted push to lessen dependence on fossil fuels, to increase the use of renewable energy sources, and even to demand the end of deepwater drilling, and these calls resonated among Democrats in Congress and within the Obama administration. But the BP spill did not fundamentally alter the stronger political consensus that the United States should continue to develop its own energy resources, including drilling for oil.[6] The risk/reward calculation for such a fundamental shift in overall US energy policy remained too great, as suggested in the weeks following the spill by the chair of BP's board, Carl-Henric Svanberg: "The reality is that the world needs energy. There's no way around it. Almost every form comes with risk. And we have learned to live with that" (Cranford 2010, 1390).[7] The spill's macroeconomic context was also important: a deeply suffering American economy was just beginning to show signs of life in the wake of the worst downturn and financial crisis the country had seen since the Great Depression. Relatively high gas prices (around three dollars per gallon) added to consumers' misery. Moreover, the oil and gas industries were a centerpiece of economic life along the Gulf Coast, and bipartisan political support for drilling never wavered (Russell 2012). In fact, in response to a temporary moratorium on deepwater drilling initiated because of the spill, Governor Bobby Jindal (R-LA), whose state was the hardest hit by the oil disaster, appealed to President Obama and the Department of Interior to expedite the review of deepwater practices and to resume drilling, declaring, "During one of the most challenging economic periods in decades, the last thing we need is to enact public policies that will certainly destroy thousands of existing jobs while preventing the creation of thousands more" (Cranford 2010, 1389).

The political environment and economic forces at the time of the spill ultimately posed a stiff barrier to any broad legislative effort at energy or climate change policy that could be perceived as stopping the oil industry from offshore drilling and bringing more oil online for the United States. Many members of Congress were faced with the electoral imperative of feeding a job-deprived economy over other policy goals. However, under Henry Waxman's leadership, the committee undertook a rigorous and probing oversight process that produced bipartisan consensus on a package of much-needed safety and industry-related reforms. But the fragile goodwill carefully crafted in committee vanished, replaced by partisan rancor on the House floor. The run at reform legislation subsequently died at the hands of Senate Republicans. Still, the committee's efforts did come to fruition in terms of policy changes—many of its recommendations were adopted administratively through new rules and regulations under the Environmental Protection Agency (EPA) and Department of Interior.

Despite the underlying necessity for political leaders to right the country's economic ship, public outrage over the magnitude of the environmental damage and the growing realization that it could persist indefinitely led to demands for the government and BP to confront the oil spill disaster. The White House responded unilaterally and placed intense pressure on BP to take responsibility for the spill's damage, investigate the cause, and ensure the safety of future drilling operations. Following the initial disaster, the administration ordered a six-month freeze on deepwater drilling before following up with an executive order that created a national commission to investigate the spill and make recommendations to prevent future accidents (Anderson and Scholtes 2010). The freeze on deepwater operations allowed the commission time to find solutions. Under intense political pressure from the White House, BP agreed by mid-June to withhold shareholder dividends and create a twenty-billion-dollar compensation fund to begin covering spill-inflicted damages.[8] BP also created a one-hundred-million-dollar fund to support unemployed rig workers, softening the political blowback on the White House from the temporary drilling freeze. In addition, the company agreed not to invoke its seventy-five-million-dollar insurance liability limit, instead agreeing to pay all reasonable claims (Schatz and Koss 2010).[9] In addition, the Department of Interior began major reorganization efforts to strengthen agencies tasked with regulating and oversight of oil drilling and exploration (Harrison 2013).

Through these clear and forceful actions, the White House sought to show that it was responding effectively to the Deepwater Horizon disaster. And BP, for its part, appeared to cooperate closely with the White House to get assistance to the region to begin the repair of massive environmental damage, even as the company struggled to find a solution to the oil breach a mile below the ocean's surface.

Congress also moved rapidly, with ten different legislative and oversight committees calling for investigatory and legislative action. Concurrently, dozens of proposed bills on safety and oversight of the oil industry circulated (Hobson 2011b). But in terms of actual lawmaking, Democrats in the 111th had only limited success, as exemplified by the passage of a narrow bill (S 3473) that provided the president with greater flexibility in withdrawing advances from the Oil Spill Liability Trust Fund to help manage the effects of the Deepwater Horizon spill.[10] The Republican takeover of the House in the 112th Congress effectively ended efforts to regulate the oil industry or move climate legislation. Not surprisingly, the new House GOP majority had strong antiregulation principles and no appetite for shackling the oil industry, especially in a time of continued "economic distress". As Kenneth Green, an environmental expert from the American Enterprise Institute, noted at the time, "I don't see Congress passing anything that looks vaguely hostile to domestic energy production (Hobson 2011b, 852). Instead, the new GOP House majority shifted the energy-related legislative agenda toward proposals that would spur drilling and domestic production. But this agenda, like the Democratic efforts in the prior Congress, failed to result in new laws. The 112th Congress did pass the RESTORE Act of 2012, which created the Gulf Coast Restoration Fund to pool revenues from administrative and civil penalties and provided allocation guidelines for such monies to the five Gulf Coast States (Harrison 2013). Congress's collective lawmaking response during and immediately following the crisis for both the Democratic 111th Congress and the Republican 112th took a similarly narrow posture, finding sufficient support only for policies targeting the allocation of funds to areas affected by the spill disaster. Thus, the BP crisis illustrates how Congress can have both very aggressive oversight and a limited legislative response.

What explains Congress's limited legislative response to the most significant environmental disaster in US history? Actions taken by the administration and BP—to the extent that they were viewed as significant steps forward in addressing accountability and preventing future spills—were certainly important in defusing some of the demand for legislative action. And the country's economic and political context made major policy change difficult. Even narrower policies aimed at safety issues in the oil industry were met with resistance, given the high-stakes political debate between energy and the environment and oil versus clean energy. This was ultimately reflected in how the politics of the spill played out in Congress. Consensus generally existed within the committee regarding its response to the crisis and the investigatory role that led to the development of substantive administrative reforms. But beyond the committee, the politics of the BP spill and Congress's collective response to the disaster became intertwined with the broader debate on energy and environmental policy and thus enmeshed in partisan conflict.

Both sides saw policy and/or partisan opportunities in the politics of the BP crisis. The Democratic leadership saw the BP spill as a way to focus public attention on the need for policy change to wean the country off of fossil fuels and onto a clean energy track. But as chapter 1 showed, the Democrats were unable to navigate the cap-and-trade bill through the Senate. Republican leaders saw a clear opportunity to use the BP spill disaster to blame the Obama administration for poor crisis management and thus blunt new legislation to regulate the oil industry. As in other cases, leadership strategy and partisan incentives were important in shaping the congressional politics of the crisis.

## The Role of Leadership Strategy and Partisanship: Political Opportunity and Danger

The politics of the spill had a couple of important dimensions. Members of the committee were immediately concerned with investigating the crisis to prevent such an accident from ever occurring again and to find ways to make affected citizens whole. From the outset, Democrats were clearly on the offensive, wanting to hold BP to account, while Republicans sought to limit political fallout for themselves and damage to their long-standing allies in Big Oil. These political forces were all on display in the committee as investigation efforts unfolded. However, another important dimension to the politics of the spill went beyond the committee and intersected with the broader legislative debate on energy and environmental policy. It is here that leadership decisions on strategy provide deeper insight into how partisanship came to affect congressional politics and the response to the crisis.

First, the Democratic leadership sought to couple the politics of the crisis with the push for broader energy and climate policy. The public outrage at the worst environmental disaster in the country's history and the spectacle of the country's need to find more sustainable and cleaner energy neatly crystallized these issues and the deeper energy policy choices at stake. For both Democrats and Republicans, the disaster became enmeshed with the larger energy and environment policy debate.

Second, the GOP leadership sought to use the BP crisis to attack the president's political standing and sink the broader Democratic agenda. Both decisions reflect the importance of electoral and partisan incentives. Candidate Obama had campaigned on freeing the country from its dependence on fossil fuels and fostering a new clean energy economy. Many Democrats were eager to deliver on such a major policy reform to energize environmental allies by notching a major policy victory that could pay electoral dividends in the upcoming midterm election. And for the GOP, similar incentives were at work. Republicans were closely aligned with the policy interests of the oil industry, which included curbing federal regulation and promoting drilling and fossil fuel development. In raw political terms, Republicans on the committee recognized that the crisis might present a perfect Katrina-like storm for the administration. By positioning the party to take advantage of executive missteps or failures in managing the catastrophe, the GOP leaders could focus public scorn on the White House for failing to stop the spill and end the environmental and economic devastation that had been unleashed on the Gulf and its communities. Republicans' political calculation was that any political toll inflicted on the president and Democrats as the crisis ensued would strengthen the GOP's electoral prospects. So policy, electoral, and partisan forces aligned with each of the parties and in opposition to one another.

Before the BP spill, Democrats remained hopeful that a broader policy agreement on energy and the environment was still possible even though the Senate had prevented a broader deal on energy and climate legislation the preceding year. Developing renewable energy sources and reducing US dependence on fossil fuels had been one of Obama's major campaign issues and retained vigorous support among most congressional Democrats. Spurred on by rising gasoline prices, Congress had moved toward a bipartisan compromise centered on an agreement to allow more drilling to increase domestic supply.[11] Just weeks before the spill, the White House announced its commitment to open up new oil and gas exploration in the Mid-Atlantic, Southeast, and Gulf of Mexico.[12] Behind the commitment to new drilling was the administration's hope for a grand bargain on energy and climate policy. Movement on new drilling was key to obtaining Republican support, and a seemingly strong advocate emerged in Sen. Lindsey

Graham (R-SC), who had promised to deliver his chamber's Republicans as long as drilling was part of the legislative package. Moreover, lawmakers and stakeholders on both sides were concerned that the absence of a legislative breakthrough on overall energy and climate legislation would result in a far worse outcome—a "nightmare scenario" that would leave the EPA empowered through the Clean Air Act (PL 101-549) to regulate carbon emissions and ensnare industries in a costly and uncertain decades-long court fight (Davenport 2010b)—than the market mechanisms contained in the cap-and-trade legislation.[13]

For all these reasons, the melding of the BP crisis oversight activity with support for broader legislation seemed to offer a workable path for Democrats. They believed that they could regain momentum in the fight toward agreement on energy and climate policy. Democratic leaders expected that the devastation wrought by the spill would strengthen their cause among those who opposed any broader effort on energy and environment policy (Koss 2010). In fact, Sen. Harry Reid (D-NV) believed that "rather than slow us up, I think [the spill] should expedite our doing energy legislation" (Schatz and Davenport 2010, 1133). House Speaker Nancy Pelosi (D-CA) offered a similar though more subdued outlook: "I don't think this is something that will stop it" (Schatz and Davenport 2010, 1133). And Waxman intended the investigatory strategy to provide a road map for enhancing drilling safety and strengthening the liability law to prevent future disasters. But he also signaled his shared vision with the Democratic leadership: the committee could use its oversight activities and forge a vigorous investigatory effort designed to renew and carry the energy and climate agenda across the finish line (Ota 2010a).

Rep. Waxman had spent decades building a sterling reputation for skill in harnessing the committee's investigatory arm to push through legislation, especially related to protecting public health and the environment (Waxman 2008). He combined the art of building a case and with pure forensic tenacity and an unyielding will to get to the truth. His investigations bludgeoned through ambiguity until only the facts remained: what went wrong and why, who was accountable, and how the problems could be fixed. Waxman believed that the most effective oversight was based on a team approach. In addition to having an expert staff with excellent command of the issues and the law, Waxman sought consensus on strategy and lines of responsibility with his senior subcommittee leaders. For example, Rep. Bart Stupak's (D-MI) Subcommittee on Oversight and Investigations would focus on the failed blowout preventer, while Rep. Markey's Energy and Environment Subcommittee tackled issues related to the effects of the spill on the environment.[14] At the first hearing on the BP spill, Waxman signaled his ultimate goal of implementing the leadership's strategy for sweeping legislation: "If we do not have the courage to take on the oil companies, we may never start down the path toward a clean energy economy" (Ota 2010a, 1392).

However, the BP spill opened fissures that made it hard to reach consensus on issues related to drilling expansion and the industry's spill liability limits. These key issues fueled bitter partisan conflict that ultimately doomed the prospects for a grand bargain on energy policy and hopes for significant progress on oil safety legislation, respectively. As a result, Congress passed only quite limited legislation despite the context of the largest environmental disaster in US history.

## The Demise of an Energy Grand Bargain and Oil Safety

Even as the House committee's investigation was generating political pressure for policy solutions, the issue of new drilling became more prominent and more complicated in the Senate as the spill's environmental enormity came into focus. Indeed, tolerance for drilling melted away among key senators as the oil plume in the Gulf grew. The position of liberal Democrats from coastal regions hardened against drilling and undermined the president's earlier commitment to expanded drilling. For example, Sen. Bill Nelson (D-FL) announced that "the president's proposal for offshore drilling is DOA" and threatened to filibuster any legislation containing new drilling. Other key Democrats, including New Jersey's Bob Menendez and Frank Lautenberg, soon followed suit as ocean currents threatened to carry the spill to their state's waters. Given these conflicting pressures, majority leader Harry Reid decided to move immigration reform before any energy and climate proposal. If taking drilling off the table was not enough to squash a larger energy and climate deal, Reid's change in the Senate agenda was. In response, Sen. Graham walked away from six months of climate negotiations, taking other potential drilling proponents with him and closing the door on bipartisanship (Davenport 2010b). Graham admonished Reid for changing the agenda: "We haven't done anything to prepare the body or the country for immigration. It destroys the ability to do something like energy and climate" (Davenport 2010b, 1094).

But the political postures of Sens. Graham and Reid were just emblematic of the larger partisan and electoral forces bearing down on members from both parties. Given strong sentiment among Republicans in Congress against any climate bill, Graham had faced pressure from his own leadership to end energy and climate negotiations, with Sen. Mitch McConnell (R-KY) warning that other Republicans would break away from any agreement during an election year. Graham was also feeling political heat from Tea Party groups and activists in his home state who bitterly opposed his bipartisan efforts on either climate or immigration (Davenport 2010b). Likewise, Reid's decision to jump immigration reform in front of climate efforts served a purpose for him at home: it would likely garner support among Nevada's Hispanic voters and brighten prospects for his tough reelection bid. Further, the majority leader's decision to prioritize immigration was also spurred in part by pressure from significant parts of the Democratic base for immigration reform in response to Arizona's controversial new law targeting illegal immigrants (Davenport 2010b).

Immense policy differences between the parties and an overall atmosphere of hyperpartisanship made a grand breakthrough on energy policy difficult. In particular, the oil spill crisis dashed hopes in the Senate that offshore drilling could foster a bipartisan breakthrough on energy policy even as the House Committee on Energy and Commerce employed its investigative efforts to build public support and political momentum for precisely such legislative action.

### Oil Safety

Partisanship also wreaked havoc on the possibility of more limited agreements on oil safety policy, especially when deep-seated conflict ignited in the Senate over the oil spill liability cap (Koss 2010). In the wake of the Deepwater Horizon calamity, both the House and Senate were considering oil safety bills that contained provisions changing federal oversight of the continental shelf to alleviate numerous legal, regulatory, and safety issues that were uncovered by the Gulf spill investigations. The House Bill (HR 3534) passed mostly along party lines (209–193) but only after Democratic leaders promised political cover to about thirty oil-patch Democrats.[15] However, a series of issues ultimately prevented the passage of the Senate bill (S 3663). For example, Republicans and moderate Democrats were very hostile to efforts by Sens. John Kerry (D-MA) and Joe Lieberman (I-CT) to include climate-related measures in the oil safety bill. But even when climate initiatives were scaled back, the Senate bill was permanently derailed over potential changes to the seventy-five-million-dollar oil spill liability cap. Democratic leaders viewed increasing the liability cap as critical to the goal of holding BP and other responsible parties accountable for economic and environmental costs.[16] The liability cap issue roiled oil-friendly southern Democrats and Republicans, who argued an increase would destroy the business of smaller independent drillers (Koss and Scholtes 2010). The Senate failed to bring either the Senate or House version of an oil safety bill to the floor (Hobson 2011a).

Other targeted legislation, including the committee's Blowout Prevention Act of 2010 (HR 5626), met a similar fate as the election winds began to heavily favor Republicans and political positions continued to harden. The spill also took place in an election year, with the bases of both parties activated, meaning that as November neared, both sides had increasing difficulty forging—let alone accepting—half victories, thus magnifying the burden of marshaling sufficient support for an agreement (Davenport 2010b). So although the committee exercised its full powers of oversight, with all the attendant media attention and activity by interest groups and lobbies with a direct stake in the outcome, to try to forge a legislative path that would prevent anything like Deepwater Horizon from recurring, Congress failed to pass such legislation.

### Political Opportunity: Blaming the White House

Political opportunity for Republicans and political danger for Democrats were both in play at the start of the BP spill crisis. In the first days, Sen. George LeMieux (R-FL) warned his colleagues, "There are those who are casting blame on [BP], there are those who are casting blame on the government. There will be time for that" (Schatz and Davenport 2010, 1135). House Republicans quickly closed ranks with a coordinated message that mixed attacks against BP with muted criticism of the White House's handling of the crisis. Republicans were careful early on to strike a balance to avoid becoming perceived as defending those responsible. One glaring exception occurred, however, when Rep. Joe Barton (R-TX), former chair of the committee, apologized to BP for its treatment by the Obama White House. Barton's actions caused immense short-term damage to the Republican narrative on the crisis. The literature on major crisis events has demonstrated that voters punish and reward individual political leaders (Gasper and Reeves 2011; Atkeson and Maestas 2012). And in the case of the spill crisis, Johnston and Goggin (2015) show that the media's portrayal of the BP spill and surrounding events proved critical in eventually linking President Obama to the crisis and saddling him with blame when it could not be ended promptly. Johnston and Goggin identify two clear phases of media coverage of the BP crisis. During the first phase (the Crisis Phase), which lasted about a month, media coverage focused almost exclusively on the spill, the urgent need to cap the well, and BP's response and cleanup operations. BP, not Obama, was perceived as responsible.

However, on May 26 BP's so-called top-kill attempt (with its "junk shot" of detritus) failed to stop the leak.[17] And the White House aided the shift in media coverage with a leak of its own at nearly the same time, with a flummoxed President Obama bursting out at a staff briefing, "Plug the damn hole!" (Johnston and Goggin 2015, 473). The leak publically exposed the president's frustration in dealing with the crisis and made his leadership more susceptible to criticism and blame from political opponents. These two events began to alter media coverage, and a spike occurred in the number of stories that joined together BP and the president in reporting on the crisis management. According to Johnston and Goggin (2015, 474), elite commentary increasingly featured discussions of how the spill would affect the Obama presidency. The failure of the top-kill effort was important because the uncertainty surrounding the continuation of the crisis shrank—no immediate end would be forthcoming. Johnston and Goggin further argue that the attempt's failure eliminated strategic uncertainty on the part of Republicans in Congress: the GOP could now explicitly blame President Obama for failure to end the spill without worrying that the crisis would soon be solved.[18] With this shift to the second phase (the Accountability Phase), the media reframed crisis-related stories in terms of a partisan or politicized assessment, pointing to Obama's failure to take effective charge. The most prominent example triggering the politicized phase of coverage occurred with Barton's "shakedown apology" to BP at a June 17 congressional hearing (Johnston and Goggin 2015). Media coverage during the Accountability Phase significantly undermined voters' confidence in President Obama (Johnston and Goggin 2015, 485). Johnston and Goggin (2015) suggest that voter attribution of blame is affected by factors such as partisanship and level of trust in the media and that the media coverage had the greatest effect on independents but also influenced Democrats to a lesser extent. Moreover, their findings suggest that voter confidence in Congress (at least among independents) was also undermined. The media framing of events can play a critical role regarding when and to whom voters attribute political blame for crises. In the case of BP, the media framing was shaped by Republicans' strategic decision to use the crisis, especially after the top-kill failure, to target the political standing of President Obama and congressional Democrats.

Thus, strategic decisions by the leadership reflect on the importance of partisanship in shaping Congress's response to the BP crisis. The Democrats' strategy of employing the committee's investigatory action to blaze a legislative path yielded little in the way of laws despite its success at an investigation and in systematically recommending policy reforms. The Republican strategy of shaping media coverage and attributing public blame on the White House worked to a degree. Voter confidence in President Obama was dramatically undermined; this, in turn, weighed down the Democratic agenda, which was already being squeezed by the electoral clock. At the same time, the committee's investigative and oversight activities held BP and the oil industry as a whole to strict account in the court of public opinion. BP paid an immense price in its reputation and the public's understanding of how it did business.

## Thursday April 29, 2010

Yesterday morning, the committee held a major hearing with Lisa Jackson, head of the EPA, on clean energy policies and reducing our dependence on oil. The most compelling point emerging from the hearing was that under the Obama administration's policies, a significant resetting of the country's oil consumption patterns has occurred. The administrator reported that as a result of auto efficiency standards, energy efficiency initiatives, clean coal, and added renewable programs, we have gone from oil consumption growth as far as the eye could see to a plateauing of oil demand through 2030 at 2007 levels. All told, this will save 1.6 billion barrels of oil per year—the highest conservation of any such program ever. She also defended, under hostile fire from the Republicans, the EPA's finding under the law that greenhouse gases endanger public health. The Republicans didn't see it that way, preferring to seize on the political opportunity offered by a rhetorical assault on "jobs-killing" energy taxes. We already have jobs-killing energy taxes in oil prices—and we pay them to Saudi Arabia.

The timing was dripping with political irony. Today witnessed the biggest oil spill in American history, unfolding about fifty miles off the coast of Louisiana—absolutely staggering in proportions (although we did not know the extent at the time) and much bigger than the 1989 *Exxon Valdez* disaster in Alaska. It comes less than a month after Obama outlined a balanced approach to energy security, allowing more offshore drilling, including in the Gulf of Mexico. That policy reflected intense pressure on the issue brought to bear since 2008 when Sarah Palin, the Republican vice presidential nominee, enraptured the party's convention with the rallying cry *Drill, baby, drill*. And that has been the four-syllable answer from the right on energy policy, endorsed by every major Republican. We were willing to buy into it to appease some conservatives—for example, Sen. Graham—the ticket we punched in hopes of getting them on board the larger energy and climate program, including carbon pricing. Graham has a gift for making himself indispensable to the legislative equation, because he telegraphs a willingness to deal on hard issues such as energy and immigration, offering Democrats the tantalizing prospect of some bipartisanship on really big bills. But when the moment comes to connect, it's like Charlie Brown, Lucy, and the football: it is always snatched away at the last moment. Well, this strategy is now busted, like the gasket on the floor of the Gulf. A terrible oil spill off Santa Barbara forty years ago closed the coast of California to drilling, and what is happening now will close the Gulf and Atlantic coasts. Who can support it in good conscience after such a catastrophe? So *Drill, baby, drill* is discredited, but it comes with a steep price. The fisheries off Louisiana are ruined, and the economic toll will be in the tens of billions. However, that does not mean more support for carbon pricing and fighting global warming. We are so stuck.

### Monday, May 3

The catastrophic oil spill in the Gulf of Mexico continues unabated, ruling the news and attention. It may be weeks before the well on the ocean floor can be capped. An entire region is on the brink of devastation. It is horrible. We will hold a major hearing next week with the CEOs of BP, the drilling company, and Halliburton, which provided construction services and which is responsible for cementing operations in the Timor Sea, off Australia, that are said to have been responsible for a huge spill there last August. Halliburton apparently performed similar cementing operations on the wellhead in the Gulf within the past few weeks. We have asked the Australian embassy to facilitate a conference call between their investigators and our staff. Tomorrow, two of the CEOs will appear in a closed-door session with the members of our two key subcommittees, Energy and Investigations. It should be a searing session.

### Wednesday, May 5

Yesterday, a lot was uncovered from the closed-door briefing with executives from BP, Transocean, and Halliburton, who lease, drill, and maintain the well five thousand feet below the surface in the Gulf. We had thought that five thousand barrels a day were spewing, but the big news the executives imparted is that (1) no one knows for sure how bad this is, and (2) it could be, under the worst circumstances, between forty and sixty thousand barrels per day. When the chair of the Energy and Environment Subcommittee, Ed Markey, extracted this little nugget of information, an audible gasp was heard in the room, and he led with this figure when he conducted the post-session press briefing. It was also clear that Florida is at grave risk as the currents in the Gulf could overtake the slick and hand it off to the Gulf Stream. This could create an oil river winding around the Florida peninsula and up the East Coast to Cape Hatteras. There is nothing to prevent this from occurring. The surest method of shutting off the leak is relief wells, and BP said they would take up to 120 days to drill. "We will do whatever it takes to control the leak," a BP executive said—as if we are to commend the company for heroic efforts following the disaster. But the real surprise, the political *shokku*, came from Joe Barton, the top Republican on the committee, who asked several questions about causality and prospects for recovery: when he got no good answers, he started lecturing the oil execs: "I am one of the industry's strongest supporters, but if this is the best you can do in explaining this to us, then you will have a very rough road." In other words, *I won't be able to save you from a shutdown of future offshore drilling, and God knows what else the liberals will do to you to restrict current offshore drilling.*

Monday, May 10

In the run-up to our hearings Wednesday on the savage spill in the Gulf of Mexico, we held a conference call this morning with community leaders across Louisiana, Mississippi, and Alabama to gauge the damage and the mood—the social, environmental, and economic impacts. This is long-term, they said, a "slow-moving disaster." Environmentally, there will be a die out of the grasses in the wetlands from the oil. Economically this will destroy a whole region of the country. The shrimpers, many of whom are Vietnamese, who fled their country during the war and resettled here, are vulnerable. They are not well educated, but they have worked so hard to build what they have; the spill is coming at the worst time, just as harvesting season is under way. They borrowed to get ready for their fishing and now are overextended. "The fabric of the community" is being torn, we were told. The call gives us ammunition for the hearings, when BP will for sure tell us everything they are doing to help affected communities—expecting to get credit for it.

## Wednesday, May 12

A terrifically powerful and successful hearing today in our Oversight and Investigations Subcommittee on the BP oil spill in the Gulf. The four CEOs of the principal companies involved all present and under oath. There is no secret to a great oversight hearing; it simply takes extremely thorough substantive work. If you have the substance, the materials, and the facts at hand, you can control the narrative. The subcommittee received more than one hundred thousand pages of documents, and early this week our staff conducted some critical interviews with company experts. What they said broke through the fog of the spill and laid out some likely causes of the catastrophe—and it was a story that had not yet been told. Specifically, the staff interviews documented pressure tests on the well taken on the day of the explosion that showed abnormalities—readings that should not have occurred. But those readings did not stop operations. Second, the so-called fail-safe blowout preventer device—the clamp that was to shut off a runaway pipeline under all circumstances—had leaks in it and could not in any event been activated fully because of some dead batteries that no one had replaced. So here were bald facts about profound issues involving the integrity of the well and the functioning of key equipment and the crew's inaction. These findings arrested the news cycle, and Henry's statement and questioning led the breaking news through the day. Phil Barnett, the Committee staff director, conceived quite an effective opening: he had Henry and Stupak (chair of the Oversight subcommittee) and Markey (chair of the Energy subcommittee) give linked ten-minute opening statements so that the narrative could be clearly told. I had not seen this done before. But we were dealing with the most complicated technology (many have likened drilling in the seabed five thousand feet below the surface and then twelve thousand feet into the rock to get the oil as on par with the Apollo mission to the moon) and we had in front of us the CEOs of the owners of that technology, so we could not afford to sound stupid. So staffers intensively studied the materials and the facts and then wove the content into a story that was told in very clear, very stark terms, without embroidery. It was just a clinical statement of what our investigators found, with the documents to back it up. It was an enormous success. There was no pushback from the executives on what they were hearing, no contradictions about what a certain piece of equipment did or what a certain pressure reading meant. This is a forte of the Waxman modus operandi, which goes back fifteen years ago to when the tobacco executives swore under oath that nicotine was not addictive. In large part, this is how Henry made his oversight reputation, and it was reinforced today.

Early this morning, Phil wanted a quote that would capture what happened and make the news. And so I sent in one sentence: *This catastrophe appears to have been caused by a calamitous series of equipment and operational failures.* That sentence led the online reports today and was featured on cable news tonight.

There was one other piece we wanted to nail. This "accident" did not occur in a vacuum. We are at a pivot point, I hope, on energy policy. And there is a lesson to be drawn from the Gulf oil spill that must not be ignored. The only answer to this is to get off oil. And so Henry ended his opening statement by saying,

> One lesson is already apparent from the catastrophe in the Gulf: we need an energy policy that emphasizes clean, renewable sources of energy. We can't snap our fingers and transform our energy economy overnight. If we do not have the courage to take on the oil companies and take decisive steps to reduce our over-reliance on oil—when the consequences of doing nothing are so clear—we may never start down the path toward a clean energy economy.

A couple hours later, President Obama reiterated a similar policy pivot in his message at the White House:

> Americans know what's at stake by continuing our dependence on fossil fuels. But the challenges we face—underscored by the immense tragedy in the Gulf of Mexico—are reason to redouble our efforts to reform our nation's energy policies. For too long, Washington has kicked this challenge to the next generation. This time, the status quo is no longer acceptable to Americans. Now is the time for America to take control of our energy future and jumpstart American innovation in clean energy technology that will allow us to create jobs, compete, and win in the global economy.

Henry's statement drove Barton nuts. He quoted the Declaration of Independence to support American dynamism, drive, entrepreneurship, freedom, and love of travel in cars from coast to coast: "We should not make a decision to fence off the outer continental shelf to drilling. It would be a mistake and disservice to the American people," he said. Drill, America, drill.

## Monday, May 17

The committee's medium-term agenda is gelling, and it is quite active and ambitious. On the oversight side, we will have several more hearings on the catastrophe in the Gulf, including a field hearing in New Orleans to hear from the people on the ground as well as those directly affected by the spill, particularly the fishing industry and others whose livelihoods depend on the marshlands, the wetlands, and the coast. We need to hear directly from the government agencies involved in regulating the industry and those cleaning up the mess. We will also be holding further hearings on Toyota and auto safety, linked to consideration of the bill to boost the budget and resources of the National Highway Traffic Safety Administration. As we did during the last stages of the health care debate, when we had oversight hearings highlighting the outrageous insurance premium increases—40 percent—imposed by Wellpoint Anthem Blue Cross in California, that led the president and the media to pay attention to the problem, we are using the Toyota debacle to keep up the pressure for far-reaching reform of our auto-safety regime. We will also do hearings on flame retardants (chemicals that leach into consumer products and cause health issues) that will help our push to advance the toxic substances rewrite. We will hold hearings on flavored cigars and expose the industry's ceaseless efforts to exploit every tiny opening they have under the new antitobacco laws to market their products to children and hook new generations of smokers. On the legislative front, we want to move the highway safety bill, funding increases for safe drinking water, a bill to ensure long-term health treatment for the responders to the 9/11 attacks in New York, and possible legislation to promote an open Internet and deployment of high-speed broadband throughout the country. This will carry us into the early summer. Not all of it is doable—the Republicans are not playing ball at all. They want to deny us any perception of achievement and responsibility. So it will be hard. But we are not just going to roll over and play dead—we will press on all fronts and make them say *No*, vote *No*, act *No*, and do *No*.

## Wednesday, May 19

A briefing this afternoon by outside energy experts who have studied the video of the oil spill in the Gulf. The scientists have no doubt: it is not five thousand barrels per day but somewhere between twenty thousand and one hundred thousand barrels per day—probably seventy thousand barrels per day. A catastrophe.

## Friday, May 21

Henry was at the White House again this morning. The president signed an executive order promoting fuel efficiency for trucks and reiterated his commitment to getting comprehensive energy and climate legislation through the Senate this year. He and Henry had a brief conversation as the president worked the line after the speech. This is an attribute of power: when you are in control, your allies get invited to the White House, meet with the president, have access and influence and suasion. So this is why we love this moment: if it's important enough to Henry Waxman, it has to be at least somewhat important to Barack Obama. It's not something to be abused or exploited—it's something to be used and optimized. We want the president to use his power on our side for good—and so does he. So, like any good exercise, the more you do it, the better you are.

Ed Markey was there, too, and when he came back, he chaired a briefing on the Gulf oil spill, this time from scientists who outlined the ecosystem of the Gulf, the marshlands, the wetlands, and the coastal waters of Louisiana. The oil spill is out of control, BP is out of control, and the goop is now coming onto the beaches of the Louisiana Gulf Coast. Immediately after the Markey briefing, Oxfam America brought in a dozen community leaders, fishermen, and representatives of faith groups who talked about life on the coast after the spill. It was the fishermen who got me. One was an older man, in his fifties, red and weather-beaten from the sun and the salt; the other was a Vietnamese woman in her forties. She and other Vietnamese refugees had re-created part of their previous life on the sea. And one member of their community, Joseph Cao, is a member of Congress—he was the sole Republican who voted for the health care bill in November. The two fishers told the same story. Boats that can't fish anymore. Debts that have to be paid. Gross uncertainty. Despair. No knowledge of when this will be over. The guy told a story of a fellow fisherman who went out a couple days ago to get some shrimp. He was in clear water. Dragging his nets, and he pulled them up covered with oil and ruined. They could not see the oil because it is in huge plumes well below the surface, invisible. Even though the water is fouled, it can look blue. The net was done, no catch, fuel burned, no hope, return to port. You see it on TV, but this guy brought it home.

## Wednesday, May 26

Henry met with the CEOs of the country's major environmental organizations to review the bidding on the energy and climate bill pending in the

Senate. There is strong consensus that the BP oil spill in the Gulf gives us a window to move forward—that "this is our moment," as one said. They urged that Henry help get the president more firmly involved in leading the effort. The industry needs the White House's leadership if it is to commit. I spoke yesterday with Phil Schiliro, and there is no doubt that the president wants to do this—but they have not yet found any Republicans to move forward on the Senate bill. I think the industry needs to go to their Republican friends and push them hard.

In the afternoon, we had a hearing on the Gulf oil spill with the EPA's chief, Lisa Jackson. John Dingell (D-MI) came out and called for a moratorium on offshore drilling. For a lion of the energy industry in this country, it was a hell of a statement, and the room rocked as he announced it.

A lousy holiday weekend for the president and the nation. The top-kill gusher-snuffing strategy for closing down the oil leak at the ocean floor failed miserably on Saturday night. When the news was announced, wherever people were, it arrived with a thud, a nasty kick in the solar plexus. The gushing continues, and likely nothing will stop it until August. So what we hoped would be a pivot point—with the well capped, the national conversation on this could turn to long-term energy policy solutions—did not materialize. The president is still held hostage to the leak. He is trying to regain stride and control with ever-more-aggressive positioning against BP. Yesterday, the attorney general announced criminal and civil investigations that can lead to massive fines and jail for the company's executives, but the limits of what even the president of the United States can do are more evident than ever. He can't catch a break. The economic recovery is jagged, and the record of legislative achievement does not ameliorate that. So across the board, the punditry is the message. Peggy Noonan (late of Reagan fame) in the *Wall Street Journal*: "Mr. Obama was supposed to be competent. . . . The disaster in the Gulf may well spell the political end of the president and his administration." And Frank Rich, who kneecaps the Radical Right in the *New York Times*: "His credibility as a champion of reformed, competent government is held hostage by video of the Gulf." And Maureen Dowd, patron saint of the Chic Left, also in the *Times*: "How does a man who invented himself as a force by writing one of the most eloquent memoirs in political history lose control of his own narrative?" So this will gush on for a while.

Monday, June 14

The Speaker met with the major committee chairs and asked them to report legislation under their jurisdiction to cope with the oil spill disaster in the Gulf. When big things happen fast and there is a need to act, there is suddenly immense fluidity and a chance to translate ideas into legislation very quickly. My memo to Phil Barnett was quite direct:

1. Immediate inspection and recertification of every offshore oil rig—at industry expense. When a major piece of infrastructure fails (the Minneapolis bridge), you have to inspect and recertify all the other relevant infrastructure, and we should do so here.
2. Pre-positioning of booms, skimmers, and other cleanup equipment in vulnerable communities—at industry expense.
3. Pre-positioning of top hats and other containment devices for all offshore sites—at industry expense.
4. There was a lot of dithering over whether to do sand berms. Why not a comprehensive program of environmental planning and assessment for sand berms for vulnerable shoreline so that they can be preapproved over the next year or so.
5. Definitive EPA study of dispersants and their use.
6. Definitive study of health effects on responders and affected communities from oil and dispersants. (This is based on our recent experience with the 9/11 responders bill).

The really big issue for us is that we generally tend to fight the last war, and the above suggestions are in that mold. But what is the next war? We need to think ahead as to what the next threats are and try to counter them. This will take shape over the next week or so. In the meantime, staffers are preparing furiously for two huge days of hearings—five major oil company CEOs testifying on the oil spill, the response, and where we go from here on our energy future and oil, plus the chair of BP, solo, on Thursday. It will be the biggest hearing of the year and an immense opportunity to focus issues, anger, politics, and policy.

A little social fun at the White House during the week—the White House picnic for members of Congress on Tuesday evening. A beautiful night with low humidity. The president worked his rope line to say hi to as many members and their kids as he could. And then I watched him, after those duties were done, thank the chefs privately, away from the crowd. You could see on their faces how much they appreciated having the president come by to express his appreciation. And no cameras to record it—this was not PR. Terrific food across the South Lawn. The theme was Taste of the States and there were lobster rolls (for New England), fried chicken (for the South), and tacos (for Texas and the West), and all American wine and beer and spirits. The senior Republican leadership boycotted. I did not see their House leadership at all or many senior Republican senators. It speaks to how poisonous the atmosphere is, how bitter, and the stakes they are all playing for in November. It has all taken a toll on the president; he looked tired. More gray in his hair and creases on his face. The pace is killing. A visit to the Gulf every week. Earlier that day, meetings with President Mahmoud Abbas of the Palestinian Authority. The unemployment numbers last Friday were not good. President Obama is getting hammered by the punditry for not showing enough emotion and grit in fighting the oil spill. The stock market was down below ten thousand. The Security Council passed sanctions against Iran, but the vote was not unanimous. Huge tensions with Israel over Gaza and that the storming of a flotilla from Turkey trying to break the blockade. And over everything in this barrage is the gushing oil, live online 24/7, an endless streaming. It is the image of the year—almost as addictive and suffocating as the oil itself. It has a huge depressant effect over everything. Obama cannot let it consume his presidency, but it is casting a cloud over everything else. Until that hole is plugged, it is just hard to get on with anything else.

### Wednesday, June 16

It is all oil all the time. The more the Gulf gushes, the more awash in it we are. Yesterday, the five top oil company CEOs were in a lineup before our committee, testifying on lessons learned. The key part of the morning was when the CEOs of Exxon Mobil and Chevron deliberately and repeatedly stated that they would not have drilled that well the way BP drilled that well. Last night, the president addressed the nation from the Oval Office, his first such address from that special setting. (President George W. Bush's first Oval Office speech was on stem cells in August 2001—how the magnitude of issues has shifted.) Obama used the speech as a pivot point. He showed that he was in control of the cleanup, fully, at long last, and shifted the discussion to what really needs to be addressed: our addiction to oil and our need to reduce our dependence on it. The pundits did not like it because he did not lay down a specific dare to the Senate. But we learned that lesson in health care: the situation in the Senate is extremely fragile, as many discussions with industry lobbyists today can attest, and if Obama overtly pressures a Senate on the brink, it will go over the edge. So everything is now geared toward increasing pressure so that it reaches maximum strength in July. We will know then whether we have critical mass to proceed. Today, prep for Tony Hayward, CEO of BP, who will come before us tomorrow. By the end, he should look like the protagonist in a Bruce Willis movie. Today, he and his chair did a perp walk before the cameras into the White House, where a four-hour meeting resulted in an agreement to have BP finance a twenty-billion-dollar compensation fund. It is just a beginning.

Friday, June 18

It was a hot grilling, a summer indoor barbeque not only of Tony Hayward but also of Barton, our top Republican on the committee. Hayward, to his credit, gave one of the best opening statements I have heard from someone in his position: sorrow, contrition, accepting responsibility. But that is where the cooperation ended. In seven hours of responding to questions, Hayward refused to acknowledge any specific mistakes. Investigations were continuing, he said, and he could not reach judgments about reckless behavior or mistaken decision making or whether corners were cut to save costs until all the evidence was in. It drove members nuts on both sides of the aisle. Yesterday was thirty-eight years to the day since the Watergate break-in and the scandal in which the word *stonewalling* resonated deeply in modern political vocabulary. And that's what Henry told Hayward: "You are stonewalling."

The astonishing thing was that the Republicans, generally pro-oil, finally broke with BP. But not Barton. He did, however do something astonishing in his opening statement:

> I'm ashamed of what happened in the White House yesterday [when BP announced the twenty-billion-dollar compensation fund]. I think it is a tragedy of the first proportion that a private corporation can be subjected to what I would characterize as a shakedown. . . . I apologize. I do not want to live in a country where any time a citizen or a corporation does something that is legitimately wrong is subject to some sort of political pressure that is—again, in my own words— amounts to a shakedown. So I apologize.

So yes, the top Republican on one of the most powerful and important policy committees in the US Congress apologizes to the man whose company caused the worst environmental catastrophe in American history. And Barton does not want any federal spending to rectify the damage—no, he wants BP to do it. But he can't countenance action by the president that sets up a system that will get billions to people who are being devastated *now*—not years from now, after endless court battles, when everything is irrevocably lost. At the hearing, Rep. Markey fired back at Barton's apology: "It's BP's spill but it is America's ocean, and it's America's citizens who are being harmed (Schatz and Koss 2010, 1507).[19]

The air was sucked out of the room. And so was Barton. The Republican leadership took him to the woodshed and told him to either apologize for and retract his apology or lose his position on our committee that same day. He crumbled. But in the process, he gave away the game on BP and the politics of the oil spill. Sometimes, you just don't know what possesses these guys on any given day. My guess is that they hate Obama and big government power so much—even when it is deployed for good—that they can't help themselves. *Bail out GM, seek to exercise control over the banks, save failing insurance companies, and now the oil industry. Where will it stop? So we have to stop Obama to save the country.*

## Saturday, June 19

The interim victories of the week are always placed in perspective during the weekend. There are reports this morning that if Republican members hear noise about Barton this weekend during their visits home, there will be renewed pressure on him to step down. Internally, we are already trying to calculate whether the need to show that he is a constructive player will mean that Barton will do business with us on some pending bills. So we may have leverage. For all the turning of the corner on the BP crisis this past week—the devastating hearings, Barton shooting himself in the foot, and the president's speech—the reality is that as the week ends, there are still a heap of political problems. The economy remains stuck, and employment is sluggish. The economy needs another big jolt of stimulus, but the mood on the Hill is retrenchment and caution. The deficits are too high and are still accelerating, and there is no end in sight. The Republicans are hammering at it, and the poor voters across the country are terrified about it. So just when we need expansion, the political imperative is contraction. So even a relatively small bill to keep teachers and firefighters employed via grants to state governments is stalled in the Senate, with the Democrats well short of the sixty votes needed to break the opposition. So going into the November elections could be more layoffs, more gloom, more uncertainty, more angst. The polls are also dark. NPR did a major survey of seventy House seats that are in play, and in those seats, the president's approval rating averages 42 percent. Below 50 percent is considered a danger zone. The poll also showed immense motivation and enthusiasm among Republican voters: they will be out there in November. For us, there is no discernible bump in energy, and there will be a real drop in turnout on our side as Obama is not on the ballot. But even if he were, the *New York Times* this morning reports that 54 percent of independents do not want him reelected. A former member of the House leadership, Bob Walker, told me earlier this week that thirty seats would shift if the election were held today. And Walker believes momentum has not yet peaked on his side.

The other real concern, though, is with energy policy. The head of GE's Washington office, Larry Boggs, told me this week that he thinks the president's speech was off base, a real missed opportunity, because he did not say—demand—a price on carbon as part of his urgent call for energy legislation. The French minister at the embassy here noted the same thing when we met yesterday. I think Obama did not press the Senate on the point right now because their mood is so fragile—if he pushes too hard, it will not happen—but Obama intends for it to happen. In health care, Obama made a similar play, laying out principles and letting Congress work. Obama ultimately conceded on the key public option to get health reform through. But this is different. An energy bill that is only on the supply and conservation side and not on the carbon pricing side is not success but failure—a true squandering of a unique moment, because of the BP Deepwater Horizon, to come to grips with our energy future. What are the dangers? Aside from losing on the policy, I think this would be a seminal political moment for Obama. If he abandons carbon pricing, I think an important part of his base goes into revolt, and it could be the beginning of a great rift of internecine warfare. Rifts could open on a host of issues from Afghanistan to the economy. And his leadership would suffer. So the president really needs to stay firm. No bill is better than half a bill.

Saturday, June 26

A week of fits and starts. Things get scheduled, then taken off. A lot of contentiousness in scheduling and priorities. We have two aggressive and ambitious subcommittee chairs, Markey and Stupak, who have both been relentlessly pursuing BP and the Gulf oil spill. The next logical step in the investigation is to get the Interior Department, which regulates the deepwater licenses, up to tell us what went wrong from their point of view and to get the former secretaries from the Bush administration in front of us, too. Well, Stupak argues, it should be his subcommittee because he did the hard work on the initial investigation and documented in fact what went wrong. *No, it should be me*, says Markey, *because I got the five oil company CEOs in front of us. No, it should be me*, says Stupak, *because I got Hayward here last week*. I suggested a joint subcommittee hearing, but then they could not agree on who chairs. So Henry called them in and said, *Settle it or I'll hold it at the full committee*. It will be settled, but we won't do the hearing until later next month.

## Tuesday, June 29

A glimpse back into the abyss? A day when Democrats shuddered quietly. The Dow was down 268 points to under 9,900 as consumer confidence declined sharply in June. Then, there were reports China's economy may slow dramatically. The unemployment numbers are out Friday and there is every indication that unemployment will climb back up closer to the death zone of 10 percent. A bill to extend unemployment benefits failed to pass the House because of concerns about the deficit, which is the overriding issue. The obsession with the deficit, a sentiment now rampant in Europe, could lead to a new wave of contraction in macroeconomic policy, further restricting the recovery. Is it the 1930s all over again, when Roosevelt and his Congress, also spooked by deficit spending, pulled back on the throttle and the recession of 1937 took hold? So Obama spends nearly a trillion dollars over the last eighteen months, and voila!, we are back in the soup with nothing to show for it. To add to the gloom, Sen. Robert C. Byrd, age ninety-two, an icon of the upper body, died yesterday morning, so our majority is now fifty-eight, and it puts passage of the conference report on Wall Street reform in doubt. And to add insult to injury, it is now clear that the genius negotiators in the conference put in the bill, at 4:00 or 5:00 last Friday morning, after twenty hours of talks, some nineteen billion dollars in fees to cover regulatory and other costs. Well, those fees have angered the four Senate Republicans who voted for reform a couple months ago. So the conference committee is now reconvened this evening to try to fix/find/replace the nineteen billion dollars and get this passed. But, god, they look bad. It can only increase cynicism and loathing—two sentiments not in short supply this year in the heartland.

And for our committee, three markups and two hearings over the next two days. Nothing earth-shattering, but we will mark up a major bill to put in law fixes for what went wrong in the Gulf oil spill. The regulators will have to triple-check safety systems and ensure they are redundant in the well and the blowout preventer—the "fail-safe" valve that utterly failed, leaving sixty thousand barrels a day gushing into the Gulf. The big question this evening is *Will the Republicans support it or oppose it? Are you for or against another Deepwater Horizon?*

## Wednesday, June 30

Contention broke out in the Energy Subcommittee at its hearings on a bill introduced by Henry and Ed Markey to require regulatory upgrades in all the key safety and performance standards that BP failed in the Deepwater Horizon well. Mainstream Democrats are for it quite strongly. But there were really interesting reactions from the Republicans and the oil-state members. The Republicans were knee-jerk predictable: *There are ongoing investigations, so how can we legislate until we know what they found?* (We had an investigation, too, and it got the goods. But never mind.) The most poignant reaction was from Charlie Melancon (D-LA), who is also running for the Senate this year: he cried about the disaster at a hearing a month ago and said, "I am standing knee-deep in oil, and I don't want the oil industry to stop." He is begging for an intelligent, workable piece of legislation. If there is a moratorium, make it limited, not permanent. If there are new safety regulations, make them smart. But he wants to work it out. And really, do the Republicans want to stop any sensible controls on offshore drilling after the biggest environmental mess in our history? Is this what they want to take into the election? So after talks through the afternoon, Henry and Ed postponed the markup, and discussions with the key players begin tomorrow. Henry put a deadline in: if there is no amicable agreement, he will bypass subcommittee and do it in the full committee. The leverage will help. One other issue that is an irritant for the oil industry. The definition of what is a dangerous well that could be subject to a moratorium or safety controls is broad—it could cover some onshore wells. There is merit in this—all wells should be safe—but also some intramural politics. Offshore drilling is generally the province of the Natural Resources Committee, not us, although we have had some say over the years. By having a bill that also captures onshore drilling, we have clear jurisdiction, which keeps us in the legislative game, where we want to be. So it is an example of how internal House politics and rules come into play in legislative issues. That's why the policymaking analogy with sausage making is so apt after all. It's definitely not filet mignon. The Energy and Commerce Committee has earned its reputation—it is respected and feared for good reason.

There was a major political screwup today. Another piece of the oil spill fix package was to provide direction to the health authorities to undertake longitudinal studies on the populations exposed to the oil, the dispersants, and the overall petro-detritus. It needs to be done. For several days, the Department of Health and Human Services was telling us they did not have adequate statutory authority to do this important work. Then, this afternoon, they tell us, *It's fine. We have authority. No problem.* Except their turn-on-a-dime moment creates a big political problem for us. The Republicans are already hammering away that this is moving too fast and we don't know all the implications of what we are proposing, and now they are handed a political gift. On this issue, they are right. So someone in Health and Human Services messed up big time in understanding the statutory authority they have to protect the long-term health of the people of the Gulf: a problem we did not need.

## Thursday, July 15

A spectacular day of success for Obama and Democrats in Congress. The Senate passed, by 60–39, the Wall Street reform bill, sending to the president for signature into law the most significant upgrade of regulatory authority over the US financial system since the Great Depression. Not amazing in one respect: What else would you expect after we went through a near-meltdown of the banking system and the economy? But also profound: sweeping reforms and the public interest generally prevailed despite every lobbying tactic that Wall Street could muster.

Another success is that in full committee, we passed, by a vote of 48–0, with no Republican dissenters (at least not publicly—some Republicans simply took a walk and did not vote) against a bill that will outlaw what happened on the Deepwater Horizon. So we are in the process of making illegal the relentless mistakes and safety errors committed by BP. So Republicans could not stand up to that irresistible political force, either. Here is what Henry said as markup convened this morning:

> The bill is designed to make sure that the problems that caused BP's Deepwater Horizon blowout in the Gulf can never happen again. This tragedy, which is the greatest environmental catastrophe in American history, can be termed an "accident" in name only. BP made a series of reckless decisions before the blowout. When drilling the well, BP took one shortcut after another in order to save time and money. BP relied on a blowout preventer that was anything but foolproof. And when the blowout occurred, BP was unprepared to deal with the consequences. Under this legislation, neither BP nor any other company would be able to make these same mistakes again.

> We found that the blowout preventer failed to perform its critical function. The bill addresses this by establishing new standards for redundancy, testing, and third party certification on blowout preventers.
>
> We found that BP made serious well design and cementing mistakes. The bill addresses this by establishing new requirements and third-party certification for safe well design and cementing.
>
> We found that BP failed to use a lock-down device to secure the wellhead. The bill requires a lock-down device.
>
> We also found that there was no CEO involvement in the well operations, despite the serious consequences of a potential loss of control of the well. The bill requires that the company CEO attest to the fact that the company will use a safe well design, have a blowout preventer that actually works, and have an appropriate and effective spill response plan.
>
> In sum, this bill ensures that the Congress is doing everything we can to prevent this from ever happening again.

At the end of the markup, Joe Barton, who made such an error a couple of weeks ago, choked up as he was talking about the spirit of bipartisanship and how this is how the committee process is supposed to work and how he wants this bill enacted. We made very few concessions to get his vote.

Later this afternoon, it appeared that BP had, on Day 88, finally put a cap on the well. This evening, there is no more oil flowing into the Gulf. So this massive stain that has suffused everything the president has done since April may finally begin to recede. There has been no air, no oxygen, for appreciation of what Obama has done, day in and day out. Just some news items from the last few days: The Russians spy on us? We arrest them—after following them for a decade and cataloging all they know—and exchange them for some of ours being held in Moscow. Israel acting up? Big successful summit with Benjamin Netanyahu in the White House. Elena Kagan about to be confirmed for the US Supreme Court. Goldman Sachs settles its indictment today with the Justice Department and will pay $550 million in fines. This is a do-nothing president, a drifting president, a failed presidency?

## Thursday, July 22

A self-inflicted wound at the end of today. Harry Reid announced that the Senate would not take up comprehensive energy and climate legislation this month. No progress on global warming. "We know where we are," he said.

"We know that we don't have the votes." So it will be a small-bore bill on the Gulf oil spill and nothing consequential in addition, and it will not properly serve as a vehicle, once it passes the Senate, for major add-ons from Waxman-Markey that we passed a year ago. This is profoundly disappointing and makes what was already a long shot virtually impossible, even in a lame-duck session. A lot of people are angry at the president for not pressing further and at Reid for not being able to corral his troops, but there are bigger culprits here. Dozens of leading US companies—GE and the like—want to vault into world leadership on green technology. And the fact is that for all their "work" on this, their CEOs have not been able to convince one Republican senator to join in pricing carbon, which ultimately is the most effective spur to renewables. So the business community, which is the base of the Republican Party, has failed in its mission to deliver Republicans. That is the failing here. And what it shows is the absolute rejectionist hard-line Republican antipathy for doing anything constructive with Barack Obama, even when our national security depends on it. It just stinks. But Obama loses because our base becomes dispirited over more temporizing on a key issue. So we can add global warming to Guantanamo, gay rights, guns, the public option, and Afghanistan, to name a few, where the president who promised change has been unable to deliver it. It hurts.

### Wednesday, July 28

A semi-sprint to the August recess, which will begin after the House adjourns on Friday night and go through mid-September: six weeks for members to spend in their districts, campaigning like hell in a nail-biting year. Yesterday, a hearing—our ninth so far—on the Gulf oil spill. This time it was on tourism. Ken Feinberg, who is in charge of the BP's twenty-billion-dollar compensation fund, testified and was his usual irascible, authoritative self. He ran the compensation scheme after 9/11 for responders and victims' families, and he has served as pay czar for the banks the government took shares in during the financial meltdown. His job is to make businesses and families a little bit more whole out of the disaster, and he will get that job done and get it done right.

### Saturday, July 31

The House adjourned last night for six weeks of campaigning at home. See you in September. A major last item of business was passing legislation to correct the failure in regulatory oversight in oil drilling in the Gulf of Mexico. There will be more inspections and much more redundancy in drilling operations, much of it informed by the work we did in investigating the tragedy and Deepwater Horizon. Our staff found what went wrong—the well was not engineered with safety in mind, and corners were cut, leading to catastrophic systems failures. The bill that passed last night is built on those findings. But even so, with all the scope of the disaster and the knowledge that surely we must learn from these mistakes, thirty-nine Democrats voted against it—the precise number that would cost us a working majority except that two Republicans voted for the bill, and several Republicans stayed away and did not vote (I think they could not in good conscience vote against the bill, as their leadership was arguing, so they took a walk instead.) So what that vote meant, on the eve of the recess, is that next year, the new House will surely have many fewer Democrats, and bills like this won't be possible—we won't have the numbers. Even if we still have control, we will have to be very clever about how we craft legislation. It means more work with the Republicans—if they deign to work with us. So less ambitious outcomes. In the last caucus before the break, the Speaker made the stakes quite clear: "Every day that the election gets closer, the choice gets clearer. Understand what is at stake: the well-being of the American people." And Steny Hoyer, the majority leader, told them how to work their districts: "When I first got here, Clarence Long was the dean of our delegation. And he sat me down and said, 'Do a lot for your people—and tell 'em about it.'" Steny hasn't lost an election since.

## Friday, August 13

Heavy into recess mode, but still plenty of notable work and events. We worked through a hearing for next week to follow up on the Gulf: an accounting of the oil and where it is or has dispersed in the environment and an assessment of the safety of seafood from the Gulf. We are out of session; Members will have to come back for the hearing. But Ed Markey, chair of the subcommittee, was insistent, and as long as we have two members—they can be of the same party—that serves as a quorum under the rules to hold the session. It is always good to be certain in your knowledge of the rules. The Republicans huffed and puffed and said they prefer it not occur. But the clear message from the Gulf today, with the well finally capped and no oil leaking, is *Don't forget us!* So a hearing on how the Gulf is coping is supposed to be deferred because we in Congress are on vacation for another four weeks? We'll hold the hearing next Thursday. But it took hours to work through.

## Thursday, August 19

Earlier today, a hearing in Rep. Ed Markey's Energy Subcommittee on the Gulf oil spill—an update on the accounting of the oil, where it has gone, and whether the seafood from the Gulf is safe. We tend to think August is dead, but newspapers and newscasts still have immense space to fill, and the press coverage was sensational, even though Ed was the only member present. The Republicans made some noise about objecting to the hearing, since the rules require two members to constitute a quorum for a hearing. There were signals that a Republican might come in, object, and leave. So I checked with the parliamentarian: if an objection was lodged, the hearing would indeed have to be adjourned. But it could be immediately reconstituted as a "briefing" without any official paraphernalia—principally the taking of a transcript—and proceed. The subcommittee has eight experts from the Gulf and Washington to testify. I sent word to the Republicans that if they want to object, fine, but the message we were hearing from the Gulf was *Don't forget about us*. So, just because Congress is on vacation, we are to take a vacation from the Gulf? As Ed said this morning in his opening statement, "Congress may be away, but the oil is not gone away." We did not get a peep out of the Republicans.

## Tuesday, September 7

Even during the recess period, we have the capability to respond quickly as warranted. Last Thursday morning, an explosion occurred on another oil rig in the Gulf of Mexico, this time in shallower waters, but with men thrown into the sea and fears of a reprise of the Deepwater Horizon, where the explosion and fire led to the massive oil leak. News reports of the incident were reported midmorning. Even with our chairs and staff dispersed across the United States, we could use email to get a letter authorized by Waxman, Markey, and Stupak to Manner Energy, operator of the rig, demanding a briefing within the next several days. The letter made the front page of the *New York Times* on Friday and the message was clear: *Don't mess with us on this. We want answers. And we will hold you accountable.*

## Wednesday, October 27

The halls are fairly deserted, the garages less than half full. Many of the staff have taken vacation time to go to Virginia and Ohio and Indiana to help out Democrats in really tough races. Calls and emails are off sharply. The mood is tense. Everyone reads the papers and scours the web and cannot miss the glaring message that our time is up. Charlie Cook, the leading prognosticator of modern times, this morning came out with his penultimate take on the House: that we lose at least forty-eight seats and likely closer to sixty. Yesterday, I met privately with Henry to share my view that I could not see us getting to a majority—just to make sure he was under no illusions. He was already there in his own thinking. Which is all to the good for what will have to be done next week and in the weeks to come to effect a transition.

For a little break in the tedium of waiting for next Tuesday, we dealt with an unresolved issue with BP: our strong desire to have a concluding hearing on the Gulf oil spill. Ed Markey had written to BP in August, seeking the appearance of their new CEO, Bob Dudley. They declined, citing his need to get the company focused on improving its business. But Markey wants the hearing and Henry supports him, and a further letter from Markey was rebuffed last week. One of BP's outside lobbyists pinged me yesterday: Was the chair shoulder to shoulder with Markey? I advised that he indeed was, that the right answer to Markey's request for a hearing was *Yes*, and that it was advisable that such an answer be forthcoming today. I also said that Waxman was not pleased with the Hayward hearing, where Hayward stonewalled the committee (and Barton apologized to BP for its ill treatment by the president!), that the committee needed to complete its investigation, and that if the CEO was indeed refocusing the company, this was the perfect opportunity to inform the Congress and tell the American people about it. Unfortunately, today, BP's senior counsel in Washington, a former assistant attorney general in the Justice Department under President Clinton, informed us that the new CEO did not want to testify this year. Tonight, Waxman and Markey sent a sharp letter asking BP to agree to testify and requesting a reply within the week. Election politics are playing a role. BP may think the Republicans are coming in and be trying to run out the clock. While our letter does not threaten a subpoena, that idea is clearly on the table—but using a subpoena during a lame-duck session could be difficult. Does it look too political if the Republicans do not support its issuance? For maximum positive effect, we are keeping the letter nonpublic for the moment; they are likely more willing to agree without the glare of news coverage. We may yet release it if they demur further over the next few days.

## Tuesday, November 2

Election Day. The last economic data was reported yesterday: real income fell 0.1 percent in September, the first decline since July 2009. Couple that with 9.6 percent unemployment and 60 percent of Americans believing the country is on the wrong track, and today's results should be dismal. The only issue is how dismal. Everyone will talk about Obama and health care and cap-and-trade and elitism and not selling the message, but this election is about the economy, and everything else is seen through what is happening with the economy.

## Wednesday, November 3

The day after. It was very important for Henry to meet with the entire staff today. There are some eighty of us, and our numbers will be halved in the transition. People are nervous, fearful, on edge. Two months in a weak economy is not much time to find another job if you are married, have children, and/or have a mortgage. So it was critical that Henry meet with the staff to tell them how proud he was of them—and he did it with aplomb. And to talk about seizing whatever opportunities we could. And to express the prospect that maybe we can get back into power in two years, which may well be possible. After all, today we are 193 Democrats versus 242 Republicans—a narrower margin than the 256–179 we enjoyed until yesterday. So 25 seats to a majority; yesterday, the Republicans won 63 seats. Then Phil Barnett outlined what can be said with certainty about the transition—which was not much. But individual conversations will be held with each staff member. It is the least we can do.

Obama held a postmortem press conference this afternoon. It was the economy, the unemployment, the jobless recovery, the fact that things were not getting better enough fast enough for enough people: this was the cause of what happened at the polls yesterday. He was right.

Late today, Bob Dudley replied to Waxman and Markey's request that he appear for a hearing and report on what the company is doing to ensure the Gulf oil spill never happens again. He effectively declined, citing the onerous pressures of getting the company reconfigured in the wake of the disaster, but he offered to appear at a private briefing. My view is that this is unacceptable. The CEO can talk to the markets, and analysts, and the media but cannot report to a committee of Congress responsible for these issues? While potentially deserving of a subpoena, a postelection compulsory process when the chair will be handing the gavel over to the Republicans in two months' time is fraught.

## Saturday, November 13

We finally decided on a course of action with respect to the long-standing request to have Bob Dudley testify. In normal times, the man would get a subpoena, given his refusal to come forward. But Henry decided that given the change that is to occur, a last-minute subpoena would not sit well as a matter of precedent or politics. We rejected Dudley's offer to appear at a closed-door briefing:

> BP's safety practices are a matter of utmost importance to the Congress and the American people. A private meeting would deny Subcommittee members the opportunity to ask questions and keep the American people in the dark about critical safety issues relating to BP's future operations in the Gulf of Mexico and elsewhere.

We intend to release all three months' worth of correspondence to show the public exactly how obstinate Dudley and BP have been. My own view is that they are cynically running out the clock to avoid testimony, counting on the fact that Henry's decency will mean no subpoena. They are correct—but that does not make them right. As soon as the letter went to London, I emailed their top Washington outside lobbyist and said simply, "Any encouragement for a positive response would be sincerely welcome and appreciated." But I'm not holding my breath.

## Conclusion

The 2010 election swept in Republican majority control of the House, but the Democrats retained control in the Senate, though by a smaller margin. With split-party control, the House and Senate of the 112th Congress went in different legislative directions. The House focused on legislation to reduce regulation and increase offshore drilling production, while the Senate labored unsuccessfully to end tax subsidies enjoyed by the oil and gas industry (Symes and Goldfarb 2011). Policy momentum in Congress for broader legislation on energy and climate or even oil safety, was gone, washed away by the midterm wave.

The 112th Congress, like its predecessor, mustered only a minimalist legislative response to the greatest environmental disaster in history. A bipartisan national commission on the BP spill led by William Reilly, former EPA director under President George H. W. Bush, and former Democratic senator Bob Graham issued a report on the performance of various actors in the spill response: the White House got a B, the oil industry received a C+, and Congress earned a D for its failure to enact any legislation to foster offshore drilling safety or advance the nation's response to spills. The report bluntly declared that Congress "provided neither lead-

ership nor support" (Russell 2012, 798). In addition, Reilly pointed out
that despite the administration's and the industry's progress in reducing the
likelihood of future spills, only legislation by Congress could ensure that
this progress cannot be undone.[20]

Decisions by party leadership and the role of partisanship were central
to understanding the politics and Congress's collective response to the BP
spill. For the Democrats in Congress, the BP oil spill represented not only
legislative opportunity but also political risk. On the one hand, the committee sought a legislative path forward by directing public attention to
the immediate crisis and provided much-needed reform recommendations
through its oversight function. These reforms were eventually adopted
through administrative channels. At the same time, the Democratic leadership worked to kick-start momentum for broader policy change. On the
other hand, the Republicans seized the political opportunities afforded
by the public's views of the White House's and congressional Democrats'
response to the crisis. The Republicans sought to use the disaster to undercut Obama's political standing, denying him and the Democrats the ability
to push their policy agenda (Lee 2009; J. H. Clark 2015; Green 2015). The
strategy paid political dividends for Republicans in Congress. The failure of
BP's top-kill operation meant that the oil leak would not be solved quickly,
and the opposition's strategy of politicizing the crisis and attributing blame
to President Obama subsequently became more pronounced. The media
responded by changing how the BP and surrounding events were covered
(Johnston and Goggin 2015). The Republicans effectively pointed public attention to the president's ownership of and degree of competence in
dealing with the crisis. It is hard to say how much impact the Republicans' tactic had on the Democrats' policy agenda, but it did significantly
reduce voters' confidence in the president (Johnston and Goggin 2015).
The literature demonstrates that a president's public standing with voters
can greatly impact the scope of his policy agenda and the likelihood of
winning legislative victories in Congress (Rivers and Rose 1985; Edwards
1989; Canes-Wrone and De Marchi 2002; Eshbaugh-Soha 2005, 2010; for
a contrary view, see Peterson 1990). And these leadership decisions offer a
window into how partisanship affected Congress's collective response.

Ideological differences take on a very prominent role in the literature
explaining partisan conflict in Congress (Cox and McCubbins 1993; Krehbiel 1998; McCarty, Poole, and Rosenthal 2006; Smith 2007). However, the
need to fix the largest environmental disaster in US history had no inherent ideological principles. Yet rather than ameliorating partisan incentives,
the crisis provided an opportunity for the political parties to exploit those

incentives. The BP spill offered the Republicans opportunities to enhance their political position through such factors as agenda control, presidential leadership, and tainting the Democrats' reputation and the government's response (Lee 2009; J. H. Clark 2015; Green 2015). These are all important and understudied sources of partisan conflict that merit further scholarly attention (Gilmour 1995; Parker and Dull 2009; Kriner 2010; Lee 2013). For example, Lee's (2009) work demonstrates that presidential leadership on issues in Congress during the past two decades has exacerbated conflict between the parties. Her work also suggests that parties in Congress as "small groups" may not face the same Olsonian dilemma of collective action as other groups do but instead may maintain a predisposition to cooperate for the good of the party (Olson 1961; Lee 2009). These factors may be conditioned by ideological conflict, but as the BP case suggests, they may also play an independent role in understanding party conflict in Congress. And their effects on party conflict or at least the degree of party coordination during the BP crisis was impacted directly by party leaders' decisions.

There is no way to know how different strategic political decisions by the leadership of both parties would have changed the committee's or Congress's response or whether an early capping of the spill would have given President Obama more leverage in pressing his energy agenda. Absent the BP crisis, could Democrats have kick-started broader climate policy in the Senate? Would Republicans have reaped electoral benefit by focusing more attention on fixing oil safety as opposed to attributing blame to President Obama? The answers to both questions may well be *yes*, but these are the roads not taken. Such is the nature of a political focus by party leadership when such a premium is placed on short-term political gains.

The BP spill portrays a classic view of Congress reacting to a crisis in terms of "fire alarm oversight" (McCubbins and Schwartz 1984). This type of oversight is typically characterized by an event-driven crisis that demands media attention and engages significant political interests. Fire alarm oversight provides legislators with valuable opportunities to take popular positions and focus legislative activity on issues that are important to voters. This approach contrasts sharply with "police patrol" oversight, which is more prevalent in Congress (Balla and Deering 2013). This form of oversight is characterized by routine comprehensive investigations of issues and bureaucratic behaviors. Police patrol oversight has high costs, which are shouldered exclusively or mostly by the members of Congress themselves. The committee's oversight powers and autonomy were on full display in the context of the crisis. The committee systematically investigated the spill and developed a consensus around a package of solution-oriented reforms. But beyond the committee room, partisanship overtook the later stages of the legislative process, preventing deeper, more sweeping reforms. The BP crisis did allow valuable position-taking opportunities on drilling and liability limits, but they exacerbated partisan differences on the House floor and in the Senate that worked to undermine rather than build support for energy and climate legislation. The BP case leads to some interesting questions for congressional scholars: How successful are cases of fire alarm oversight in producing legislation, and how do such explanations compare to legislative outcomes from police patrol oversight?

In addition, despite the crisis, pure partisanship resulted when a zero-sum incentive drove congressional politics (Lee 2013). Such partisanship is never the sole jurisdiction of the majority or minority. But in this instance, the crisis generated immense media attention and illustrated that the minority party can use the occasion to shape political dialogue and issue salience and thus degrade the president's political standing. The BP spill provided a legitimate and salient stage for oversight from which the minority could heighten the political stakes and the level of criticism not only about presidential leadership but also about the smaller day-to-day management of the issues, such as the politically embarrassing issue of whether the Department of Health and Human Services possessed the requisite legislative authority to protect residents in the Gulf.

In its oversight role, the committee undertook investigative efforts that brought to light numerous significant technical, safety, legal, and even moral concerns (see the appendix). That said, Waxman has argued that key oversight elements are essential to create a legislative imperative for Congress. At the top of the list of these elements are staff expertise and rigorous, fact-based analysis, supplemented by the creation and sustaining of a story line, compelling antagonists, and dramatic conflict (Waxman and Green 2009). The successful legislative effort to regulate Big Tobacco fully reflected these features. However, the BP crisis was different. Over the course of the disaster and its aftermath, the public lost the focus on the BP disaster that could have transformed political pressure into energy and climate legislation. The Democrats' loss of majority control of the House also significantly changed the investigative agenda. The BP spill did send political tremors through Congress, but the public attention and pressure were not sustained. As Charles Ebinger, the director of the Brookings Institution's Energy Security Initiative, put it, "Once the spill moved from the everyday headlines and the terrible pictures of the wildlife and seashore devastation, it went out of the public mind" (Hobson 2011b, 853).

Another lesson here may relate to the executive's preference for grand bargains or sweeping give-and-take policy compromises, especially under unified party control. However, Congress seems to have a less expansive horizon. The electoral imperative for individual members naturally inclines them to focus more on the immediate and short term. This is exacerbated by party leadership and the pursuit of the party's goals. More aggressive agendas make for more opportunity by the opposition to target the president's political position (Eshbaugh-Soha 2010). This is also a factor in understanding why serious, significant reform can often take several Congresses to achieve.

# SIX

# When Ideological Fidelity Trumps the Common Good

## The Politics That Ended the Grand Bargain

This chapter provides a historical framework for understanding how the debt-ceiling process served different purposes for Congress over time and for exploring the interbranch politics that surrounded such decisions. In 2011, the issue of raising the debt ceiling resulted in a political near-crisis, calling into question the US government's ability to manage its fiscal affairs responsibly.

The chapter looks at some of the key motivations and events shaping leadership decisions to explain the breakdown of the extensive efforts by President Barack Obama and Speaker of the House John Boehner to effect a "grand bargain" on overall debt and budget issues and the subsequent passage of the Budget Control Act of 2011 (BCA), which brought a rapid yet fluid conclusion to the crisis. The grand bargain also highlights the challenges presidential and congressional leaders face in forging a supportive coalition. Fiercely divisive congressional politics, especially among Democrats, and the sweeping nature of the proposed deals meant that the president had to work not only the Republicans but sometimes members of his own party in the ultimately unsuccessful effort to overcome congressional opposition. The pressure to succumb to lowest-common-denominator party consensus won out, trumping a larger common good that could have been secured with a grand tax-and-spending deal to address long-term structural budget issues (F. E. Lee 2013).

During the spring and summer of 2011, the president and the Speaker sought to move beyond their respective political bases to dramatically alter the federal government's fiscal path. Over drinks after a June golf outing at Andrews Air Force Base, Boehner floated the prospect of using the debt crisis to spur a legacy-making deal for both men that would package the necessary increase in the debt ceiling with the tough medicine of restructuring federal spending, entitlements, and sweeping tax reforms (Bai 2012). Still deeply in the shadow of the worst financial crisis and recession since the Great Depression, the 2010 midterm election had primed the moment for Madison-style cooperation between the two leaders. Moreover, the midterm results were widely perceived as signaling that the public was ready for such a deal—at least in theory. Despite their different viewpoints, both Obama and Boehner believed that it was time to either go big and reap the political rewards of making history or hunker down for the next election. And they were prepared, at least at the outset, to go against elements in their own parties to reach such a deal.

But the grand bargain died, crushed between the default clock and politics that conspired against both sides. Obama and the Republican House ended the debt-limit showdown just hours before the government would have defaulted (Schatz 2011, 1756). But little more was accomplished. Even the close brush with the debt limit had serious reverberations for the economy. According to the University of Michigan's tracking of consumer sentiment, which is of the most reliable and extensively used indicators of economic health, the economy had previously gained ground under President Obama but slumped dramatically during the summer 2011 debt-limit crisis. The worry that Congress would cause US default was enough to shake markets and the American public, sending shock waves through an already teetering economy (Sides, Tesler, and Vavreck 2016).

### A Historical Primer: The Statutory Debt Limit and Congressional Politics

Article 1, Section 8 of the US Constitution places control over the federal government's purse strings—spending, taxing, and borrowing—squarely in the domain of Congress as a core constitutional responsibility and power. For the first 130 years after the adoption of the Constitution, Congress micromanaged the country's debt by passing specific authorizations that allowed all of the Treasury's borrowing actions (Cranford and Schatz 2011). However, with the significant increase in spending spurred by the US entry into World War I, Congress decided to delegate much of its role to the Treasury, empowering it with wide-ranging discretion over the federal government's mechanisms for financing debt. To achieve these aims, Congress passed the Second Liberty Bond Act of 1917, which set statutory limits (though they could be raised or lowered) on the borrowing authority of the US Treasury (Austin 2015). The statutory debt limit or debt ceiling was stable for its first decade at $43.5 billion, but US borrowing rose with the Great Depression, and reached $300 million with the massive military spending required to win World War II.[1] From the last year of the Eisenhower administration (1953–60) to the last year of the Carter administration (1977–80), the debt ceiling increased threefold from about $284 billion to nearly $909 billion. It then tripled again during the Reagan administration, reaching nearly $3 trillion by President George H. W. Bush's 1989 inaugural year. The debt ceiling nearly doubled under the Clinton administration and doubled again under President George W. Bush, topping $12 trillion just a month after President Obama took office and surpassing $18 trillion by 2015.

Congress has chosen to vote more and more frequently on the debt limit with shorter extension periods.[2] From 1960 through 2015, Congress raised the debt limit more than eighty times. Congress has never failed to raise a debt limit, but since the 1970s it has allowed the debt-ceiling deadline to lapse on a number of occasions, forcing the Treasury Department to use extraordinary measures to extend the federal government's borrowing capacity. Moreover, because of Congress's intransigence about paying debts already incurred, it has also defeated debt-ceiling measures from time to time. Not surprisingly, most experts have long since concluded that the statutory debt limit has outlived its usefulness, and in 1979 the General Accounting Office urged Congress to completely revamp its process (Cranford and Schatz 2011). Decades later, experts are still of a similar mind. As an example, David Walker, comptroller general and head of the General Accounting Office (1998–2008) opposed the continued existence of the arbitrary and outdated debt limit and concluded that any new process should include "fail-safe mechanisms" that triggered automatic spending cuts and revenue increases when a specified debt-to-GDP ratio was breached (Cranford and Schatz 2011, 1550).

This economic rationalist view of the debt ceiling, however, has in modern times never been able to transcend efforts to use the debt ceiling and its extension to score political points with the public. These issues go back to the founding of the republic: Alexander Hamilton sanctioned debt to build the republic, while Thomas Jefferson worried that debt would give financiers undue leverage over the government (Kowalcky and LeLoup 1993). Although the public widely perceives otherwise, the debt-ceiling question routinely put in front of Congress is not inherently ideological; it is not steeped in conservative (or liberal) principles and does not involve the size or role of the federal government (F. E. Lee 2013). In fact, Congress's specific decision point regarding whether to raise the debt ceiling reflects the consequences of its past decisions—the forced recognition that the spending it has already approved has come home to roost. In pure fiscal management terms, the issue of the debt limit reflects how much money Congress authorizes and appropriates to be spent, taking into account the revenues the government receives; it is a simple mathematical exercise in driving to a number that adds to the national debt. Yet members of both parties have quite effectively fed the public perception—a congressional sleight of hand—that action on the ceiling somehow forestalls deficits or could be employed to manage the debt. Renowned congressional scholar Norman J. Ornstein of the American Enterprise Institute put it bluntly: "What I find utterly absurd is, the House voted for a budget that itself increases the debt by trillions over the next 10 years and is now refusing to increase the debt ceiling to accommodate its own budget" (Cranford and Schatz 2011, 1548).

Members of Congress's responses to debt-ceiling votes have had a regularized partisan component since Roosevelt's New Deal. However, voting patterns became increasingly partisan during the 1960s, especially in the House (Kowalcky and LeLoup 1993). The overwhelming picture of congressional voting in the past several decades has been highly dependent on party control of Congress and the president.[3] And in recent Congresses, the votes on the debt limit have become almost perfectly partisan (F. E. Lee 2013, 780). During unified government, when one party controls both the White House and both houses of Congress, members of the House minority rarely vote in support of extending the debt limit, and the Senate minority has proven nearly as united. Under divided-party control, the majority party typically provides more votes in support than the minority but pressures the party of the president, who is burdened with the responsibility of governing, to supply a substantial number of its members to support and pass the debt ceiling. So the pattern in recent Congresses has not differed for Democrats or Republicans. The president's opposition party in Congress employs the opportunity afforded by the debt limit debate (and eventual vote) to pummel the sitting president's economic policies and "freewheeling" spending that has brought the country to the brink of insolvency—or worse.

Why would Congress choose to make more frequent conflict-ridden decisions on the debt limit, in effect forcing brinksmanship decisions when it could otherwise end such risky spectacles? The statutory debt limit does not live in the Constitution—it is not a constitutional requirement to reduce or eliminate the nation's debt, and the debt has continued its unabated growth (with the exception of the emergence of budget surpluses in the last years of the Clinton administration) irrespective of congressional posturing on the public record.[4] By the 1970s, there was an important collective realization that the statutory debt ceiling offered no practical means of controlling spending and that stronger tools were needed. As a result, Congress dramatically changed the budget process via the Budget and Impoundment Control Act of 1974, which significantly centralized the budget process, giving party leaders greater control over macro budget management. It also required a budget resolution that specified the amount of the future debt limit that would be needed, with the idea that going on record as supporting the need to raise the debt ceiling before the fact would induce pressure to reduce spending and hence borrowing. Under the old process, deficit-producing fiscal decisions occurred before the ceiling was raised. Despite great hopes, the 1974 reforms fell short of changing these dynamics and producing more responsible management of the debt ceiling and did nothing to curb the growth in federal borrowing or mitigate the looming risk of default (Kowalcky and LeLoup 1993).

So after nearly a century, why does Congress continue this less-than-decisive process of raising the statutory debt limit? The answer is that regardless of which party controls the House or Senate, legislation regarding the debt limit has served the changing goals of members of Congress. David Mayhew (1974) argues that the existence of congressional institutions depends on how well they help members of Congress achieve their individual political goals. Mayhew focused on the electoral imperative for ease of theoretical tractability: "The organization of Congress meets remarkably well the electoral needs of its members. To put it another way, if a group of planners sat down and tried to design a pair of American national assemblies with the goal of serving members' electoral needs year in and year out, they would be hard pressed to improve on what exists" (1974, 81–82). Mayhew's argument helped to explain many congressional institutions, among them the committee system, seniority rule, and even institutional norms of deference and reciprocity. Despite the enormous footprint of electoral needs of members, multiple goals can be served by congressional institutions and can vary over time (Fenno 1978). The regularized process of the statutory debt limit gave Congress the opportunity to react to changing political pressures and achieve multiple goals. For example, prior to the 1974 budget reform, the debt limit actions offered a valuable opportunity for congress to oversee the budget and to question the president's management of budgetary affairs. Members argued that the oversight afforded by the debt limit represented a real (or at least symbolic) check on the executive's borrowing discretion and thus fed public concern that a strong congressional watchdog was hard at work keeping the pressure on the president (Kowalcky and LeLoup 1993). The debt limit has also increasingly served as a legislative vehicle to overcome policy gridlock. The greater frequency of divided government has meant that must-pass legislation like the debt ceiling has carried controversial policies (through both germane and nongermane amendments) as a strategy to increase chances of passage. Congressional leaders have hitched a myriad of difficult domestic add-ons (e.g., Social Security, taxes, spending) as well as foreign policy riders to debt limit packages. These efforts have had rather mixed success, but taking a position has afforded members significant political value regardless of policy outcome (Kowalcky and LeLoup 1993; F. E. Lee 2013).

During President Obama's first term, the debt-limit debate has become an invaluable opportunity to draw sharp contrasts between economic philosophies and to reveal partisan policy priorities affecting federal spending, taxes, and debt. The underlying motivation in elevating the debt limit to an issue of major national importance is simple: no member of Congress wants to go on record as supporting the new astronomical ceiling (Cranford and Schatz 2011)—and thus be in line for blame. Attacks on a "tax-and-spend" Congress or a Congress whose spending is "out of control" are the bread-and-butter of modern congressional campaigning. Moreover as F. E. Lee argues, the problem with the debt limit is ownership: "Delay, procrastination, and buck-passing are the order of the day" (2013, 780). Although Congress owns the debt limit in the sense that its spending decisions, past and present, ultimately drive the amount of the national debt, those in Congress who are leading the charge on these issues often seek to create the perception that the president and his party have fomented the conditions bringing the decision to a head. The president sends an annual budget to Congress that lays out overall spending, tax and debt parameters. The president is obligated in his role as chief implementer (through the Treasury) to pay for federal programs, so in this sense he owns the consequences of debt limits and naturally supports increases to pay for those ongoing obligations. But those numbers do not become real until Congress enacts specific spending and tax legislation. Thus, partisanship has motivated the opposition party in Congress to seek to utilize the debt limit debate to hammer the president, his economic policies, and his party.

## A Summer of Opportunity: How the Grand Bargain Turned Small Ball

Rahm Emanuel, President Obama's chief of staff, famously opined, "Never let a serious crisis go to waste; do things you could not do before" (Kenen 2011, 1613). The spring and summer of 2011 represented one of those rare windows of political opportunity. The 2010 midterm election had been a one-sided thumping of the president's party, and control of the House had shifted to the Republicans, with the sixty-three-seat wave constituting the largest GOP landslide since 1938. The 112th Congress also left Democrats holding a much narrower Senate majority. Grassroots and the Tea Party Republicans had done more than just win seats in Congress: they had changed the political debate by channeling populist anger at out-of-control federal spending, skyrocketing deficits, and Obama-led policy reforms. Noted one veteran policy expert, "I think it's fair to say that the Republicans have been very successful in changing the whole nature of the discussion of the level of cuts" (Kenen 2011, 1613). Moreover, in the wake of the worst economic downturn in generations and in the midst of a fiscal morass, the ominous reality of a US default crisis loomed just on the horizon.

The prospect of a government shutdown coupled with a default on the national debt was not a mere episode in a game of political chicken filled with hollow rhetoric; by any reasonable standard, it was a crisis with national and even global economic ramifications (Austin 2015). The hyper-partisanship of Washington politics had finally reached a stage where it threatened Armageddon—a combined government shutdown and default by the Treasury on the full faith and credit of the United States—and some people found that catastrophe desirable to force revolutionary reform on Washington.

In May 2011, Treasury secretary Timothy Geithner announced that the United States had breached its statutory debt limit and the Treasury would begin taking extraordinary measures to prolong borrowing capacity until August 2 (Austin 2015). If Congress allowed that August deadline to pass without resolution, markets would likely become unhinged because Uncle Sam would be signaling that the world's largest economic power was no longer good for its debt.[5] US credit cost and fluidity affect American consumers and industry in a host of areas, among them mortgages and housing construction, car and student loans, credit card rates, and new business startups (Cranford 2011). During the summer (and at the height of debt-limit negotiation), credit watchdog Standard and Poor's took the unprecedented step of downgrading the US debt, citing significant uncertainty regarding the country's creditworthiness. Standard and Poor's cited the "gulf between the political parties" as undermining confidence in the "effectiveness, stability and predictability of American policymaking and political institutions" (Applebaum and Dash 2011). At nearly the same time, the country's business leaders urged both President Obama and Congress to put aside partisan considerations and raise the debt limit for the good of the country (Schatz and Krawzak 2011).

In this setting, the GOP leadership eagerly sought to flex its newly acquired muscle and fully embraced the strategy of using the debt crisis as a bludgeon to leverage spending cuts and policy concessions from the White House. Even prior to the election, Senate minority leader Mitch McConnell (R-KY) had declared that the debt crisis would not be averted unless his party received some concessions (Cranford and Schatz 2011). And in the House, hard-right conservatives and Tea Party members united behind the same demand. But Boehner, newly installed as Speaker of the House, was an establishment-favored probusiness conservative who had difficulty handling the powerful Tea Party faction. The Republican majority deliberately discarded an important but little-recognized tool, the Gephardt Rule, which both parties had for decades used to protect the House from some of the brinksmanship of the debt limit.[6] In addition, the House had also sacrificed earmarks (highly specific appropriation riders for projects in members' districts), long a cherished tool of coalition builders, on the altar of fiscal piety (Cranford and Schatz 2011). Moreover, although Boehner had a reputation as one of the Hill's better deal makers, his lieutenants were far less predisposed to come to an agreement with the Democratic leaders or President Obama. In fact, Barry Jackson, Boehner's chief of staff, suggested that both Eric Cantor (R-VA) and Paul Ryan (R-WI) actively undermined Boehner's quest for a deal with Obama (Lizza 2012). According to one account, in front of a group of Republican congressmen, Jackson said "They see a world where it's Mitch McConnell—as Senate Majority Leader—Speaker Cantor, a Republican President, and then Paul Ryan can do whatever he wants to do. It's not about this year. It's about getting us to 2012, defeating the President, and Boehner being disgraced" (Lizza 2012, 6).[7] At the same time, the House Democratic caucus was much smaller and had lost several of its more moderate members in the midterm elections. The Democratic caucus was thus more liberal and hence less inclined to compromise on bedrock Democratic issues like Social Security and Medicare.

Even though both the president and the Speaker were therefore hamstrung in dealing with these most fundamental and intractable structural budget issues, both men seemed to recognize that a grand opportunity was at hand and to be willing to take considerable political risk for the chance to reset the country's fiscal management. Both leaders were serious about accomplishing something truly important—a landmark deal on spending and taxes. Reflecting on that moment nearly a year later, Boehner said, "I look at what happened last summer as the biggest disappointment I've had as speaker" (Bai 2012, 23). Each demonstrated a willingness to take on issues that were political kryptonite in his own political party. As the former director of the Congressional Budget Office put it, "I think [Obama] has crossed over that line into seriousness. He's willing to bite the bullet as long as someone else is biting it with him" (Kenen 2011, 1613). Boehner started with a willingness to embrace hundreds of billions in new tax revenue, while Obama signaled an openness to cutting hundreds of billions in spending on popular federal programs and cutbacks to entitlements that could deliver huge federal savings.[8] On that point, President Obama said, "I think it is important for [Social Security and Medicare] to remain as social insurance programs that give people some certainty and reliability in their golden years. But it turns out that making some modest modifications in those entitlements can save you trillions of dollars" (Kenen 2011, 1614).

During the spring and summer of 2011, the threat of US default loomed over Washington and Wall Street. A number of bipartisan groups worked earnestly to find a solution to the mounting deficits and debt. At the end of 2010, the National Commission on Fiscal Responsibility and Reform (known as the Simpson-Bowles Commission), a special bipartisan group created by President Obama earlier that year, charged with developing policies to improve the country's fiscal situation, presented a landmark report suggesting ways to achieve long-term fiscal sustainability. But as was the case with Obama and Boehner a few months later, the commission ultimately failed to get even its own members to agree on final recommendations.[9] The commission did, however, set a precedent in that members of both parties opened some of their pet policies up to debate, encouraging the president and his team to engage substantively on previous taboos like indexing spending on entitlements to the rate of inflation (e.g., the chained consumer price index) (see Ferris 2016). In addition, Vice President Joe Biden and majority leader Cantor headed up talks on a shorter-term budget compromise. House Republicans demanded that budget cuts equal the amount of the increase to the debt limit—about $2.4 trillion.[10] Although the two sides found common ground to cut about $2 trillion in spending, the discussion ran aground on the issue of taxes toward the end of June: Cantor and the Republicans, especially the Tea Partiers, refused to acquiesce to any tax increases whatsoever. In addition, Biden refused to move on spending cuts without new revenues on the table (Bai 2012).

In July 2011 the so-called Gang of Six Senate working group launched another attempt at finding common ground, picking up the Simpson-Bowles Commission's work to develop a bipartisan consensus deficit-reduction plan.[11] At the same time, the White House and Boehner engaged in secret talks that grew out of the June golf outing and that involved not only spending cuts but also sweeping entitlement and tax reforms. However, Cantor's absence from the initial negotiations created White House uncertainty: it was not clear whether Cantor—and hence Boehner's rank and file—would go along with what was becoming a nearly four-trillion-dollar megadeal that included revenues. The plan imploded after Cantor let House Republicans know that he had been left out of the talks and then pushed the Speaker to call off the talks in early July (Ferris 2016). Boehner's office revived the effort in mid-July by countering an earlier White House proposal with an offer that contained an unexpected eight hundred billion dollars in new revenue—the first real move toward new revenues to accompany Boehner's demands for spending cuts.[12] The counteroffer thus dovetailed with other tax policy considerations (Bai 2012).[13]

For one crucial but fleeting moment, it was clear that the two leaders still were serious about a grand bargain. Boehner wanted something enduring from his time as Speaker, while Obama wanted not merely to end the default crisis but also to signal his resolve to tackle deficits in a move that would renew—and possibly redefine—the Democratic Party and tame the hard right headwinds that worked against his every move. Both men believed that going for a big deal was the best practical strategy to get others to take on otherwise politically unpalatable policies. As Biden said, "There's no point in dying on a small cross" (Bai 2012). The negotiations continued in earnest, with the Boehner team asking for about $450 billion in cuts to Medicare and Medicaid as well as savings from changes to Social Security (Bai 2012). There's no doubt that this turn toward entitlements was a bitter pill for Democrats, but the ongoing negotiations suggested that the White House team had conceded that they were on the table.

But these negotiations on a megadeal did not unfold in a vacuum. The Republican House leadership wanted to keep sending messages not only to the White House but to the party's political base and the country as a whole that the GOP was serious about using the leverage afforded by the need to raise the debt limit to permanently get Washington spending under control. To this end, House Republicans rolled out the Cut, Cap, and Balance Act (HR 2560) in late July (Carter and Lesniewski 2011). The legislation offered ambiguous language on spending cuts and provided that the debt limit would be raised only after a constitutional amendment to balance the budget was approved. The near-perfect party-line vote allowed conservatives to placate antispending interests and relieve hard right anger over a possible deal with the White House (Schatz and Krawzak 2011, 1556). The dynamics in the Senate, under Democratic control, were completely different. There, Cut, Cap, and Balance died with a simple 51–46 motion to table the bill as soon as it arrived (Cohen 2011, 1612; Austin 2015). The House action on such messaging legislation at a critical juncture may have done greater harm to practical coalition-building efforts by creating unworkable expectations that contrasted sharply with the sacrifices and compromise a true grand bargain would require.[14]

But a perhaps bigger turn of events occurred when the Gang of Six surprised observers by going public in mid-July with a roughly four-trillion-dollar proposal that threw cold water on the tantalizingly close negotiations between the White House and House Republicans.[15] The move placed the Senate squarely in the public spotlight and drew support from ideological adversaries such as Dick Durbin (D-IL) and Tom Coburn (R-OK), which caused a large number of senators on both sides to fall into line. Just hours after the morning presentation in the Senate, President Obama endorsed the plan, which may have been a tactical error: adding another alternative made the already painstakingly difficult negotiations between the president and the Speaker even more chaotic (Wallsten, Montgomery, and Wilson 2012).

At the same time, there was blowback from House Democrats. The president had already shown a willingness to cut sacred programs, and the Senate's Gang of Six blueprint would leave House Democrats unable to present themselves as protectors of entitlements in the 2012 elections. House minority whip Steny Hoyer (D-MD) pointed out the dilemma: "We have made it very clear that we have no intention of supporting cuts to beneficiaries' benefits"; however, he continued, "I think the overwhelming majority of Democrats—overwhelming—are for a grand bargain" (Kenen 2011, 1614). The Speaker, too, found himself in a pinch: about twenty GOP senators had expressed support for the Gang of Six plan, which included $1.2 trillion more in new revenues than the original grand bargain proposal had contained.[16]

The Gang of Six proposal shook up the Obama-Boehner negotiations. The president subsequently asked for a reformulation of the revenue to increase the $800 billion in revenue to just under $1.2 trillion, equaling the entitlement cuts that the Speaker had requested. The Speaker had viewed the original $800 billion as a ceiling—he could not go any higher (Bai 2012). Other problems also remained within the grand bargain framework. With the August 2 deadline quickly approaching, too little time remained to hammer out the details of new revenue generation—the tax reform piece of the bargain would have to come later. To ensure that both parties would work faithfully toward this goal, the White House suggested two triggers. To keep Democrats on board, the Bush tax cuts for those with the highest incomes would be reinstated if agreement on tax reforms could not be reached. For Republicans, the failure to reach a tax reform agreement would automatically result in $425 billion in Medicare and Medicaid cuts over ten years. Boehner rejected both. Instead of the second trigger, Boehner wanted the mandate that required individuals to purchase health insurance—the centerpiece of Obamacare—to be stricken. It was the political scalp that Cantor and the hard right had long demanded. The president was unwilling to cede such a trophy (Newton-Small 2011; Bai 2012; Wallsten, Montgomery, and Wilson 2012).

Thus, the grand bargain, so close on so many fronts, was stuck on two critical points, revenues and triggers. Nevertheless, despite the outcry from their respective political bases, Obama and Boehner took one more stab at striking a deal. The president offered the Speaker a choice: the original package with eight hundred billion dollars in new revenue, or the larger proposal containing more revenue but also more entitlement cuts. Obama told his congressional leaders, Rep. Nancy Pelosi (D-CA) and Sen. Harry Reid (D-NV), that he needed their commitment on both packages to move forward and they fell into line, though reluctantly and aggrieved (Bai 2012).

But it remained unclear whether Boehner could deliver House Republicans' votes on a grand bargain.[17] Even prior to the chaos caused by the Gang of Six, when the Speaker had estimated that about 150 of the House Republicans would support a grand bargain, Cantor and other congressional leaders had suggested that fewer than half as many would go along (Bai 2012). More important, the GOP leadership itself was split. Cantor had never wanted the revenue piece on the reform table; it had killed his earlier talks with Biden. Not only did it contradict his ideological stance, it could undermine his strength with the hard right wing of the party, the Tea Party freshmen, and their powerful supporters. Cantor was too heavily invested in cutting and dismantling federal programs as the hard right's voice in the House leadership and the eager hand of the Tea Party grassroots. Since the beginning of the 112th Congress the majority leader had launched the "You-Cut" program, which sent the week's most popular spending target to the House floor for a vote. He felt he could not turn tail and accept any revenue increase. Boehner thus faced the prospect of both losing his majority leader and staring down a House GOP conference that would be badly split against him.[18] Boehner ultimately could not accept the White House's proposed revenue increases. With the deal dead, Boehner and Obama retreated to their respective corners and began pointing fingers of blame at each other.

Congressional leaders then moved quickly to beat the approaching default deadline by bringing up a last-ditch procedural option they had devised as a contingency for precisely this scenario. McConnell had initiated a proposal and worked with Reid on a framework compromise that built consensus and garnered support among Senate Republicans.[19]

The BCA coupled deficit-reduction measures with a series of planned increases in the debt limit up to the president's $2.1 trillion request but with some special procedures that highlighted the sensitivity of votes to raise the debt limit. The deficit-reduction efforts included items as discretionary spending caps triggered by automatic spending reductions via sequestration.[20] The BCA also established a supercommittee—the Joint Select Committee on Deficit Reduction—to make budget-cutting recommendations to Congress and mandated a congressional vote on a balanced-budget constitutional amendment.

The BCA placed the perceived burden of raising the debt limit on the president's shoulders (Schatz and Krawzak 2011).[21] The debt limit would be raised three times over the ensuing six months—enough fiscal headroom to punt the debt limit issue until after the 2012 presidential election. In each instance, the president would certify that the debt was within its one-hundred-billion-dollar limit. Congress could then pass a joint resolution of disapproval of the president's actions to increase the debt limit, which the president would of course veto, enabling the debt limit to be raised.[22]

The BCA thus solved the crisis via a mix of substantive fiscal and procedural fixes. The House passed the final revised legislation, 269–161, the Senate approved it 74–26, and the president signed it into law (PL 112-25) on August 2 as the default clock approached zero hour.[23]

In classic form, the BCA allowed Republicans to bludgeon the president (and his economic policies) while not having to vote in favor of raising the debt limit at least three times. The statutory debt limit rose by $400 billion when the BCA passed in August, by $500 billion in September, and by $1.2 trillion in December. According to Sen. Coburn, this final resolution of the great debt-ceiling crisis of 2011 was "a political answer" (Cranford and Schatz 2011, 1550).

Congress stepped away from what would have been a historic grand bargain and instead accepted a small-bore compromise that allowed for public posturing and left the perceived ownership of the debt in the president's hands. As this endgame was unfolding, some Democrats in Congress believed that the president could exercise power to unilaterally raise the debt limit under the provisions of the Fourteenth Amendment.[24] Rep. Jim Clyburn (D-SC) and other House leaders urged President Obama to use an executive order to bridge the crisis on the grounds that the Fourteenth Amendment provided the president with constitutional authority to protect the government from financial catastrophe if the debt limit was breached and the government defaulted because of Republican refusal to raise the debt limit (Seitz-Wald and Jilani 2011). In 2013, similar and even more vocal arguments resurfaced, supporting unilateral action by the president to override the statutory debt limit in the face of unprecedented brinksmanship by Republicans in Congress that again brought the country to the edge of cataclysm. However, the White House refused to act unilaterally, instead pressuring Congress to fulfill its constitutional obligations (Liptak 2013; Schoenberg and Farrell 2013; Wilentz 2013).[25]

## Shutdown Politics: A Storm Is Brewing

### Tuesday, February 22, 2011

The buzzword in Washington today is *Shutdown!* Will the Republicans force the government to close on March 4 because of an inability to reach agreement on funding for the balance of the fiscal year? Will they reprise 1995, when a hard-line approach led by Newt Gingrich (R-GA) led to stalemate and the government closing its doors for several days? At that time, the issue was long-term spending: the Republicans wanted huge cuts, President Clinton sought a more balanced approach, and the deadlock led to a shutdown. The public revolted at losing access to needed services, and many observers believe that Clinton's victory in the standoff led to his strong reelection in 1996. So Democrats do not fear Republican budget zealotry. However, times are different now. The deficit and debt problems are orders of magnitude larger, and the public is not enamored with Democratic management of the economy and the budget. Turning gridlock into a political victory may not be as easy this time. Nevertheless, the conventional wisdom is that the Republicans in the House have more to lose and that their Tea Party base makes them prone to radicalism. Everyone is professing not to want a disaster—easier said than done. Reid, the Senate majority leader, said today that he wanted a simple thirty-day extension to provide time to work things out. Speaker Boehner and Cantor, the House majority leader, indicated yesterday and today that a simple extension without interim spending cuts is a nonstarter. So we may get to the brink that everyone says they want to avoid.

## Tuesday, March 15

William Daley, the president's new chief of staff, came to visit with the House Democratic caucus this morning. The session started slowly, with questions about aid to low-income districts, pleas not to let spending cuts kill the economy, and observations that we need to do better on our budget message. We've likely run the course on these short-term extensions of government spending for the current fiscal year, Daley said. And he promised that the president will be directly involved and vocal as the issue moves toward confrontation and (hopefully) resolution with Republicans. Daley was pressed on this: *What is our strategy? What is the role of the President? What is our message?* Daley said that we would change the contours of the debate and get the public's focus on our points as we get to the endgame. But the real character of Daley that shone through during the session came when a relatively senior California Democrat took the floor to lash into Obama's strategy on the budget and government spending measures and asked whether he was really taking on the Republicans. The congressman went on for a few minutes, and Daley, who had earlier in the session had been pretty self-effacing ("I've learned that my title means more *staff* and less *chief*") and who conveyed a complete sense of being pragmatic and just getting the job done, was willing to just let the representative vent. He hated what the member was saying—the president is out there every day talking about the budget and our priorities and where he wants to take the country—but just let him go on. Daley nodded when the member was finished and then turned to the next question. I hope he enjoyed himself and the talking he gave Daley, because that congressman will get no more favors from this White House.

## Friday, April 1

So we continue laboring in the dark ages. And the day became even darker yesterday when the House took up, on an emergency basis—no hearings, no testimony, and no amendments permitted—the Government Shutdown Prevention Act. Essentially it said that if the House does not receive a message from the Senate by next Wednesday, April 6—two days before the government spending authority expires and a shutdown begins—continuing resolution HR 1, with its sixty billion dollars in budget cuts and dozens of policy riders on abortion, the Environmental Protection Agency, and the Federal Communications Commission, comes into effect. This is one of the bigger atrocities to hit the floor in anyone's memory because the House cannot deem anything to take effect as law without the Senate approving exactly the same language and the president signing it into law. The idea would be laughable except that the people who came up with it were serious. Henry was quite worked up in a statement for the floor:

> Madam Speaker, either this is April Fool's Day or the Republicans are trying to fool the House of Representatives and the country by attempting to pass this legislation. There is no truth in labeling whatsoever in H.R. 1255, the "Government Shutdown Prevent Act of 2011." It will prevent no such thing, it will accomplish no such thing.
>
> Section 2 of the bill says that if the House has not received a message from the Senate stating, by next Wednesday, April 6, that the Senate has passed a spending bill for the balance of this fiscal year, then "the provisions of H.R. 1, as passed by the House on February 19, 2011, are hereby enacted into law."
>
> Who are the authors of this bill kidding? The House passed H.R. 1. It lies defeated on the Senate floor, unloved and unwanted. The Senate voted against H.R. 1, 44–56. It did not even get 50 votes, much less 60. So what, exactly, is the point of this exercise today? It is obviously not to enact H.R. 1, because that is futile.
>
> With the vote of this bill today, we will in effect be passing H.R. 1 a second time. This is getting to be a pattern. Instead of finding bipartisan solutions to our pressing national problems, this Republican House seems stuck on a pointless partisan treadmill.
>
> H.R. 1 contained five amendments to defund the Affordable Care Act. Yesterday, the Energy and Commerce Committee passed

five bills to remove funding for public health and doctor training programs under the Affordable Care Act.

The majority defunded all of public broadcasting in H.R. 1, and then defunded NPR on the House floor a couple weeks later.

On this April Fool's Day, do you want to know the truth about all this frantic legislative activity? After three months on the job, we have not created one job—because of one simple fact. In three months, the Republican leadership has not passed one major bill of any consequence that has been enacted into law. That is the simple truth. They have failed to enact anything of consequence.

And so with that shameful record, they come to the floor today with an illusion, a joke, a diversion, a cover-up for their failure. The Republicans have the votes to pass a bill that says their spending cuts and ideological amendments are hereby enacted if we pass this bill. But we are not enacting this bill, because under Article I, Section 7 of the Constitution of the United States, this bill has to go to the Senate and be passed in identical form and then signed by the President.

Madam Speaker, this is April Fool's Day, and this is a bill for fools. But the American people will not be fooled.

It passed, but the Republicans lost fifteen of their colleagues—fifteen souls who did not want to participate in such a farce. But this passes for substantive legislative activity in these dark days. Nevertheless, just as our committee was at the center of the president's legislative success in the 111th Congress, so it is now the fulcrum of the Republican agenda.

### Wednesday, April 6

As all this is occurring, there is a major contretemps over continued funding of the government and the threat of a shutdown on Friday night. This is highly charged. Can the Republican Speaker reach a deal with Obama? The president clearly wants to, but it would inevitably not be as stringent as what passed the House: Will the Speaker's Tea Party troops accept it? The president was in excellent form at the White House yesterday as negotiations faltered, and I sent a message in: *More bully in the pulpit.* And late tonight, negotiations broke, but Obama reported progress and said there would be no excuse for failure to reach a deal. It was a high-road bully pulpit and a good framing of the situation should the worst occur.

Also yesterday, the Republicans announced their draconian budget. The meeting in the Democratic caucus was quite resolute. The leadership and virtually all members believe that the Republican budget, in its harshness, is a gift on a silver platter—the most radical budget we have ever seen. The party will hammer Paul Ryan's budget on three criteria: Does it help the economy? Does it put people back to work? Does it reduce the deficit in a way that reflects priorities? The messaging will be quite straightforward: *Their choices are wrong for America. They extend the Bush tax cuts while they cut education and terminate Medicare. They keep tax breaks for big oil and gut Medicaid. Seniors, the disabled, children—they are the biggest targets of the Ryan budget. This does not reflect the priorities of America. This is not reform—this is the same old Republican agenda. Under their Medicare, they force seniors into the private insurance market. Seniors will be hit with increased health care costs, and they are on their own. They ration health care and choice of doctor by income. This is a bonanza for the private insurance industry.* So this evening, at a fund-raiser for House Democrats, Steve Israel (NY), chair of the party's Congressional Campaign Committee, said that these issues would cut for us in November 2012—that we had lost the seniors' vote in 2010 over health care after winning it decisively in 2006 and 2008. Their budget, Israel said, will help us get seniors and independents back.

### Friday, April 8

It was such a peculiar day, with the government shutdown looming because of the budget deadlock. Last night, as the president and congressional leaders were about to meet, I sent a memo to staff in the White House: "What a Fly on the White House Walls Might Have Heard during the Night":

> John [Speaker Boehner], I want a deal and I want it tonight. We're virtually there on the dollars. You have won more than 50% of what you wanted. So let's finalize it and lock it in. But I am not taking the riders. And if you want to shut down the government on these riders please go right ahead.
>
> Because I will go to the country and say that once again the Republicans are wrecking the economy out of ideological fervor. You did it 15 years ago and that sad history is repeating itself. The Republicans' job-killing riders are going to throw more Americans out of work.
>
> You know I won an election too. And so did Harry. And I will explain to the country that we have orderly, constitutional legislative

processes to resolve abortion and health care and carbon and the Internet. Let the House and Senate take as many votes as they want on these issues—but not on this bill.

So yes, I will explain how you are holding our economic recovery hostage—instead of banking the largest spending cuts in modern history. Deal?

I heard that I was right: that was indeed the conversation on Wednesday night! But all day long, people on the Hill were obsessed with what might happen: it was on a par with a blizzard that would shut down everything for days. It appears that Obama has agreed to thirty-eight billion dollars or so in cuts, much more than half of what the Republicans sought, but was balking—properly—on the riders regarding abortion, the environment, and the open Internet. On the floor in the afternoon, members were amazed that the Republicans might shut down the government over funding for women's health programs. At the same time, the thirty-eight billion dollars in cuts looked pretty steep—very mixed feelings about it.

### Saturday, April 9

I don't think the president dug in hard enough. A shutdown of the government was averted by an agreement sealed an hour before midnight last night. Thirty-nine billion dollars in cuts—six billion dollars more than was on the table a day or so ago. Yes, no riders on women's health services, but the Senate will be forced to vote on whether to repeal the health care reform bill. Boehner emerges with a clear win. And because we did not go into shutdown over social policy issues and had the largest spending cuts in modern history, Boehner looks stronger today and the Democrats have tangible things they have lost. Obama looks OK to middle America—he was the adult at the table who did what needed to be done to make sure the government kept functioning—but there were no countervailing wins like last December, when some very progressive things on tax cuts for working Americans were put in place. So the bottom line is that Obama probably helped himself with independents for the time being, and Republicans helped themselves as well in terms of cementing control over Congress in next year's elections. Mainstream Democrats lost. But this is not the main game. In the coming weeks, the fight will be over the harsh Republican budget, its savaging of Medicare, and the games the Republicans will play on the vote to raise the debt limit and extend the full faith and credit of the United States. Those two issues are the really high stakes.

## Wednesday, April 13

So today was the Ryan budget. The Democratic caucus this morning was tepid. There is no enthusiasm for the round of cuts to be voted on tomorrow but no real enthusiasm for what we will offer either. But there is a lot of energy in opposing the Republicans for their "Medicare Massacre"—a real feeling that this is an issue where Democrats can recapture seniors and independent voters and improve prospects for the House elections next year. This afternoon, the president weighed in with a sharply partisan speech on the causes of the current deficit crisis and the effects of the Republican nostrums. So he came to them on their creation of the problem and the unacceptable solutions they offer. Obama called for protecting Medicare and Medicaid but still making significant cuts, driven principally by efficiencies to be enacted. It will be hard. The two sides are bitterly divided. Obama said that revenues—taxes—have to be part of the equation, and that is anathema to the Republicans. He called for a summit, chaired by the vice president, to work through the macro issues. This will happen in May and June. Might the Republicans boycott the talks? To up the ante, those discussions run right into the drop-dead date for extending the debt limit. So it will be a summer of high-stakes budget politics. I hope Henry will be one of the eight House interlocutors. With Medicare and Medicaid so much a part of the issues here, it is hard to see how he can be cut out.

## Saturday, April 16

Republicans won the week—again—but hit some potholes. The deal for the 2011 budget passed on Thursday, but with fifty-nine hard-line Republicans against the legislation. It was not tough enough for them. Indeed, the Congressional Budget Office, which is the official scorekeeper of spending and which drove us nuts from time to time with their evaluation of the health reform law, came up with a doozy just before the vote: The bill doesn't save $38 billion, as Republicans claim, but only $358 million—1 percent of the expected savings. And in fact, the Congressional Budget Office went on, total spending in 2011, after the bill, will be $3 million higher than all of 2010. Go figure.

But another interesting development may have important consequences to the future. In the end, Boehner could not pass his vaunted spending cuts without Democratic votes. And the Democrats split almost down the middle—108 against, 80 for—but the Democratic support enabled Boehner to carry the day. This split was reflected in our leadership, with Pelosi against and Steny Hoyer, who is emerging under Republican rule in the House more and more as a very strong voice of the Democratic minority, voting for the agreement. By yesterday morning, Pelosi had had enough, and she said something really interesting: the agreement last Friday night was predicated on the idea that there would be no Democratic votes—that the Republicans had the votes to pass it. They are wrong, she said. There have now been two votes—first on a short-term bill to extend the spending authority while the big deal was being negotiated and now the final agreement—where they needed our support to get these things through. So we have leverage. And in the future, we have to get something for pulling their fat out of the fire. She said that House Democrats were not in the negotiations and that there was absolutely nothing in the agreement for us. This will come back as the really big showdown on the debt limit gets under way.

## Monday, May 31

The Republican stunt of a "clean" vote to raise the debt limit succeeded, at least for now with the bill going down to defeat by a 318–97 vote. It was a crass ploy: shoot down what the Democrats and President Obama have consistently said what they wanted—an up or down vote to increase the debt limit, without conditions, to do the right thing and keep the markets from panicking. But all the Democrats who voted for this bill would be subject to an attack ad saying that they supported adding two trillion dollars to the debt while doing nothing about the deficit. Our caucus was split, and an intense, spirited, and fascinating hour-long discussion occurred just before the vote. The leadership had reached the conclusion over the weekend that a *No* vote was the safest possible vote. Hoyer said that Democrats should vote *No*—it's a joke, don't legitimize it, it is not a bipartisan effort. Chris Van Hollen (D-MD), the ranking member on the Budget Committee, who is at the table with Obama and the Republicans to negotiate a megadeal on the debt limit and deficit reduction, concurred. Members piped up. *They're presenting a trick. A complete charade, and it's a mistake to give credibility to it.* And this sentiment was carrying the early part of the discussion over a differing view by several liberals that the correct vote was *Present*, which would say *We are not playing your game. We don't buy into this process.* But the fear was that it was too hard to explain—a nuance in a trillion-dollar poker match. And so as the vote neared, the voices of other liberals who wanted to vote *Yes* because it was the right vote to make, became louder. "A *No* vote equates us with the Republicans, and it's very dangerous," one said. There was also a lot of concern that even though Republicans were telling Wall Street that this was not a serious vote and that there was no need to panic when the Internet headlines blared, *House defeats debt limit extension*, the markets would indeed go nuts. A lot of members recalled what happened in 2008, when the first post-Lehman-collapse bailout failed and the Dow collapsed eight hundred points in a day; Congress blinked and revoted and passed the damn thing. It was harrowing. And the debt limit is a much bigger issue than that one because it is the full faith and credit of the United States, not just some banks.

I at first advocated a vote of *Present* to Henry, but by the end of the discussion, I finally recommended a *Yes* vote: My final recommendation is *Yes*. The debt limit is not to be gamed or messed or trifled with. It's too serious given the consequences of what is at stake. Bruce Josten of the US Chamber of Commerce said in the *New York Times* this morning, "Wall Street is in on the joke"—the Republican ploy. But the Chinese may not get it. And that would be a catastrophe. So in the absence of party position for *Present*, I believe the best vote is *Yes*.

So Henry was one of 97 Democrats who voted *Yes*; 82 voted *No*, and only 7 voted *Present*. No one was in disagreement on the fundamentals: the Democrats oppose what the Republicans are trying to do on the debt limit. And the right vote would have been a consensus party view to go *Present*—we are not playing your game. But that would have taken one more day and some earnest discussions—time we did not have because the Republicans moved up the vote twenty-four hours, so it was right against the Memorial Day holiday. They play hard and smart.

## Saturday, June 4

Yesterday was terrible. Only fifty-four thousand jobs created in May, a fraction of the worst-case estimate by economists. Unemployment back up to 9.1 percent. The average unemployed person in May has been out of work for over thirty-nine weeks, the longest since records began to be kept in 1948. It's like hitting a brick wall. And suddenly Obama and the House Democrats are exceedingly vulnerable. There is nothing left in the locker to fight the fire. We are out of dough. The debt is over fourteen trillion dollars. The debt ceiling must be raised. The two are linked, and the price of sanity will be high. Taking the air out of the economy will not help on the jobs front, which plays right into the Republicans' hand and how they want sentiment in the country to be a year from now. A responsibly positioned conservative Republican can tap into this extremely well—Tim Pawlenty rather than Sarah Palin; Jon Huntsman rather than Newt Gingrich.

## Saturday, July 9

Another devastating unemployment report out yesterday morning. Only eighteen thousand net jobs created and unemployment crept up to 9.2 percent from last month's 9.1 percent. Unemployment has been above 8 percent for twenty-nine months—virtually all of Obama's term. The economic recovery is faltering. But we have a choice of having an issue—Medicare, Medicare, Medicare—or an economic program. Since we have no weapons left in the arsenal, the only thing that can get the economy moving again with investment and growth is certainty and stability. And that means a very significant debt-reduction deal. This was the backdrop for a midday party caucus. With the exception of one brave (or foolhardy) moderate from the Pacific Northwest, the mood against cuts in Medicare, Social Security, and Medicaid was quite hostile—both on the substance and on how the politics could play out. Many were upset with what might happen to Medicaid, and Democratic leaders are urging Democratic governors to call the White House.

Members expressed vociferous support for entitlements and real concern for being wedged by Obama in the final negotiations. The caucus mood was captured with voices like these:

*We have to protect Medicare, our values as a party, and our candidates for 2012.*

*We will have to find our way as House Democrats to differentiate ourselves if necessary—I hope we don't have to go there.*

*If we want to get seniors who left us last year back again, we better help them.*

*We must have revenues. Cuts only is a no-go.*

*Sometimes you have to stand up to your president and fight.*

*We all saw the jobs figures this morning. Every cut we make will make the economy worse, which is exactly what the Republicans want.*

*At some point the president has to know that we are prepared to say no to a bad deal. . . . I desperately want to vote for something, but I won't vote for just anything.*

I have felt all year we will not win the House back and we will surely lose the Senate. And that means that if we are to ensure that what we did in the 111th survives, we need to make the grand bargain and let a rising economic tide lift President Obama to a second term. But that probably means that the cuts are deeper than most Democrats in the House can abide and thus that a split party gives Obama a victory standing on the shoulders of the House Republicans. This is a pretty nasty political calculation.

### Tuesday, July 12

Obama is pressing the Republicans hard to come clean and play straight on the debt limit, and he is getting under their skin, because he is taking the high road—"This is something we can do. Now." And they insist on cutting support for Medicare but not requiring the richest among us to pay a penny more to cushion some of that pain. In the caucus this morning, Pelosi said that the president was "magnificent"—that he was there for working families and seniors. We will continue to push the issues of Medicare and no tax breaks for the rich: a fair deal for the American people. We want to see skin in the game from the Republicans as far as revenues are concerned. After a decade of tax cuts, there were no jobs. Are we going to have fairness to the middle class or not? Our caucus is united on no short-term debt limit. The president is hanging tough, and we've got to give him the leverage.

The White House should enjoy the backing while its got it. Mitch McConnell, the Senate Republican leader, who last year said quite memorably that he wanted to make Obama a one-term president, put the knife in this morning in the Senate: "After years of discussions and months of negotiations, I have little question that as long as this president is in the Oval Office, a real solution is probably unattainable."

### Wednesday, July 13

Today, at long last, a massively important letter from the business community on the imperative of raising the debt limit and ending the growing crisis. Hundreds of business leaders—many of them Republican supporters—and companies signed:

We believe it is vitally important for the US government to make good on its financial obligations and to put its fiscal house in order. With our nation on a sound fiscal footing, we are confident that America's businesses and entrepreneurs will foster generations of high value, well-paying jobs and contribute to a prosperous future. To this end, we believe now is the time for our political leaders to act. . . . Now is the time for our political leaders to put aside partisan differences and act in the nation's best interests. We believe that our nation's economic future is reliant upon their actions and urge them to reach an agreement. It is time to pull together rather than pull apart.

McConnell proposed a procedural fix, allowing Obama to raise the debt limit subject to a resolution of disapproval by Congress, which the president could veto: given the makeup of the House and Senate, the veto would stick. At the same time, he would have to propose spending cuts of the same magnitude as the debt-limit increase (*So you want to raise the debt limit by two trillion dollars? Well, show us two trillion dollars in cuts*) but they would go through the normal appropriations process. So Obama can raise the debt limit—and then take full responsibility for it. And he has to show his hand on all the pain of the spending cuts without the Republicans proposing some equities in terms of new revenues. So it's kind of a neat political parlor trick, but it is procedural, not substantive. It will not produce the grand four-trillion-dollar megadeal that would really get us on the road to solving the debt problem. But Washington loves procedures—they're so much easier to parse and argue over than the hard substance. So if the debt negotiations get really stuck, this god-awful nonfix will become the way out. For what it's worth, I suggested to Phil Schiliro that Obama start secret negotiations with Speaker Boehner on a megadeal or smoke out the Republicans by putting on the table the entire four-trillion-dollar package of cuts and revenues and letting the country judge who is really trying to solve problems and do so in a balanced way and who is playing pure politics.

## Monday, July 25

We are now at an impasse in the debt-ceiling deficit-reduction fight. Both the president and Speaker Boehner addressed the nation on TV, and what was abundantly clear is that we are completely stuck. Before the speeches, the House Democrats met. While there was confusion and doubt as the discussion got under way at 5:30 pm, there was clarity and resolve coming out. As one of our leaders said (and many others agree), "The Boehner plan takes us into the deepest depths of hell."

Other members were insistent: *We don't want the Boehner plan to get to the president's desk. Our objective has to be that they fail to get 218 on their side for Boehner. We cannot give them any votes. We don't want the president to be in a position of either vetoing or signing a bad bill. That would be terrible to have him in that position. Let's understand that the Republicans want a bad economy and this crisis to continue, because it weakens the economy. The Boehner plan is their campaign plan.*

The Boehner plan is all cuts and no taxes, plus it's only a short-term debt-limit extension until next February, the beginning of the political campaign year. So it not only doesn't solve the problem but in fact makes it worse by simply perpetuating the crisis—and the uncertainty and paralysis that are killing the country—for the next several months. And this suggests that there is a motive here: to keep the economy from recovering and benefit the Republicans in 2012. It is the president who wants to get the economy moving again, the president who is willing to take on the sacred cows in his party and put the national interest above partisan interest, the president who has been willing to go more than halfway by tough spending cuts and minimal tax provisions.

I believe that Obama reached the nation and that Boehner reached his base. The key thing to watch is whether the Republicans can pass their plan in the House on Wednesday. If they lose thirty Tea Partiers and no Democrats cross the aisle, they lose. Then the leverage will shift to Reid and the Senate. But if they win, then there will be a test vote in the Senate. I find it hard to believe the Senate can pass the Boehner plan. So—impasse.

### Tuesday, July 26

Morning-after misgivings on the president's speech. He called for a balanced approach and excoriated cuts, but he also endorsed the Senate Democratic proposal that just has cuts. So has he given away the game? And then, word came this afternoon that a Tea Party revolt was under way among House Republicans and that there were growing doubts that the votes were there to pass the Boehner proposal. If we hold all our votes, they can afford to lose only twenty-five of theirs and still prevail, and the reports are that dozens of Republicans are leaning against what Boehner is doing—because it does not make enough cuts! And then word came from the Congressional Budget Office that the Boehner bill fell short by hundreds of billions of dollars. Late tonight, Boehner pulled the bill, and the vote is now scheduled for Thursday. But now we have an opening to get back to a grand bargain with revenues: if Boehner fails in his own House, then it is clear that the only way to pass something is with Democratic votes, and revenues are our price. Obama may yet be redeemed.

Wednesday, July 27

My fears about what has been given away were crystallized this morning in the *Wall Street Journal* lead editorial:

> Thanks to the President's overreaching on taxes, Mr. Boehner now has the GOP positioned in sight of a political and policy victory. If his plan or something close to it becomes law, Democrats will have conceded more spending cuts than they thought possible, and without getting the GOP to raise taxes and without being able to blame Republicans for a debt-limit crack-up or economic damage. If conservatives defeat the Boehner plan, they'll not only undermine their House majority. They'll go far to re-electing Mr. Obama and making the entitlement state that much harder to reform.

This editorial and other pressure from Republican leadership began to have an impact as the day progressed, and by tonight, my sense was that Boehner has the votes to get his package through. He changed his proposal to ensure that it had more savings, eliminating the Congressional Budget Office problem, and then leaned on his members heavily in a caucus this morning: "Get your ass in line," he reportedly said. Several Democrats are quietly furious, believing that Obama has given away the game—there is simply now no vocal insistence on taxes and balance. The fight now is simply about whether you raise the debt limit in one big leap or two. Now, two is terrible for the economy, because we will remain obsessed with this stupid game for months and it will kill the economy. But how to translate that into a winning issue with the public? Taxing the wealthiest to spread the burden around—people understand that. But not whether we extend the debt limit for six months or eighteen months. Hoyer said that he understood Boehner to be thirty or forty votes short and that if Boehner is beaten, Reid is the only alternative, and we will have to go for it. Van Hollen said that if Boehner fails, Reid is strengthened enormously and McConnell has more room to work with Boehner.

Several members were now concluding that the president has to invoke constitutional authority on the debt ceiling. *He has not told us this, but I have to believe it's an option on the table. . . . A lot of lenders may believe that a large cloud hangs over such an order and that it may not help much with respect to the markets.* Clyburn then said he wanted to say something about the Fourteenth Amendment. He said that if the president gets a short-term extension, he should veto it and use the same pen to sign an Executive Order raising the debt limit based on the Fourteenth Amendment: "Anything less than something bold is a LOSER for us." We will lose the next election and he will be retired to Chicago.

It seems to me that the only positive options are predicated on Boehner failing. With respect to the president invoking the Fourteenth Amendment, I believe that will bring on impeachment. But, if the White House can be assured—and I mean 100 percent assured—that Congress is hopelessly and irreparably stuck because of Republican intransigence and that such action will avoid both default AND a downgrade—well, then let us have the mother of all election campaigns on these issues in 2012.

The House votes on the Boehner plan tomorrow.

### Thursday, July 28

Five days until default. Rather remarkable developments late this afternoon: word from the Republican leadership that they were delaying the vote on Speaker Boehner's draconian cuts and debt-limit bill. Word quickly filtered through that they have lost twenty-seven of their ranks, putting them four votes short of a majority. Hoyer announced that no Democrats would vote for Boehner and produced a letter from fifty-three senators that the Boehner plan was dead in the Senate. So why walk the plank in a vote that is going nowhere? It is a real shocker for Boehner, and late tonight, after rumors that he would tweak the bill further to recoup Republican support, votes were postponed indefinitely. So Boehner may not be able to pass a bill, which gives the Democrats in the Senate more flexibility and running room to craft a compromise that Obama can sign.

### Saturday, July 30

Boehner won on the floor last evening, but even with his constitutional twists and perversions, there were still twenty-two Tea Party defectors, and a couple more would have sent him down once again. What was so interesting was that when they crossed the 217-vote threshold, there was no applause, no whooping and foot stomping—the exact opposite of the reaction on the floor when we passed Waxman-Markey and the health reform law. Those were also squeakers, but they felt like a landslide. This was a whimper. To put down the rebellion, Boehner added a provision that said that the next debt-limit extension could only occur if Congress has passed and sent to the states a constitutional amendment for a balanced budget. First, we do not know what the text of that is. Second, this Congress, as constituted, is not going to pass a balanced budget constitutional amendment. It requires two-thirds of both bodies, and the votes are not there. So the Boehner measure means an automatic default in six months. This is how they are legislating in the House today. This is the best proposal they can come up with to pass something without Democratic votes—in other words, not compromise.

Henry was asked by the leadership for a statement on the floor, and he had at it once more:

> I have never witnessed such a legislative and political travesty. The Republican majority is threatening to take the entire economy hostage unless we write their draconian budget—which would end Medicare and Medicaid—into the Constitution.
>
> Throughout this week, the Republican leadership and Republican caucus have been operating in a world of unreality. The Speaker and his team have persisted in passing legislation that everyone in the real world knows is dead on arrival in the Senate. Today, we have moved from unreality to fantasy.
>
> We are being told that if we do not pass a constitutional amendment to end Medicare and Medicaid, then the debt limit will not be raised . . . the United States of America will default . . . and the American people will suffer grievously.
>
> And under a balanced budget amendment, Congress will be placed in a straightjacket and the government will not be able to respond to compelling humanitarian and public health needs in times of economic downturns.
>
> This is not the moment to engage in fantasy. This House must take its responsibilities seriously and do its proper duty for the nation.
>
> The bill before us, with the poison pill of a balanced budget amendment, is a vicious assault on Medicare, Medicaid, Social Security, along with public health, scientific research and environmental protection. I urge the defeat of this rule and the terrible consequences that will flow from it.

## Monday, August 1

One day until default. The deal came together last night, with the president saying on television that congressional leaders in both parties from both houses had reached agreement. There are $2.5 trillion in cuts, 1 trillion of which go into effect now. The new super joint committee will outline by Thanksgiving another $1.5 trillion in cuts, and if Congress fails to enact, automatic cuts go into effect, although Social Security, Medicare, and Medicaid will be spared. The agreement covers the debt ceiling through the next election, so we will not have this horrible blackmail at least until 2013. Early this morning, I cleared a note to Henry with Phil Barnett and gave my advice:

> Bottom line: I'm against it. They won—big—on taking the country and the budget hostage to their extreme demands, and in defining the playing field. We lost—badly—on revenues and balance. Lowering discretionary spending levels to the Eisenhower era is nothing to be proud of. The spending cuts will work to weaken the economy through this decade, even though ending the uncertainty of this crisis should provide a lift to psychology and hopefully business investment and consumer spending. The sequester does not go into effect until 2013, which means immediate spending cuts are limited. All of this is positive because the economy is dead in the water today in large part to this crisis in Washington. But overall, the deal is consistent with the Republican political agenda of weakening the economy in order to hurt the President and congressional Democrats next year. The only two mitigating factors on closer examination are the joint committee and the sequester. The joint committee can do revenues, and it will most likely be in the form of tax reform that closes loopholes and ends tax expenditures and lowers rates. This would be a positive outcome that would not be possible without the special rules that guarantee unimpeded votes on the committee's work. The Bush tax cuts expire on 12/31, and that can give Obama leverage with the Joint Committee in structuring the tax package. The sequester, if it is triggered, hits defense and it exempts Medicaid and Social Security; for Medicare, the cut is limited to 2% and affects providers (but that will hurt the supply of providers to the system). So there is some equity in the sequester. My overall recommendation is to vote against it. This is not what we were sent

here to do. It is not what the President was elected to do. But, if your vote is needed today or tomorrow to avoid a default—then I think that is the higher need, because a default will punish everyone worse than even this tragic package.

But first, there was a meeting of the Democratic caucus with Vice President Biden. The mood was grim, unhappy, and very subdued but not angry. In reconstructing the day, it is clear that this meeting was pivotal—that Biden, by fronting the caucus the way he did, by listening for over two hours, and by quietly outlining why there are good things in this deal, clearly convinced a lot of Democrats to go along with it:

> The deal is not the preferred deal. The whole debate and debacle is not about the debt limit or the deficit. It's about fundamentally altering how government functions. They are using the deficit they created to decimate the social structures in this country. You have educated us all as to how far out these guys are. There are 100 in the House and 10 in the Senate who would take this country over the cliff.
>
> Yes, we could have done some things differently six months ago, and two months ago, and a month ago: but this is where we are.
>
> Our objectives:
>
> Rationally begin to reduce long term debt without eating our seed corn. Preserve the ability to keep investments and grow the economy. Protect Medicare and Medicaid. If we could get some stimulus up front too (e.g. continue the payroll tax holiday).
>
> It was clear when Cantor walked out we could not get revenues. And Boehner walked out twice. So if we default, a double dip recession is likely and we would hurt the people we care most about.
>
> Because of you, the terms of the debate have changed: polls show the public wants revenues. The credibility of the Tea Party with the nation as a whole has expired. Assuming this passes, I believe we can go forward from now until the joint committee finishes its work in beating the hell out of them on revenues.

I had expected Democrats to split 2:1 against the deal and told the White House staff and the VP's chief of staff that's what I thought would happen. But they divided evenly instead because the consequences of default were too terrible to bear, even if the price was giving in to this extortion.

Indeed, Boehner said in an interview this morning that Republicans got 98 percent of what they wanted. And they did! So all this is a measure of how hard they play, how vulnerable we are to such scorched-earth tactics, and how they were unwilling to play with the fire of default. The vote was 269–161—a huge margin. I thought the leadership would only get two-thirds of the Republicans (160 votes), but they did a bit better—174. Henry voted no. There was a magic moment in the voting. The Democrats were holding back during the fifteen-minute roll call, making Boehner show how much strength he had in his caucus. When they crossed 160, the Democrats started voting, including Gabrielle Giffords, who was almost fatally attacked in January and who came back specially to cast her vote—in favor—on the most important bill of the year. The place erupted in cheers and whoops and applause that went on for the balance of the roll call, and her vote in favor undoubtedly helped lift the tide.

## Concluding Thoughts

So, the Budget Control Act of 2011 passed and the debt crisis subsided, at least temporarily. But as Thomas Miller of the American Enterprise Institute warned, "If you dodge the debt ceiling bullet, there's another one coming" (Kenen 2011, 1614). Miller's prediction has been right on point: for the remainder of Obama's presidency, Republican leaders proved themselves unable to resist the tactical advantage presented by the debt limit, provoking a series of fights over deficits and spending to keep the government running (Debonis 2016). Minority status in the House freed Democratic members to criticize President Obama for failing to express sufficiently strong support for the party's base. In addition, even with control of the White House, House Democrats found that they had less bargaining ability relative to the majority in such areas as control over the congressional agenda. In addition, the grand bargain dynamics illustrated how bargaining leverage could switch from the House majority to the Senate when the House majority party failed to coalesce around a policy alternative.

There are certainly competing narratives about the demise of the grand bargain. Both sides agree that a deal was struck on a general framework, but there are differing views on the reasons that the grand bargain unraveled. From the Speaker's perspective, after the two sides had reached a handshake deal, Obama moved the goalposts on revenues (Schatz and Goldfarb 2011; Bai 2012). Indeed, Boehner remarked at a news conference that bargaining with the White House was like "dealing with a bowl of

Jell-O. . . . There was an agreement with the White House for $800 billion in revenue. It was the President who walked away from this agreement" (Wallsten, Montgomery, and Wilson 2012). The White House, of course, sees things differently: Speaker Boehner crumpled under pressure from the far right of his own party and was just looking for an escape hatch from the negotiation because he couldn't deliver his own conference. In the words of one White House aide, the Speaker "probably could not deliver a pizza" (Wallsten, Montgomery and Wilson 2012). The truth no doubt lies somewhere between the two views.

Regardless, a wide-ranging consensus holds that the demise of the grand bargain squandered a monumental opportunity to reset the country's fiscal path and shattered any lingering vestige of trust between President Obama and the GOP (Ferris 2016). The negotiations were the biggest of their kind, historic in their scope and parameters. The magnitude of the numbers probably makes sense only to a small circle of budgetary experts and staffers who understand the intricate assumptions and conditions involved. Health policy analyst Jack Hoadley remarked at the time, "The real impact will depend on the details that don't get in the newspaper headlines" (Kenen 2011, 1614). However, the negotiation was at least as much about political perception as about the intricacies of public policy. The seismic implications of the grand bargain resulted not from the hundreds of billions or trillions of dollars at stake but from political perceptions. Would financially strapped seniors be stripped of benefits? Would the middle class suffocate under a mound of debt, or would corporate America be crushed under the burden of taxes? Who would win, and who would get gored?

There is no way to know whether different decisions would have changed the tide. In this respect, both Obama and Boehner made choices at various junctures but ultimately found themselves trapped by bedrock political constraints that foreclosed prospects for a grand bargain. All of these constraints seem to connect back to partisanship. For example, the president's decision to embrace the Gang of Six plan was meant to put added pressure on the House GOP, but a plan with significant Republican support in the Senate only backed the more extreme House party further into its own corner. Similarly, President Obama's decision to reformulate the revenues and additional spending cuts in the creation of the bigger grand bargain further complicated the Speaker's position—how could he get his conference on board to support even more revenues—while risking House Democrats' support?

The Speaker's decisions, too, were critical and illustrate the underlying motivations of partisanship. The Speaker held out for a quid pro quo—

repeal of a key provision of Obamacare, the individual mandate—as a symbolic prize for the hard right. This decision seems to have been less about the budgetary bottom line and more about taking an ideological trophy. But President Obama—and a significant number of House Democrats—would never have accepted that price. The Speaker's quest for ideological unity in his coalition cost him the bigger prize in the grand bargain—perhaps an apt illustration of what Riker viewed as a strategic mistake of leadership overpaying for coalitional unity (1962, 211–15). The Tea Party Republicans who delivered to Boehner the Speaker's gavel proved a curse as well, he ultimately could not cajole them or the majority leader along for the ride. Rather than staging a "profiles in courage" moment and bringing the grand bargain to the floor, Boehner chose an increasingly common—and safe—strategy in an era of zero-sum partisanship, prioritizing keeping peace within the party over policymaking (Sinclair 1983). In such a hyperpartisan climate, the negative effects of allowing Obama anything that could be perceived as even a partial political victory would outweigh the policy benefits of correcting the country's fiscal ship—a major Republican policy objective—because of the costs of chaos in the conference. Boehner was unwilling to gamble with the Speaker's gavel and the party's prospects for the next election.

Democrats, too, prioritized party and would have faced a difficult choice if the grand bargain had made it to the floor for a vote. It is possible that Democrats would have refused to support the grand bargain in the interest of delivering a jolting defeat to the Speaker and his party. It is important to avoid underestimating the political utility of winning. As the eminent political scientist Bill Riker has pointed out, "What the rational political man wants is to win" (1962, 20). Nevertheless, it is likely that Democrats would have held their partisan fire and supported the deal because the president had clarified the stakes and had the united backing of the Democratic leaders. But the grand bargain never came to a vote. To strike a deal on the grand bargain, both sides would have to share ownership of the common good and the painful political decisions necessary to achieve it. Without that balance, sufficient incentive for a deal did not exist. Thus, the 2011 debt-limit crisis illuminates an increasingly difficult challenge for presidential and congressional leaders: allowing party considerations to continue to trump the common good (F. E. Lee 2009).

# SEVEN

# Beyond the Historic
# 111th Congress

During the early years of the Obama administration, the House Energy and Commerce Committee played a central role in shaping congressional politics and decision making with regard to some important legislative battles. In some policy areas, such as tobacco regulation, the committee operated fairly autonomously; in other arenas, such as the passage of the Affordable Care Act and energy and climate legislation, the committee was more responsive to the political parties. Even on issues not formally under the committee's jurisdiction, the White House relied on the committee's chair, Rep. Henry Waxman, to take the president's message to the House floor and win the support of reluctant rank and file members.

But what has happened since the 111th Congress? How does the 111th Congress compare to its successors in terms of legislative productivity? Did the committee remain important to the GOP's House majority? And how have partisanship dynamics changed in light of the internal conflict that now affects the Republican Party. Moreover, the Republican majority has imposed institutional changes in the House: How and why did it do so, what do those changes tell us about the new majority party's policymaking power, and what implications do they hold for understanding congressional politics?

## Policymaking under Divided Government and the New Republican Majorities, 112th–114th Congresses

The 112th Congress featured a large number of new Tea Party members, giving Republicans control of the House of Representatives for the first time during the Obama presidency. Divided government is a key factor in explaining a president's level of legislative success in Congress, and GOP House control dramatically altered the legislative paths of Obama's first two years in office (Bond and Fleisher 1990; Edwards, Barrett, and Peake 1997). The president found his legislative agenda largely stymied in the House after losing many of the strategic advantages that resulted from having members of his party chairing committees and working to promote the administration's legislative agenda. As Beckmann (2010) has argued, presidents can achieve legislative success when party leaders design agendas to advantage executive initiatives or to limit the opposition's incentives. Our work illustrates how the committee and its leadership controlled important legislative initiatives of President Obama and the Democratic majority during 2009–10. But the president's legislative agenda was significantly curtailed beginning in 2011, especially after the failure of the grand bargain, and by 2013 was all but frozen. President Obama signed fewer new statutes in that year than did any other president since before World War II (Hawkings 2014). And the support he did muster came almost solely from within his own party (Ethridge 2014).[1] Creating legislative coalitions became more difficult, as evidenced by a 2013 Pew poll indicating that 42 percent of Republican primary voters said that congressional Republicans compromised too much (Dimock, Doherty, and Kiley 2013). In the Senate, majority leader Harry Reid (D-NV) and the diminished Democratic majority became a critical backstop, preventing a stream of House-passed bills from reaching the president's desk.[2]

Figures 7.1 and 7.2 provide some empirical context regarding the significance of political party and divided government on the level of presidential support on roll-call votes in the House and Senate. In figure 7.1, the upper dashed line represents the average level of the president's party support on roll-call votes he took positions on, while the lower line represents the average support of the opposition party in the House from 1953 to 2015. The figure illustrates the growing gap in support from members of the president's party and from members of the opposition party. Although the gap had been widening for decades, it became particularly pronounced after the 2010 midterm election and the switch in House party control, reaching historically high differences in the most recent congresses. Figure

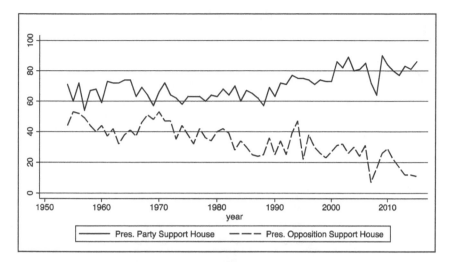

Fig. 7.1. Average House support, president's party and opposition, 1953–2015

7.2 shows a similar pattern for the Senate, although the differences are less sharp as in the House. When Republicans took control of the House, their control of the agenda highlighted differences in coalition support for the president.

In addition, observers suggested that presidential outreach strategies in Congress would not help the president win future legislative victories. According to Larry Sabato, President Obama "could run an open, free White House bar from early morning, starting with bloody marys to martinis late at night for all members of Congress, and it wouldn't make any difference" (Ethridge 2014, 177). In the new context of divided government and entrenched partisanship, the White House had less incentive to engage in legislative deal making and congressional outreach. Instead, the administration focused on election politics designed to replace some of those members in the 2014 midterm (Shear and Weisman 2013). In addition, the loss of the House and the dramatic reduction in legislative capacity forced the White House to rely more heavily on unilateral tools such as executive orders. The administration also utilized less visible strategies, such as Office of Legal Counsel memoranda, agency directives, and agency rulemaking. To some extent, then, the White House pivoted away from a legislative presidency, dependent on winning congressional coalitions, to a more muscular regulatory and administrative presidency designed to influence and where possible implement public policy.

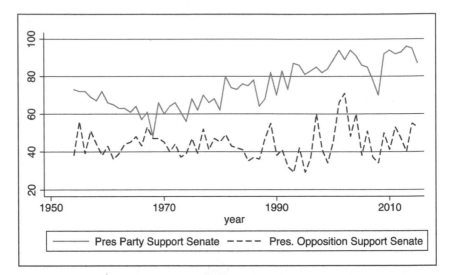

Fig. 7.2. Average Senate support, president's party and opposition, 1953–2015

How did these changes in political context and strategy affect lawmaking in Congress? Lawmaking output during the 112th and 113th Congresses fell to some of the lowest levels seen in modern times. Longtime Congress watcher Norman J. Ornstein (2011) labeled the 112th the Worst Congress Ever, at least in part because of its dearth of legislative accomplishments. Without the passage of legislation to avert fiscal disaster (HR 8, the tax-rate-extension bill), the final House roll-call vote of the 112th, the Congress would have scored even lower. As GOP moderates in both chambers all but disappeared, members sought support from the motivated and vocal political bases at home and from the cash-flush, ideological PACs that increasingly shape national political debate. In keeping with this focus, House and Senate party leaders loaded the floor agendas with proposals to galvanize party cleavages rather than attract votes from across the aisle. In 2012, nearly 73 percent of House roll calls were party-unity votes, the highest percentage ever in a presidential election year (Sanchez 2013).[3]

The 113th Congress rated slightly better than the 112th but had many similarities and passed only about a dozen more laws than its immediate predecessor.[4] And the 113th House earned its own notoriety for having the highest percentage of party-unity votes in the chamber's history—74.5 percent of roll calls (Newlin 2014, 1344). Moreover, the primary defeat of majority leader Eric Cantor (R-VA) triggered a leadership race, elevating establishment-favored Kevin McCarthy (R-CA) to that post and conserva-

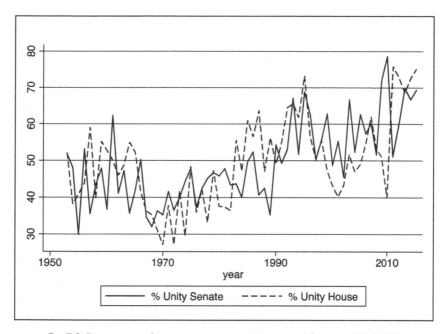

Fig. 7.3. Percentage of party unity votes in House and Senate, 1953–2015

tive favorite Steve Scalise (R-LA) to majority whip. The leadership shuffle exposed a long-simmering divide between the Tea Party wing of the House GOP and traditional business-friendly establishment Republicans (Ethridge, Phenicie, and Wright 2014).

Despite the intraparty tension in the Republican House, partisan conflict continued unabated and even rose. The frequency of party-unity votes on the floor of the House and Senate hit high-water marks. Figure 7.3 shows the growth in the percentage of party-unity votes on the floor of the House and Senate. The House peaked at 75.8 percent in 2011, while the Senate high of 78.6 percent occurred under Democratic majority control in 2010. The levels of party-unity votes during the Obama administration have been higher than those of most other congresses over the past seven decades.

How does the legislative productivity of the 111th Congress compare with that of other recent congresses? Table 7.1 offers some useful historical perspective on lawmaking and the role of the House Committee on Energy and Commerce, demonstrating that the 111th Congress was the most productive of the Obama years but was less productive than most of the other Congresses since the late 1980s. However, looking only at the number of laws passed does not take into account the significance of the legislative achievements of the 111th Congress (see Appendix). The 111th enacted some of the most important legislation in decades, including historic health care legislation and financial reform. Moreover, Energy and Commerce has remained one of the House's preeminent policy committees (Davidson et al. 2016), even under the GOP majority. Despite being one of twenty-one House standing committees that compete for floor time for legislation that falls under their jurisdiction, Energy and Commerce accounted for more than 12 percent of all successful legislation during the 113th Congress.

Figure 7.4 offers one last empirical view regarding presidential success over time by illustrating the percentage of roll-call votes in which the president's position prevailed on the House and Senate floors. For both chambers, the highest percentage of presidential victories in roll-call votes occurred in 2009: 94 percent in the House and 99 percent in the Senate. The House reached that level on only one other occasion in the years presented here: in 1965, under Lyndon B. Johnson. However, the Obama years also witnessed historic lows in 2015 (the 114th Congress), when GOP majorities controlled both chambers, falling to 15 percent in the House and 17 percent in the Senate.

The Republican gains in the 2014 midterm elections seem to have exac-

TABLE 7.1. Public Laws by Congress and Lawmaking Activity of House Energy and Commerce Committee, 100th–114th Congresses

| Congress | Number of Public Laws | Laws Referred to House Energy and Commerce |
|---|---|---|
| 114th (2015–16) | 329 | 9.7% ($n = 32$) |
| 113th (2013–14) | 294 | 12.2% ($n = 36$) |
| 112th (2011–12) | 282 | 6.0% ($n = 17$) |
| 111th (2009–10) | 382 | 7.6% ($n = 29$) |
| 110th (2007–8) | 459 | 10.0% ($n = 46$) |
| 109th (2005–6) | 482 | 7.7% ($n = 37$) |
| 108th (2003–4) | 498 | 7.4% (n=37) |
| 107th (2001–2) | 377 | 7.7% ($n = 29$) |
| 106th (1999–2000) | 580 | 5.3% ($n = 31$) |
| 105th (1997–98) | 394 | 8.9% ($n = 35$) |
| 104th (1995–96) | 333 | 13.8% ($n = 46$) |
| 103rd (1993–94) | 465 | 4.9% ($n = 23$) |
| 102nd (1991–92) | 590 | 5.4% ($n = 32$) |
| 101st (1989–90) | 650 | 6.8% ($n = 44$) |
| 100th (1987–88) | 713 | 7.7% ($n = 55$) |
| TOTAL | | AVG. 8.0% |

Note: Public laws collected from www.Congress.gov

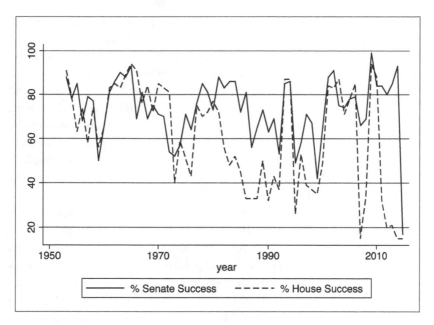

Fig. 7.4. Presidential success in House and Senate, 1953–2015

erbated the intraparty fissure between the hard-right and establishment Republicans, especially in the House. Speaker John Boehner's (R-OH) 247-seat majority was the Republicans' largest in more than eight decades, but this advantage has not led to more (or easier) legislative victories, as the early 2015 struggle to pass the Department of Homeland Security appropriations measure illustrates.[5] Boehner and other House leaders relied heavily on Democratic votes to narrowly adopt a clean appropriations bill and to end an intra-Republican standoff that nearly resulted in a government shutdown. The stalemate resulted from conservative Republicans' demand that the funding bill contain policy riders that choked off monies necessary to implement President Obama's executive orders allowing illegal immigrants brought to this country as young children to stay in the United States. The policy riders lacked the support to pass the Senate, forcing the House GOP to pass a funding measure without the riders or to face blame for shuttering Homeland Security, a vital department. Speaker Boehner's reliance on Democrats became a prominent pattern on major must-pass legislation as the GOP establishment and hard right disagreed about a legislative and political strategy for pushing back against the Obama administration's agenda.

Nevertheless, the first year of the 114th Congress (2015) defied expectations in terms of lawmaking. Despite very high levels of party voting (figure 7.3), complete lawmaking gridlock was not present. Even with the House GOP voting with the president at record low levels, 2015 was much more productive than the first years of the 112th and 113th Congresses.[6] For his part, President Obama embraced the opportunity to cut deals with the Republicans, remarking, "Every battle I've had with Congress over the last five years has been uphill, but we keep on surprising you by actually getting some stuff done" (CQ Weekly Feb. 8, 2016 "2015 Vote Studies: Presidential Support Hits Low for Obama," http://library.cqpress.com. proxy.lib.miamioh.edu/cqweekly/weeklyreport114-000004830476).

The tensions within the Republican Party resulted in a major revolt against Boehner that became the first test of the new House majority in early 2015. In hopes of regaining some discipline, the Speaker removed two party rebels from his House Rules Committee. The tensions nevertheless persisted, and in October 2015, Boehner not only resigned as Speaker but left the House entirely. In the ensuing leadership vacuum, Rep. Paul Ryan (R-WI), chair of Ways and Means, jumped over the existing leadership hierarchy to become House Speaker.

This surprising increase in lawmaking resulted from two important developments. First, GOP majority control in the Senate changed the mix of issues on the agenda. Moreover, after Ryan became Speaker, he and Senate majority leader Mitch McConnell (R-KY) embraced a different strategy, wanting to demonstrate their capacity for governing—that is, to show that Republicans could pass legislation rather than simply blocking the policy process, as had previously been the case. For much of 2015, Boehner deftly circumvented the hard right Republicans and reached out to build coalitions with Democrats, outmaneuvering the extremists to pass clean continuing resolution funding measures with Democratic support to avoid government shutdowns. Boehner relied on Democrats' support to pass critical legislation and clear the barn of many other intraparty controversies, including a two-year budget deal that helped smooth Ryan's transition to wielding the gavel.[7] Ryan followed a similar strategy on some legislation by garnering necessary Democratic support to pass reforms to No Child Left Behind and a highway bill that angered conservatives as corporate subsidy.

Although 2015 was indeed more productive, that year proved to be just a temporary reprieve. Gridlock returned with a vengeance in 2016—a presidential election year—with even noncontroversial bills encountering roadblocks as members of Congress weighed reelection politics over legislative compromise. The 114th Congress ended with very little in the way of legislative accomplishment, barely topping its two immediate predecessors and their record lows of numbers of laws passed.

So far this discussion has provided a little empirical context to better understand the stark levels of partisanship in recent Congresses and the connection with the president's reliance on members of his party for legislative support. And we saw from Table 7.1, that although far fewer laws were passed during the congresses following the 111th, the role of the Committee was undiminished. In fact, the House Committee on Energy and Commerce continued to play a central role in terms of the legislative output of Congress. This is not surprising given the argument we set out in Chapter 1 that the size and salience of the Committee's jurisdiction would be vital to policies important to the political parties.

Now we turn to take one final look at the new House Republican majority and changes they implemented in House standing rules in the last couple of congresses to see what implications this has for understanding party theories of congressional politics. To get some better understanding of this, we will look briefly at changes enacted during the 104th Republican Revolution in the House in comparison to recent rules changes by House Republicans.

### Speaker Gingrich and the Revolutionary 104th

In 1994, partisan guerrilla warrior Newt Gingrich (R-GA) delivered on his promise, wresting control of the House from Democrats and ending the longest period of single-party control in the institution's history. It was a shift in party fortunes of proportions rarely ever seen in American politics, with equally seismic impacts on the House's operation and institutions (Aldrich and Rohde 1997–98). The Republicans' fifty-four-seat increase combined with its gains in the 1992 election cycle to create an ideologically cohesive class of conservative activists who sought policy change on a wide array of fiscal, social, and cultural issues. One member of the wave, John Shadegg (R-AZ), reflected on his new colleagues, "The freshmen aren't interested in coming here to be reasonable and to settle for what they can get. They don't want to go along to get along" (Shear 1995, 602). The GOP majority empowered its leadership by changing institutional structures and processes in ways that would promote policy change. Gingrich, the new Speaker, not only served as the party's formal leader but also was widely viewed as the ideological architect of the Republican revolution. According to one of the insurgents, Rep. Sam

Brownback (R-KS), "Basically, he's using us to institute the revolution" (Doherty 1996, 916). The most important changes involved stacking the leadership of key House Committees with party loyalists to ensure that committee leaders would be responsive to the goals and policies of the leadership.

### The Tea Party Arrives: A Limited GOP House Alliance

The 2010 electoral tsunami was no less profound, shaking up the House and infusing the new GOP majority with a powerful Tea Party faction. In fact, the sixty-three-seat gain represented the largest GOP increase since 1938 and gave the party a majority that was about a dozen seats larger than Gingrich enjoyed. But as Denny Hastert (R-IL), who served as Speaker from 1999 to 2007, noted, a larger advantage does not necessarily make building party coalitions less challenging:

> When you have a thin majority—with an advantage of just five or six seats—that means you can't lose anybody. But it's almost easier to stick together. . . . Everybody can see the casket and the grave. You don't have to preach to everybody. When you get more of a margin, that's when it gets to be more difficult. That's when some people start to tell the press that they won't vote for something. (Ota 2010b, 2528)

Unlike the flamboyant Gingrich and his histrionics, Boehner was a more restrained Speaker (Schatz 2010). The formal leader of the GOP majority, Boehner was a classic probusiness Republican, not the conservative movement's leader or culture warrior. He never possessed the same "one of us" bond with the freshmen that Gingrich enjoyed. Said one former Republican aide, "The new crop of freshmen is not going to be deferential to the leadership, so its going to be much harder to be like Moses and demand fealty" (Schatz 2010, 2520). Boehner campaigned very effectively and raised immense amounts of money for party candidates but largely delegated the development of the Young Guns and the new contract, Pledge to America to his lieutenants (e.g., Cantor, Ryan, and McCarthy). The Republican's Pledge to America was not embraced as widely during the 2010 campaigns as was the original Gingrich contract and was more a set of general principles rather than a list of specific policy promises. The inherent ambiguity in the pledge's principles allowed creative policy prescriptions instead of anchoring the party conference to particular policies.

Because the party consequently could not be judged by the success or failure of those policies, there was much less sense of a binding contract than had existed during the Gingrich era.

Many of the new members were elected by the grassroots Tea Party movement and were thus less dependent on the traditional party establishment. Boehner instructed his leadership team to embrace the Tea Partiers but admitted, "They didn't know who I was, or whether they were for me or against me" (Schatz 2010, 2520). As a probusiness conservative, Boehner faced a difficult balancing act. Many of the traditional Republican interests (e.g., government contracts, free trade, tax breaks, defense spending) were at odds with the libertarian stream of the Tea Party. Outside groups kept pressure on the leadership to deliver on Tea Party priorities. As the former chair of Freedom Works—a powerful conservative advocacy group, Dick Armey, reminded Republicans, "The electoral broom sweeps both ways" (Ota 2010b, 2528). From inside the House, these newly elected members found their interests more closely aligned with the hard right than with the traditional establishment Republicans, particularly with regard to reducing government spending and dismantling Obama-led regulations and reforms in health care, the environment, and the financial industry. The Tea Party members quickly integrated with the Republican Study Committee (RSC), whose 176 or so members accounted for three-quarters of the House GOP conference. The establishment-dominated leadership and hard-right members of the Study Committee found relative agreement primarily on this smaller subset of issues. Indeed, Speaker Boehner declared that he "felt just as strongly about spending and debt and Obamacare as any tea partier in America" (Goldfarb 2011, 378). Nevertheless, the president's veto power and the lack of a sixty-vote Republican majority in the Senate meant that the efforts to repeal these aspects of the Obama agenda would remain ineffective no matter how relentlessly they were pursued.

The range of issues on which the House GOP agreed during the 112th Congress was much more limited than had been the case in the 104th. Many more issues thus offered the potential for division, complicating the leadership's role in advancing an agenda while minimizing intraparty conflict. Rep. Charlie Dent (R-PA), a longtime Boehner ally, quipped, "We really don't have 218 votes to determine a bathroom break over here on our side. So how are we going to get 218 votes on transportation, or trade, or whatever the issue. [Party leadership] has not done a good job of managing expectations. There are too many folks with unrealistic expectations" (Parker 2015, A1).

## The 112th Congress: Institutional Change
## and House GOP's Intraparty Challenge

Speaker Boehner seemed to design his House leadership in a characteristically un-Gingrich-like manner. Freshmen members made up less than 20 percent of his leadership transition team, whereas 50 percent of Gingrich's transition team were freshman. More important, Boehner publicly rejected the centralized leadership models of the recent past, vowing to conduct the House in a more open and transparent manner and giving committees freedom to do their work unshackled from leadership control. Upon taking the gavel for the first time, he said, "The House works best when it is allowed to work its will" (Gettinger 2011, 961).

Under the Gingrich revolution, the party's institutional changes focused on enhancing the leadership's power, often at the expense of the committees. In the 112th, by contrast, the leadership did not circumvent party rules to stack committees as occurred during the 104th Congress. Instead, the GOP's Steering and Policy Committee went by the book in selecting committee chairs. Even so, the hard right exerted notable pressure to choose more reliably committed conservative candidates for posts on the Appropriations and Energy and Commerce Committees. But the 112th Congress lacked the same level of intense tension that existed between committee chairs and revolutionaries during the 104th Congress (Aldrich and Rohde 1997–98). Committee chairs played an important role in spearheading the party's policy priorities—in other words, employing positive agenda powers designed to replace the status quo on a relatively narrow range of policies preferred by the majority party. However, the leadership did not succumb to pressure to jump seniority or waive the three-term tenure limits to install more extreme conservatives as chairs. There was no need to break conference appointment rules because nearly every prospective chair as well as the leaders played the same card, vowing to cut government spending and roll back Democratic achievements on health care, financial regulation, and the environment (Goldfarb 2010, 2868). For example, Ryan, who chaired the House Budget Committee, pledged to cut federal non-national-security spending back to FY 2008 levels, and Fred Upton (R-MI), who chaired Energy and Commerce, took a hardline stance against Environmental Protection Agency regulations. In these cases and others, such promises on key party issues would be sufficient. As a result, the Energy and Commerce Committee (as well as the Appropriations Committee) targeted issues such as fighting Obama administration reforms on health care and the environment and on drastically cutting federal spending, issues on which relative agreement existed throughout the GOP conference.

The narrow range of issue agreement in the GOP House majority as well as budgetary constraints imposed by mandatory spending caps presented challenges for authorization committees developing new policies. However, this climate magnified the role of the appropriations process in policymaking. As one longtime Republican staffer said, appropriations had become "the only game in town" (Hallerman 2014, 540). Hitching policy riders to the appropriations train to encourage (or discourage) agency spending or create new policy is the big business of lobbyists and lawmakers. Party leaders view the appropriations process as a powerful tool to deliver on a range of GOP priorities, including what McConnell called "Obama's overactive bureaucracy" (Scholtes 2015, 18). But the leadership also recognized that such party priorities have to be balanced with the risk of paralysis, as the chair of the House Appropriations Committee, Harold Rogers (R-KY), noted: "Appropriations bills are not a luxury, they are a necessity. We have to pass them" (Zeller 2014, 1384). Moreover, stopping the president's agenda with appropriations carried real risks, and the political stakes of shutdown politics are exceedingly high: in Rogers's words, "Don't take a hostage you can't shoot" (Zeller 2014, 1384). The Republican leadership has thus walked a fine line, utilizing appropriations on issues that unite the majority party but doing so in a way that demonstrates competence in governing and ensures that the appropriations train runs on time.

Members of the rank and file empowered party leaders to change standing House rules to ease the process of reducing federal spending. One such change was the spending cut lockbox, which applied to floor amendments to appropriations bills. Any cuts in spending would go to a special account to reduce the size of the spending bill, in effect creating reverse earmarks: existing programs could be targeted for cuts. Another example was the GOP House majority replaced the Democrats' pay-as-you-go rule with cut-as-you-go, requiring that mandatory spending be offset by cuts to existing programs, although the rule does not apply to tax cuts and provides some other exemptions for GOP priorities. One practical implication of this rule change was that a bill containing a new spending program could not be brought up under suspension of the rules unless the bill contained an offset that eliminated another federal program of equal or greater size. The 114th House rules changes also added mechanisms to cut funding in appropriations while protecting the GOP majority from difficult votes. For example, the 114th outlawed amendments to spending reduction accounts in appropriations as well as amendments to appropriations bills that would propose an increase in budget authority unless they were considered en bloc with other amendment(s) proposing equal or greater decreases in budget authority. These most recent changes in the appropriations process (similar to those from the 112th) prohibited certain types of amendments that would be politically difficult for the GOP conference and provided political cover with en bloc amendments. The Republicans have made many other changes as well, but these standing rules changes illustrate the larger point that because the GOP majority was unified primarily around reducing spending and key Obama reforms, the leadership focused on changes to the appropriations process that would help deliver on these limited policy goals.

Instead of taking on larger authorization bills from the standing committees, where intraparty fights were more likely to erupt, the GOP leadership used the appropriations process to reduce spending and undo Obama administration policies or prevent the White House from implementing such policies via administrative strategies.[8] This was a very different strategy from that pursued during the 111th Congress, when party leadership relied heavily on the chairs of key authorizing committees such as Energy and Commerce to develop and coordinate the passage of major policies on the Democratic agenda. This leads us to our last important question, what do these recent institutional changes tell us about party theories and understanding congressional politics? In particular, how might the 111th and recent GOP majorities add to our understanding of party theories?

## Party Theories and Final Thoughts on Congressional Politics

For decades, students of Congress have debated various theories of legislative organization and congressional process, behavior, and institutional change (Mayhew 1974; Cooper and Brady 1981; Kingdon 1989; Krehbiel 1991; Rohde 1991; Sinclair 1995; Binder 1996; Cox and McCubbins 2005). Here we look more closely at the cartel and conditional party government (CPG) arguments in light of our discussion regarding recent institutional changes (Aldrich and Rohde 1997–98; Cox and McCubbins 2005). In focusing on these perspectives, we assume individual members of Congress have multiple goals (e.g., reelection, policy, power) and that members place varying weights on these goals (Fenno 1978). We also assume that institutions affect legislators' attainment of these goals. Party leaders share similar individual goals but also balance collective goals of the party, such as maintaining majority control and working to deliver directly (or indirectly) on individuals' goals. Institutions and procedures represent a critical tool leaders use to strike such a balance. The cartel and CPG theories are in relative agreement about such a framework, but there are some differences in emphasis on positive and negative agenda control.

The core feature of cartel theory is that the majority party is empowered as a "procedural cartel" with the ability to control the floor agenda in the House of Representatives (Cox and McCubbins 2005). The primary mechanism of this power is negative agenda control—that is, the ability to keep off the agenda policies that would be antithetical to the party's preferences (or goals) or would create a significant cleavage within the party (Cox and McCubbins 2002). Critical manifestations of this power revolve around leadership agenda powers, committee gatekeeping, and the Rules Committee, which controls a bill's access to the floor. Cox and McCubbins (2005) have demonstrated that since the adoption of Reed's Rules, the majority party in the House has maintained an extraordinary winning advantage on roll-call votes across a variety of legislative stages from the committee to the floor (procedures through final passage). Cox and McCubbins show that the majority party's advantage has very little variation. According to cartel theory, the negative control is unconditional, an ever-present power that does not change regardless of the size of the majority's advantage or members' preference homogeneity. Like his immediate predecessors, Speaker Boehner began his tenure in 2011 with a preference for or predisposition toward minimizing intraparty strife by bringing to the floor only bills that a GOP majority preferred—in keeping with what is known as the Hastert Rule.[9] However, strategic necessity eventually forced Boehner to abandon the Hastert Rule to forge coalitions with Democrats on many significant legislative initiatives and on must-pass legislation to prevent government shutdowns.

In the context of the current House GOP majority, therefore, leadership strategy plays an important role in affecting the House's negative agenda power. Boehner's strategic necessity derived from the majority party's political goals (e.g., party reputation, preserving the majority), which outweighed the costs of dividing the conference over policy. Boehner (and subsequently Ryan) thus faced the challenge of demonstrating party responsibility in governing at the same time that he was fighting a powerful part of his conference that preferred more aggressive political strategies (like government shutdown). In this sense, Frances Lee's (2009) emphasis on the shared political goals that constitute partisanship helps us better understand congressional politics in the current environment.

In contrast, a major plank of CPG is that the power of the majority party is conditional on the cohesion within and disparity between the two parties' policy preferences. That is, the power granted to party leaders and the willingness of party members to collectively support the exercise of such institutional power hinge on the distribution of preferences not only within the majority party but also between the majority and minority parties (Rohde 1991; Aldrich and Rohde 1997–98). The distribution of preferences of the majority and minority parties is largely determined exogenously through elections. A key hypothesis from CPG is that as intraparty preference homogeneity and interparty conflict grows, members of the majority party will increasingly have the incentive to empower leaders with resources and control over institutions to pursue goals shared by the party (e.g., policy). The CPG perspective has placed greater emphasis on the majority party's ability to exercise positive agenda control to effect policy outcomes (Rohde 1991). Positive agenda control is the ability to place proposals preferred by the majority party on the floor agenda (Finocchiaro and Rohde 2008).

However, the majority party's inclination to employ institutional or procedural powers at least partly depends on the governing context of the majority party and its relation to existing policy status quos (Finocchiaro and Rohde 2008). If the party has just won majority control in the most recent election, its new governing role might be expected to target many existing status quo policies, depending how long it had been out of power. The particular issues and breadth of the majority party's desired policy change(s) would be conditional upon the intra- and interparty preference distributions of the political parties, as CPG suggests. If, however, the recent election simply returns the existing majority to its governing role, the majority party would be expected to seek fewer changes to existing policies and have fewer opportunities for policy change. And according to CPG, although the hunger for policy change would likely be muted or narrowed, the push for positive policy change would be conditional upon the distribution of the parties' policy preferences.

On the surface, our findings seem to provide some evidence for the CPG perspective, as we have highlighted some key distinctions between the 104th and 112th Congresses. In 1994, Speaker Gingrich's party and his frontline troops had been in the political wilderness for decades and desired to alter existing policies across a broad range of social, economic, and cultural issues. In contrast, the 2010 GOP takeover ended a relatively short four-year hiatus from power in the House and featured somewhat narrow agreement on policy change (e.g., reducing spending to 2008 levels, overturning regulations and Obama reforms). Where relative agreement on policy change existed, especially in the area of federal spending, the majority party changed the standing rules of the House (especially in the 112th Congress but also in the 114th) to enhance the leadership's control over spending decisions and the party's ability to institute spending cuts.

However, the range of policy issues on which the party was in agreement was relatively limited, encompassing Democratic reforms in health care, financial and environmental regulation, and especially federal spending. This helps to understand why the House Energy and Commerce Committee remained vital to the GOP majority. The GOP takeover of the Senate for the 114th Congress likely raised expectations for policy change, but the structural limitations of the Senate's supermajority requirement and the ever-present prospect of a White House veto did not change. Given that federal spending was a key area of relative agreement between conservatives and the Tea Party faction and was a priority in the Republicans' Pledge to America, the majority party enhanced its control over spending decisions of the House, as CPG predicts.

We suggested in Chapter 1 that the House Energy and Commerce Committee represented a key committee that Democratic leaders used to carry out the majority party's agenda and that of President Obama during the 111th Congress. Chairman Waxman and the committee were a vital part of the majority party's team. We argued that the policy issues and jurisdictional characteristics of Energy and Commerce, much like the Appropriations Committee, uniquely situate it to be of significant importance to party leaders in achieving the collective policy and political goals of the political parties. There was variation of course. The Committee did show greater autonomy in some policy areas, while being more responsive to partisan interests in other areas. Moreover, the data on lawmaking output from Table 7.1 is only suggestive, but it does show that the role of the House Energy and Commerce Committee remained relatively important in terms of lawmaking even with the switch to Republican House control in the most recent congresses. Taking into account the heightened partisanship in Congress and the almost lockstep voting within the two parties on major issues, the outcomes of battles over a president's legislative agenda appear to depend primarily on whether the House and Senate majorities are of the president's party as well as on the quality of the working partnership between the president and the leaders of his party in Congress, including the chairs of the key committees with jurisdiction over the president's legislation. Our study has not tested whether the Boehner/Ryan model would have been as productive under a Republican president as the record Obama and the Democrats compiled during the 111th Congress. Based on early returns from the Trump presidency, we think not, primarily because of the inability of the Republican White House and Republican leaders (at least so far in the 115th Congress) to translate their high-level policy objectives into legislation that can attract winning coalitions on the floor of the House and Senate. Obama and congressional Democrats regularly cleared this hurdle.

Despite the existence of some policy differences, the Democrats during the 111th Congress had greater policy agreement on a wider range of issues than did the recent GOP majorities. This level of policy agreement, along with the president's ability—with the help of party leaders—to coordinate around certain policies produced exceptionally productive legislative achievements. Moreover, Democrats had been out of power for many years, resulting in an abundance of policies that Democratic legislators and the president wanted to enact. In contrast, the recent GOP majorities swept in after only a relatively short time out of power. And although the Republicans enjoyed large majorities, the growing hard-right and Tea Party factions did not cohere with establishment Republicans in terms of both policy and a collective party strategy to challenge the Obama agenda. In both of these respects, the Democratic majorities in the 111th were more united. In this sense, the 111th Congress illustrates the importance of presidential leadership and presidential power in helping the majority party build the coalitions necessary for passing policy. In this case, presidential leadership produced incentives for members of the Democratic majority to cooperate in passing legislation important to the party. In terms of the theoretical notions of collective action and party organizations, presidents can employ their power to foster party cooperation, affecting individual members' political calculations in a way that can create a predisposition toward supporting the party (F. E. Lee 2009).

Looking at the Energy and Commerce Committee, the benefits of having a chair who had forged policy on so many issues over decades of leadership are clear. But without the greater power of the president and the House leadership, the legislative achievements would have been modest indeed. So even a chair as effective as Waxman was only a sufficient condition for success; the necessary condition was the consistent support of the president and the Democratic leaders in Congress. In the 111th, this alliance succeeded most of the time, as the historical record attests. But in key instances—particularly energy and climate legislation—the leaders' efforts were inadequate, and they ultimately could not marshal the votes to pass crucial legislation. This analysis also demonstrates that at least in the House, committee chairs now have less power relative to party leaders and the president than in the past.

We will not see the likes of the 111th Congress again for many years. In 2017, the GOP controls the White House and both Houses of Congress. It remains to be seen whether Trump and Republican party leaders will devise innovative strategies for breaking the gridlock that has long plagued the capital. The Republican Party faces existential issues, and it is not yet clear whether it can see the virtues of working toward bipartisan solutions on the nation's key structural problems: the budget, health care, entitlements and taxes, immigration, and infrastructure. Indeed, over the past three decades, the Republican Party in Congress has become increasingly radical, tribal, and contemptuous of the traditional norms that make the institution—and American democracy—work best (Dionne, Ornstein, and Mann 2017). It remains to be seen, in the wake of the Trump presidency, if enlightened leadership within the Republican Party can emerge and change these dynamics.

But this volume shows that there are moments when political forces can come together in Congress to drive historic change. When it happens—under Presidents Johnson, Reagan and Obama—it is something special to behold. We believe that President Obama ultimately will be seen as a very consequential leader, that his stature will rise as the 2016 campaign fades into the past. We believe history will treat him very kindly, seeing him as a visionary who set an enduring agenda for America for the first half of the twenty-first century and as a president with the temperament and ethical values that most Americans want to see in their president.

We also believe—particularly because of the frontal assault that President Trump and the Republicans in Congress have launched against what Obama accomplished—that the Obama legacy will become an exemplar of what the government in Washington should do to benefit the American people and the country as a whole. And as the telling of our story has shown much of that legacy results from the legislative accomplishments of the 111th Congress. President Obama achieved historic levels of legislative success in the 111th Congress and all during a remarkable period of challenges facing the country. Those accomplishments—a $787 billion stimulus package, overhauls of health insurance and Wall Street, tobacco regulation, and many more—overshadow most other modern Congresses of modern times. Moreover, we believe Henry Waxman's stature as one of the most effective legislators of modern times and as a model of lawmaking and oversight will grow among students of Congress and political junkies alike.

Political parties have historically played the dominant role in forming coalitions in Congress (Poole and Rosenthal 1997). Their role will not soon subside, and their significance for coalition building has grown even more vital over the past several decades. Frances Lee's (2009) work suggests that presidential leadership of the legislative agenda has significantly sharpened the zero-sum conflict between the political parties. This heightened conflict increases incentives for individual members of Congress to cooperate with party leaders to achieve the parties' collective goals. Lee demonstrates that legislation from the presidential agenda is far more partisan than non-presidential agenda items. In addition, she shows that presidential leadership on legislation increases cohesion among members of the president's party and similarly unites the opposition party against the president. As Lee has suggested, presidents repel as well as attract members of Congress to coalitions. We may very well have entered an era of congressional politics where the political benefits from policy change are marginal compared to the political benefits from challenging or thwarting the agenda of an opposition president. If so, there are implications for members' incentives to specialize and for committees' policymaking roles. In addition, disuse could mean that Congress loses the legislating muscle that comes from year-in, year-out work on solving policy problems.[10] And if these types of congressional incentives and roles are undermined, it could signal a further erosion of Congress's institutional position of power relative to the executive. We hope not, as our work shows Congress's importance as a bulwark of our democracy.

History is replete with presidents blessed with astounding political gifts—Washington; Lincoln; Franklin Roosevelt; Lyndon Johnson, who could intimidate and persuade like no other; and the Great Communicator himself, Ronald Reagan. Although such political gifts have proven vital and probably indispensable, they cannot replace having congressional votes. And as partisanship has intensified, partisan control of Congress is increasingly vital to passing the president's legislative priorities. This book has provided a rich array of insights regarding how congressional leaders navigate the policy and political process and regarding the importance of the president's party in passing his agenda in Congress. The House Energy and Commerce Committee was central in crafting the Obama administration's legislative legacy.

## Signing Off

### Monday, December 5, 2011

My great friend Phil Schiliro announced his departure from the White House today. He called this morning in advance; he really wanted to leave a year ago, but the president told him he couldn't, and he stayed on for this eventful and difficult year. I told him it's not often that you get to see your own obituaries, so enjoy it.

Office of the Press Secretary
For Immediate Release

December 05, 2011

Statements on the Departure of Phil Schiliro

WASHINGTON, DC—The White House today released statements on the departure of Assistant to the President and Special Advisor Phil Schiliro. Schiliro was announced as Assistant to the President and Director of Legislative Affairs on November 15, 2008 and served in that role from the beginning of the Obama administration until January of 2011. During that time he presided over the passage of a series of critical pieces of legislation including the Recovery Act, the Affordable Care Act, Wall Street reform and New START, as well as the confirmations of two Supreme Court justices. Since then, he has served as Assistant to the President and Special Advisor, providing counsel to the President on a wide array of issues. He will stay on in that role until the end of the year.

President Obama said, "As my advisor and chief liaison to Congress during one of the most productive legislative periods in our history, Phil Schiliro helped shepherd through a series of historic accomplishments on behalf of the American people, from health care reform that will make coverage more affordable and accessible to Wall Street reform that will protect consumers and our economy. The White House will not be the same without Phil, but more importantly, the country would not be the same without his steady leadership and tireless effort over the past three years."

White House Chief of Staff Bill Daley said, "Phil Schiliro has been an integral member of the President's team. Regardless of the issue at hand, Phil's thoughtful counsel, sound judgment, and unparalleled understanding of and relationships with Congress have made his advice invaluable. His presence will be sorely missed at the White House, but his tremendous contributions to the American people will live on long beyond his departure."

More than anyone else, Phil is responsible for my being in Washington for a large part of the first Obama term. We've been talking for over thirty years, and I suspect we'll be talking for a few more.

## Saturday, January 28, 2012

The Democrats held their annual issues and strategy retreat over three days at a resort in Cambridge, Maryland, near the Chesapeake Bay. They were in a good mood. The raw pain of defeat in 2010 that had suffused the first months of last year has eased; it is now just a dull, chronic ache. But they are encouraged by the openings presented by the Republicans' extreme agenda and hard-line politics. Rep. Steve Israel (D-NY), who heads up the Democratic Congressional Campaign Committee, was bullish on the prospects of claiming the twenty-five seats necessary to take back the House in November. There are fifty competitive seats in play, he said, and perhaps up to seventy-six. Redistricting a wash—so far, we have a net Democratic gain of two seats. Fund-raising at parity with the Republicans—unprecedented for a party in opposition. Moreover, GOP favorability steadily declined through every crisis last year: the first government shutdown threat; the Ryan anti-Medicare budget; the debt-ceiling debacle; the Supercommittee failure; the payroll tax victory in December. Republican approval for control of the House has fallen from 49 percent last January to 39 percent in December. And in generic polling—the single-strongest indicator of what will happen in November—today the Democrats are up 4 points over the Republicans (the Democrats were down 5 in June 2010). So there was a mood among the members of optimism that maybe, really they would come back. And if belief that you are going to win is at least half of the deciding component in any political equation, then they are coming in fired up. Also encouraging are the continuing reports that the economy is improving. Fourth-quarter growth was reported at 2.8 percent yesterday morning—higher than anticipated and seeming to put away the threat that we would slide into recession.. The president's approval rating is at 48 percent—higher than it has been over the past several months but still 6 points below a year ago. Unemployment is at 8.5 percent—better. And while 60 percent of Americans believe the country is on the wrong track, that is down from 69 percent a few weeks ago.

And so it was with this background music that the Democrats warmly welcomed first Vice President Joe Biden and then the president yesterday to conclude their retreat.

The VP was in full vintage Biden mode. He can connect so easily with the gut of Middle America, and he will be instrumental in winning back the independent voters who deserted us so decisively in 2010, when we lost nine million from 2008: *Nancy Pelosi will not be remembered for being the first woman Speaker; she will be the second woman Speaker, and she will go down as one of the most significant Speakers in the history of the United States of America. . . . It is absolutely clear that the decisions we made are working. And the public understands they are working. . . . The American people understand that the Republicans have rejected the notion of compromise. That's not the way the American people want us to do business. . . . We can't straighten them out, but the American people will in November. . . . Boehner, Cantor, and McConnell made it clear: it's about obstructing President Obama and his agenda. I know where this ends next year, next January 20: Barack and I are standing with a majority in Congress. We will win based purely on the merits of our position. America is going to get an absolutely clear comparison this year. It's a stark, stark, stark, contrast. . . . Osama bin Laden is dead and General Motors is alive.*

And then President Obama arrived and spoke in the early afternoon: *The critical debate, the defining question, is whether we will restore the American Promise. . . . We are moving in the right direction. A lot of that had to do with tough decisions you took. People understand the job's not done. We have to make sure American manufacturing is strong. . . . We need American energy. . . . Skills for American workers. The question is: Are we creating opportunity for everybody? Even as we are out there making our case about the brightness of our future if we work together, there is still work we can do together right now. . . . There are folks out there who are still counting on us, who are still hurting. Where the Republicans obstruct, where they are more interested in party rather than country, we've got to call them out on it. . . . We can't wait. . . . We are always more successful when we do it together. . . . What matters is when we have a sense of common purpose and common resolve. . . . That is at the core of what it means to be an American.*

Obama had just come from three days of travel across the country, selling his State of the Union address from last Tuesday night. He looked fresh, replenished, and there is always an energy, a spring, in his step. He worked the crowd after the speech, and we shook hands. His eyes settle on you, very clear and direct and warm. "All strength to you Mr. President," I said. And he smiled and nodded and went on.

# Appendix

*Committee on Energy and Commerce Major*
*Accomplishments of the 111th Congress*

## Committee Legislation Enacted into Law

*Omnibus Legislation*

**American Recovery and Reinvestment Act (PL 111-5):** This law provides funds to develop renewable energy sources, investments in clean energy, and energy efficiency ($19.1 billion), increase funding for Medicaid to address the effects of the recession ($87 billion), improve health care technology ($19 billion), and expand broadband Internet access for businesses and households in underserved communities ($7 billion).

*Health Laws*

**The Patient Protection and Affordable Care Act (PL 111-148):** This law enacts comprehensive health reform that guarantees universal access to health insurance while curbing insurance company abuses, controlling costs, expanding the Medicare prescription drug benefit, and reducing the deficit.

**Health Care and Education Reconciliation Act (PL 111-152):** This law contains health-related financing and revenue changes that amend provisions of the Patient Protection and Affordable Care Act.

**Children's Health Insurance Program Reauthorization Act (PL 111-3):** This law provides $74 billion over ten years to fund health coverage for millions of low-income children and their parents.

**Family Smoking Prevention and Tobacco Control Act (PL 111-31):** This law grants the Food and Drug Administration authority to regulate the advertising, marketing, and manufacturing of tobacco products.

**FDA Food Safety Modernization Act (PL 111-353):** This law grants the Food and Drug Administration comprehensive new authority to protect the nation's food supply and consumer health, including the authority to set new safety standards for fresh produce, recall contaminated food, and monitor imports.

**Ryan White HIV/AIDS Treatment Extension Act (PL 111-87):** This law authorizes more than $9 billion in funding over four years for medical and support services needed by people living with HIV/AIDS.

**James Zadroga 9/11 Health and Compensation Act (PL 111-347):** This law provides nearly $6 billion in funding through 2020 for health care for the responders to the 9/11 terrorist attacks.

**Medicare and Medicare Extenders Act (PL 111-309):** This law averts a 25 percent cut in physician fees under Medicare by maintaining current levels of physician fee reimbursement for 2011.

**Combat Methamphetamine Enhancement Act (PL 111-268):** This law requires retailers and distributors to meet strict training requirements before they handle precursor chemicals for the production of methamphetamines.

**Secure and Responsible Drug Disposal Act (PL 111-273):** This law amends the Controlled Substances Act to direct the Justice Department to establish safe procedures for the collection and destruction of unused or expired medications.

**Early Hearing Detection and Intervention Act (PL 111-337):** This law reauthorizes the existing newborns and infants hearing-loss program and expands the program to include more diagnostic programs and efforts to recruit and train qualified personnel.

**National Alzheimer's Project Act (PL 111-375):** This law directs the Department of Health and Human Services to create a national plan to address Alzheimer's.

**Reauthorization of Johanna's Law (PL 111-324):** This law reauthorizes Centers for Disease Control programs to educate women and health care providers about gynecological cancers.

**Stem Cell Therapeutic and Research Reauthorization Act (PL 111-264):** This law reauthorizes the C. W. Bill Young Cell Transplantation Program, which includes the National Registry for adult donors of bone marrow and related programs.

### Energy and Environment Laws

**Consumer Assistance to Recycle and Save Act (PL 111-32):** This law, known as Cash for Clunkers, provides $3 billion in incentives for consumers to trade in old, gas-guzzling vehicles for newer, more efficient ones.

**Diesel Emissions Reduction Act (PL 111-364):** This law provides $500 million over five years to reauthorize a program established in the Energy Policy Act of 2005 to provide loans and grants to reduce diesel air pollution from trucks and to conserve diesel fuel.

**Reduction of Lead in Drinking Water Act (PL 111-380):** This law amends the Safe Drinking Water Act to reduce allowable lead levels in faucets and plumbing fixtures from 8 percent to 0.25 percent.

### Consumer Protection Laws

**Dodd-Frank Wall Street Reform and Consumer Protection Act (PL 111-203):** Title X of this law establishes a new Consumer Financial Protection Bureau to protect consumers from abuses by financial institutions.

**Formaldehyde Standards for Composite Wood Products Act (PL 111-199):** This law establishes national standards to reduce formaldehyde emissions from trailers, furniture, and other wood products.

**Truth in Fur Labeling Act (PL 111-313):** This law eliminates consumer confusion by requiring labeling of all articles of apparel containing fur.

**Pedestrian Safety Enhancement Act (PL 111-373 ):** This law directs the National Highway Traffic Safety Administration to establish a motor vehicle safety standard for electric vehicles to alert blind and other pedestrians of their presence.

**Restore Online Shoppers Confidence Act (PL 111-345):** This law prohibits the use of "negative option" sales over the Internet, making it unlawful for any person to use the Internet to charge consumers for goods or services without their express informed consent.

### Communications Laws

**Twenty-First Century Communications and Video Accessibility Act (PL 111-260):** This law requires smartphones and other devices that connect to the Internet to be accessible to users with disabilities; requires all equipment used for voice communications, including voice communications over the Internet, to be compatible with hearing aids; and expands the use of closed captioning on television and the Internet.

**The Commercial Advertisement Loudness Mitigation (CALM) Act (PL 111-311):** This law prohibits broadcasters from raising volume levels when television programming goes to a commercial.

**Local Community Radio Act (PL 111-371 ):** This law expands the Federal Communications Commission's ability to license low-power FM radio stations and enhance local programming.

**Satellite Television Extension and Localism Act (PL 111-175):** This law reauthorizes and amends provisions of the Communications Act of 1934 regarding satellite retransmission of television broadcast signals.

**Digital Television Transition Extension (PL 111-4):** This law extends by four months the deadline for the transition from analog to digital television to avoid disruption to viewers.

**Truth in Caller ID Act (PL 111-331):** This law prohibits spoofing, where a caller falsifies the caller ID information during the transmission of a phone call.

## Committee Legislation Passed by the House

*Health Legislation*

**Melanie Blocker Stokes Mom's Opportunity Access Health, Education, Research and Support for Postpartum Depression (HR 20):** This legislation would have promoted greater coordination between the Department of Health and Human Services, the National Institutes of Mental Health, and the National Institutes of Health on postpartum depression and postpartum psychosis.

**Wakefield Act (HR 479):** This legislation would have authorized grants under the Emergency Medical Services for Children Program for the acquisition of state-of-the-art emergency medical care for ill or injured children and adolescents.

**Vision Care Act for Kids (HR 577):** This legislation would have authorized grants to states for comprehensive eye examinations and other vision treatment and services for children.

**National Pain Care Policy Act (HR 756):** This legislation would have supported programs through the Institute of Medicine to address pain care issues, including training, education, and awareness.

**Pediatric Research Consortia Establishment Act (HR 758):** This legislation would have provided for the establishment of up to twenty national public research consortia in the field of pediatric health.

**Dental Health Emergency Responder Act (HR 903):** This legislation would have promoted the use of dental professionals in hazardous and emergency response plans.

**Heart Disease Education, Analysis, Research, and Treatment for Women Act (HR 1032):** This legislation would have required the inclusion of women in clinical trials related to heart disease submitted to the Food and Drug Administration; required reporting by gender of patient-safety data; and required the Department of Health and Human Services to develop education programs about heart disease and women.

**Arthritis Prevention, Control, and Cure Act (HR 1210):** This legislation would have authorized the Department of Health and Human Services to develop a National Arthritis Action Plan.

**Acquired Bone Marrow Failure Disease Research and Treatment Act (HR 1230):** This legislation would have authorized the Department of Health and Human Services to fund research and treatment of acquired bone marrow failure diseases.

**Dextromethorphan Distribution Act (HR 1259):** This legislation would have prohibited the possession of unfinished dextromethorphan, a cough suppressant sometimes used as a psychedelic drug, by persons who are not registered or licensed under federal or state law.

**Concussion Treatment and Care Tools Act (HR 1347):** This legislation would have directed the Department of Health and Human Services to establish guidelines to prevent and manage concussions in school-aged children.

**National Neurological Diseases Surveillance System Act (HR 1362):** This legislation would have directed the Department of Health and Human Services to establish national surveillance systems for multiple sclerosis, Parkinson's disease, and other neurological diseases and disorders.

**Josh Miller Helping Everyone Access Responsive Treatment in Schools Act (HR 1380):** This legislation would have established a grant program administered by the Department of Education for automated external defibrillators in elementary and secondary schools.

**Family Care Accessibility Act (HR 1745):** This legislation would have provided liability protections for volunteer medical practitioners at public health centers.

**Diabetes in Minority Populations Education Act (HR 1995):** This legislation would have authorized the Department of Health and Human Services to conduct additional research on diabetes in minority populations.

**Scleroderma Research and Awareness Act (HR 2408):** This legislation would have authorized the National Institutes of Health to increase research into scleroderma and the Department of Health and Human Services to increase public awareness of the disease.

**Methamphetamine Education, Treatment, and Hope Act (HR 2818):** This legislation would have established public education and treatment programs to prevent methamphetamine addiction in pregnant women and mothers.

**Veterinary Public Health Amendment (HR 2999):** This legislation would have amended the Public Health Service Act to authorize grants to schools with veterinary public health programs, such as programs to prevent infectious diseases that spread from animals to humans.

**Emergency Medic Transition Act (HR 3199):** This legislation would have directed the Department of Health and Human Services to establish a program to help veterans with emergency medical training obtain state licenses as emergency medical technicians.

**Nationally Enhancing the Wellbeing of Babies through Outreach and Research Now (HR 3470):** This legislation would have established pilot programs at the Department of Health and Human Services to combat infant mortality in areas with high rates of infant mortality.

**Eunice Kennedy Shriver Act (HR 5220):** This legislation would have authorized funding to expand activities in support of the Special Olympics and to establish Eunice Kennedy Shriver Institutes for Sport and Social Impact.

**Gestational Diabetes Act (HR 5354):** This legislation would have authorized the Department of Health and Human Services to provide funding for research, diagnosis, treatment, and prevention of gestational diabetes.

**Birth Defects Prevention, Risk Reduction, and Awareness Act (HR 5462):** This legislation would have directed the Department of Health and Human Services to establish programs to increase public awareness and promote prevention of birth defects.

**National All Schedules Prescription Electronic Reporting Reauthorization Act (HR 5710):** This legislation would have reauthorized funding under the Public Health Services Act for state programs to track drug prescriptions to prevent overuse and illegal diversion.

**Training and Research for Autism Improvements Nationwide Act (HR 5756):** This legislation would have authorized the Department of

Health and Human Services to make grants to universities with programs in developmental disabilities to improve services to children and adults with autism.

**Neglected Infections and Impoverished Americans Act (HR 5986):** This legislation would have required the Department of Health and Human Services to report to Congress on parasitic diseases among poor Americans.

**Directing the Secretary of Health to Review Diabetes Screening (HR 6012):** This legislation would have required the Department of Health and Human Services to report on the utilization of diabetes screening benefits.

*Energy and Environment Legislation*

**The American Clean Energy and Security Act (HR 2454):** This legislation would have enacted a new comprehensive energy policy for the United States, creating clean energy jobs, reducing the nation's dependence on foreign oil, and curbing global warming pollutants.

**Home Star Energy Retrofit Act (HR 5019):** This legislation would have authorized the Department of Energy to provide $6 billion in funding over two years to encourage energy efficiency investments in homes across the country.

**Grid Reliability and Infrastructure Defense Act (HR 5026):** This legislation would have authorized the Federal Energy Regulatory Commission to issue emergency orders to protect the electric grid from cyberattack and other vulnerabilities and to approve standards to protect bulk power infrastructure.

**Chemical and Water Security Act (HR 2868):** This legislation would have reauthorized the chemical security program at the Department of Homeland Security, required chemical plants to evaluate the use of safer technologies, and directed the Environmental Protection Agency to extend the program to drinking water facilities.

**Assistance, Quality, and Affordability Act (HR 5320):** This legislation would have reauthorized the Safe Drinking Water Act, authorized $5 billion over five years for revolving loans to states to upgrade and maintain water systems, and directed the Environmental Protection Agency to require updated testing for endocrine disruptors.

**Consolidated Land, Energy, and Aquatics Resources Act (HR 3534):** This legislation would have incorporated key provisions from the Blowout Prevention Act (HR 5626), which would have required the use of safe control technologies when drilling high-risk oil and gas wells in the United States.

**American Medical Isotopes Production Act (HR 3276):** This legislation would have directed the Department of Energy and the Nuclear Regulatory Commission to take steps to promote a robust domestic supply of molybdenum 99 produced without the use of highly enriched uranium.

**Radioactive Import Deterrence Act (HR 515):** This legislation would have prevented the Nuclear Regulatory Commission from issuing licenses to import low-level radioactive waste except for military or national security uses.

### Consumer Protection Legislation

**Data Accountability and Trust Act (HR 2221):** This legislation would have directed the Federal Trade Commission to require companies that hold personal information to ensure that it is properly protected, to allow consumers an opportunity to ensure its accuracy, and to notify consumers of breaches.

**Informed P2P User Act (HR 1319):** This legislation would have prevented the inadvertent disclosure of sensitive personal information by file-sharing programs by requiring notification and informed consent by consumers that their computers are subject to search when such programs are downloaded and activated.

**Carbon Monoxide Poisoning Prevention Act (HR 1796):** This legislation would have amended the Consumer Product Safety Act to require residential carbon monoxide detectors to meet performance standards.

**Calling Card Consumer Protection Act (HR 3993):** This legislation would have required disclosure to consumers of the terms and conditions of prepaid calling cards and services.

**Guarantee of a Legitimate Deal Act (HR 4501):** This legislation would have required companies that offer to pay consumers for the value of the precious metals in their jewelry to obtain affirmative acceptance of the amount offered for such metals before they are melted down.

**National Manufacturing Strategy Act (HR 4692):** This legislation would have required the president to prepare a quadrennial National Manufacturing Strategy.

**Clean Energy Technology Manufacturing and Export Assistance Act (HR 5156):** This legislation would have established a clean energy technology export assistance fund in the International Trade Administration.

### Communications Legislation

**Radio Spectrum Inventory Act (HR 3125):** This legislation would have required the National Telecommunications and Information Administration and the Federal Communications Commission to develop a spectrum inventory.

### Major Bill Passed by the Committee

**Motor Vehicle Safety Act (HR 5381):** The bill would have established a new Center for Vehicle Electronics and Emerging Technologies within the National Highway Traffic Safety Administration; directed NHTSA to promulgate new safety standards to protect against unintended acceleration and to require electronic data recorders; made more accident data accessible to the public; and strengthened penalties for safety violations and created a small vehicle safety user fee.

### Oversight Hearings and Investigations

During the 111th Congress, the Subcommittee on Oversight and Investigations conducted major inquiries within the committee's jurisdiction, holding twenty-four hearings. with a principal focus on:

> **Health Insurance Industry Practices:** The subcommittee examined several activities and practices by the private health insur-

ance industry, including the termination of individual health policies by insurance companies; the issue of underinsurance that leaves consumers without adequate coverage; enormous premium increases in the individual health insurance market; and the high costs of health insurance for small businesses. As a result of these hearings and investigations, Congress passed the Affordable Care Act (PL 111-148).

**Food Safety:** In late 2008, an outbreak of salmonella associated with peanut butter sickened more than six hundred people in forty-four states and Canada. The Centers for Disease Control and Prevention identified the Peanut Corporation of America has having manufactured tainted peanut products that were sold to elementary schools, nursing homes, and hospitals. The company voluntarily recalled the tainted products on January 13, 2009. Additional hearings were held on salmonella in eggs and the role of the Food and Drug Administration. As a result of these hearings, the House of Representatives passed the Food Safety Enhancement Act (HR 2749), on July 30, 2009. In December 2010, Congress took final action in enacting the Food Safety Modernization Act.

**BP Deepwater Horizon Oil Spill:** In the wake of the April 20, 2010, explosion of the Deepwater Horizon oil rig in the Gulf of Mexico, the subcommittee conducted an investigation that revealed numerous key safety decisions that increased the risk of a blowout and identified important concerns about equipment failure and human error on the rig. The investigation supported legislative activity initiated in the Energy and Environment Subcommittee that resulted in the full committee's passage of the Blowout Prevention Act of 2010 (HR 5626).

**Toyota Recall:** On August 28, 2009, a fatal crash of a Lexus vehicle in San Diego brought public attention to the problem of sudden unintended acceleration. Following that crash, Toyota issued several accelerator-related recalls covering millions of vehicles. After Toyota announced its recalls, National Highway Traffic Safety Administration (NHTSA) launched a broad review of electronic throttle systems. Subcommittee hearings thoroughly examined the issues and the regulatory response, and the committee subsequently passed the Motor Vehicle Safety Act (HR 5381).

*Health Insurance*

**Terminations of Individual Health Policies by Insurance Companies.**
Oversight hearing (June 16, 2009) on rescissions, which occur when insurance companies cancel individual health insurance policies after providers submit claims for medical services rendered.

**Terminations of Individual Health Policies by Insurance Companies: State Perspectives and Legislative Solutions.** Oversight hearing (July 27, 2009, New Albany, Indiana) on rescissions.

**Insured but Not Covered: The Problem of Underinsurance.** Oversight hearing (October 15, 2009) on underinsurance and medical debt.

**The High Cost of Small Business Health Insurance: Limited Options, Limited Coverage.** Oversight hearing (October 20, 2009) examining business practices in the small business health insurance market.

**Premium Increases by Anthem Blue Cross in the Individual Health Insurance Market.** Oversight hearing (February 24, 2010) on the proposed increases in premium rates by Anthem Blue Cross, a subsidiary of WellPoint, by as much as 39 percent in California's individual health insurance market.

*Food Safety*

**The Salmonella Outbreak: The Continued Failure to Protect the Food Supply.** Oversight hearing (February 11, 2009) on the salmonella outbreak associated with products manufactured by the Peanut Corporation of America.

**The Salmonella Outbreak: The Role of Industry in Protecting the Nation's Food Supply.** Oversight hearing (March 19, 2009) examining the actions and obligations of manufacturers and retailers that purchased tainted peanut products from the Peanut Corporation of America.

**The Role and Performance of FDA in Ensuring Food Safety.** Oversight hearing (May 6, 2010) on the safety of food imported into the United States and the adequacy of the Food and Drug Administration's efforts to protect Americans from unsafe imported food.

**The Outbreak of Salmonella in Eggs.** Oversight hearing (September 22, 2010) on the salmonella outbreak associated with eggs produced by Wright County Egg and Hillandale Farms of Iowa.

*BP Deepwater Horizon Oil Spill*

**Inquiry into the Deepwater Horizon Gulf Coast Oil Spill.** Oversight hearing (May 12, 2010) examining the causes of the explosion on the Deepwater Horizon drilling rig and subsequent oil spill.

**Local Impact of the Deepwater Horizon Oil Spill.** Oversight hearing (June 7, 2010, Chalmette, Louisiana) on the local impact of the Deepwater Horizon oil spill on the Gulf region.

**The Role of BP in the Deepwater Horizon Explosion and Oil Spill.** Oversight hearing (June 17, 2010) continuing the examination of the causes of the explosion on the Deepwater Horizon drilling rig and subsequent oil spill.

**The Role of the Interior Department in the Deepwater Horizon Disaster.** Oversight hearing (July 20, 2010) on the Interior Department's actions before and since the Deepwater Horizon drilling rig explosion and oil spill.

*Automobile Safety*

**Response by Toyota and NHTSA to Incidents of Sudden Unintended Acceleration.** Oversight hearing (February 22, 2010) on the response to persistent consumer complaints of sudden unintended acceleration in vehicles manufactured by the Toyota Motor Corporation.

**Update on Toyota and NHTSA's Response to the Problem of Sudden Unintended Acceleration.** Oversight hearing (May 20, 2010) on the continued response of the Toyota Motor Company and National Highway Traffic Safety Administration to incidents of sudden unintended acceleration in Toyota vehicles.

*Public Health*

**Institutional Review Boards That Oversee Experimental Human Testing for Profit.** Oversight hearing (March 26, 2009) on whether institutional review boards and the federal government are adequately protecting human subjects of biomedical research.

**Regulation of Bottled Water.** Oversight hearing (July 8, 2009) on federal regulation of bottled water: safety, contamination, and recall issues.

**Federal Oversight of High Containment Bio-Laboratories.** Oversight hearing (September 22, 2009) on the proliferation of biological research laboratories and the status of government oversight of labs that handle dangerous diseases.

**H1N1 Preparedness: An Overview of Vaccine Production and Distribution.** Oversight hearing (November 18, 2009) on production and distribution of the H1N1 vaccine.

**Direct-to-Consumer Genetic Testing and the Consequences to the Public Health.** Oversight hearing (July 22, 2010) on sales and reliability of direct-to-consumer personal genetic tests.

*Environmental Safety*

**Secrecy in the Response to Bayer's Fatal Chemical Plant Explosion.** Oversight hearing (April 21, 2009) on Bayer CropScience campaign of secrecy to withhold information and provide misleading information to emergency responders, government officials, and the public.

*Commercial Issues*

**Commercial Sales of Military Technologies.** Oversight hearing (June 4, 2009) on the commercial sale of sensitive technology with military applications and to provide the results of a Government Accountability Office undercover investigation on this issue.

**GM and Chrysler Dealership Closures and Restructuring.** Oversight hearing (June 12, 2009) on auto dealership closures announced by Chrysler and General Motors stemming from the 2008 financial crisis and during a time when the companies received funds under the Troubled Asset Relief Program.

### Consumer Product Safety

**Crib Safety: Assessing the Need for Better Oversight.** Oversight hearing (January 21, 2010) on whether there is a need for stronger mandatory federal safety standards for infant cribs.

# For Further Discussion

## Chapter 1 Questions to Consider

1. What were some of the similarities and differences between the congressional reforms under the Democratic Party in the 1970s and the reforms that came later under the Republican Party?
2. How did the reforms affect congressional politics and the operation of the House and Senate?
3. What makes committees in Congress powerful? What different forms of power can committees exercise? Explain.
4. What are the three theoretical views about the role of committees in Congress? What predictions do the different views make about the behavior of committees? How well does the House Energy and Commerce Committee relate or fit into the different theoretical views? Why?
5. How did the realignment of the South affect the political parties and congressional politics?

## Chapter 2 Questions to Consider

1. What features of committee power were at work in the passage of the cap-and-trade bill in the House?
2. Why did cap-and-trade ultimately fail to become law? What role(s) did partisanship play? Explain.

3. What are some of the lessons learned about congressional politics from this chapter's accounting of cap-and-trade legislation?

## Chapter 3 Questions to Consider

1. What made the Affordable Care Act (ACA) different from cap-and-trade in terms of the policy and political challenges?
2. What aspects of committee power were key to coalition building and the passage of the ACA?
3. What were some of the key strategies used by party leaders to help the passage of the ACA?
4. How were procedures used to help build a winning coalition and to affect the final outcome? Give some examples and explain what the procedures accomplished.
5. How did the membership makeup of House Energy and Commerce influence coalition building, especially with regard to the Blue Dog Democrats?
6. What are some lessons from the passage of ACA regarding the role of the president and White House in the legislative process?
7. What are some of the lessons learned about congressional politics from this chapter's accounting of the ACA's passage?

## Chapter 4 Questions to Consider

1. Why is committee oversight important to the legislative process? What does legislative oversight of tobacco illustrate about committee power?
2. How do public opinion and major political interests shape legislation in Congress?
3. What were some of the key roles and strategies Henry Waxman used during committee oversight and the legislative process to pass tobacco regulation?
4. What regional politics historically constrained tobacco regulation? How were these constraints finally overcome in the passage of tobacco legislation?
5. What does it mean that a committee's work doesn't end with the passage of legislation? How does the tobacco legislation inform us about this work?

6. What are some of the lessons learned about congressional politics from this chapter's accounting of tobacco legislation?

## Chapter 5 Questions to Consider

1. What role did committee oversight play in the overall response to the BP disaster? How did the committee exercise its oversight powers, and to what effect?
2. How did the broader economic and political environment constrain congressional action in dealing with the disaster?
3. Why was Congress largely unable to respond with legislation? What does the BP disaster illustrate about the president's role and powers in affecting the outcome of the federal response?
4. The authors suggest that the committee was able to act more independently and was less constrained by partisanship on tobacco (chapter 4) and in response to the BP drilling disaster (chapter 5) than in the cases of cap-and-trade (chapter 2) and the ACA (chapter 3). Why? In addition, how did partisan conflict play out in Congress's response to the BP spill?

## Chapter 6 Questions to Consider

1. What is the debt-limit decision, and why has it been a perennial crisis for decades?
2. Historically speaking, what are the typical congressional dynamics surrounding debt-limit decisions between the majority and minority party and between the president and Congress more generally? What role does partisanship play in the process?
3. What are some of the lessons learned about the congressional politics of debt-limit decisions from the account of the 2011 crisis and failure of the grand bargain?
4. What role did congressional factions play in undermining the grand bargain?
5. What were some of the key leadership decisions made by President Obama and Speaker Boehner that affected the outcome of the grand bargain? How did they have that effect? What role did partisan interests play in these decisions?

## Chapter 7 Questions to Consider

1. What is one specific example of committee power from each of the policy chapters?
2. Chapter 1 outlined three different theoretical views on the role of committees in Congress. Which view seems the most relevant to each policy story in the book? Why?
3. What are the key distinctions between the partisan theories of conditional party government and cartel theory? What different predictions might these two theories make about congressional policymaking under the new GOP majorities in Congress?
4. Looking at the empirical patterns presented in the chapter, how has the average House and Senate party support levels of the president changed over time and especially since the 111th Congress? And, how has presidential success in the House and Senate changed since the 111th Congress?
5. What similarities and differences do you see in the politics and legislative process of the passage of the ACA (chapter 3) and the American Health Care Act, which passed the House in 2017 but failed in the Senate? Do you observe differences in the roles of the House Energy and Commerce Committee or of party leaders? What role did congressional factions play in the coalition-building process in 2017? Are they similar to or different from the role factions played in the passage of the ACA? Did the Senate's role differ in the two cases? How has the role of presidential leadership changed or remained the same?

# Notes

CHAPTER I

1. The 2008 election added 21 seats to the Democratic House majority and 8 seats to the Democratic Senate majority. This gave Democrats a 257-seat majority in the House and a 60-seat Senate majority.

2. There is persuasive empirical evidence supporting such a claim of legislative effectiveness of Obama's team, at least early on. Teodoro and Bond (2017, 343–44) use an innovative sabermetrics model to compare presidential success and show that President Obama scored considerably more wins over average expectations in the House during the 111th Congress (2009–10) but fell below average expectations after the 2010 midterm election.

3. For example, Phil Schiliro, the president's chief legislative liaison, worked for more than twenty-five years as top aide to Rep. Henry Waxman (D-CA) and served as policy director for Sen. Tom Daschle (D-SD) (Friel and Young 2010). Schiliro also assembled a liaison team comprising some of the very best leadership staffers in the business.

4. In the first months of the Trump presidency, Ryan increasingly turned to legislative processes that bypassed the normal work of the committees. The early attempts at repeal of the Affordable Care Act, for example, led to legislation being brought to the floor without hearings, without a vote by the relevant committees, and without key inputs from the Congressional Budget Office.

5. A special rule is a privileged resolution from the House Rules Committee. In effect, special rules control the House agenda by pulling a specific bill from the legislative calendar to be considered on the floor. Among other things, special rules establish the conditions governing a bill's debate and amendment (Bach and Smith 1988; Oleszek 2004).

6. During this period, the House Rules Committee had no written procedures,

so when Smith objected to legislation, he could kill it simply by using his discretion to prevent any action on it (Oppenheimer 1977, 97). He could also readily convince conservative colleagues on his panel to deny a special rule.

7. On signing the Civil Rights Act of 1964, President Johnson reportedly said to his press secretary, Bill Moyers, "We have just lost the South for a generation" (https://en.wikiquote.org/wiki/Lyndon_B._Johnson).

8. For a more complete treatment of historical changes shaping the relationship between the Rules Committee and the majority party, see Robinson 1963; Marshall 2005.

9. This went beyond a veiled threat. In fact, the liberal rank-and-file members of the Democratic caucus removed three sitting chairs in 1974 for being out of step with the party (Deering and Smith 1997). Both parties and chambers eventually placed this power with the party conferences, further diminishing the importance of the seniority rule and increasing committee responsiveness to their parties.

10. For a more complete examination of congressional reforms, see Sinclair 1989; Rohde 1991; Deering and Smith 1997; C. L. Evans and Oleszek 1997; Rae 1998; Fischer 2000; Adler 2002; Mann and Ornstein 2006.

11. At least two notable exceptions exist, however. Similar to moves instituted by the Democratic Party, in 1986 Republicans provided their party leader with the power to appoint members to the Rules Committee. Likewise, in 1988 House Republicans strengthened their leadership by providing top leaders with weighted votes on the GOP panel that recommends committee assignments.

12. Speaker Gingrich passed over more senior members to install Thomas J. Bliley Jr. (R-VA) and Henry Hyde (R-IL) as chairs for Energy and Commerce and Judiciary, respectively (Deering and Smith 1997, 137).

13. When the Democrats regained control of the House in the 110th Congress (2007–8), they did not adopt all of the Gingrich-era changes, such as term-limiting chairs, and consequently restored some autonomy back to the committee system. But the overall trend toward more powerful party leaders relative to committees continued.

14. Krehbiel's (1991) informational theory posits the idea of majoritarianism: the chamber majority controls both policy and procedure in the legislature.

15. Committee jurisdictions are codified in House and Senate organizing resolution(s) passed at the beginning of each Congress. The jurisdictions tend to remain relatively stable over time except when committees are created or eliminated, forcing jurisdictional lines to be redrawn. However, jurisdictions are also shaped by precedents established by bill referrals, thereby allowing entrepreneurial members to gain influence over new issues (Deering and Smith 1997).

16. For the rise of the Tea Party in reaction to the enactment of Obamacare,

which helped drive the Republican capture of the House in the 2010 election, see chapter 6.

17. Dingell kept a photo of the earth on the wall of the committee office to remind his staff of the committee's expansive jurisdiction.

18. Dingell and Waxman had spent more than a decade battling over environmental issues on the committee before working out an agreement on critical environmental issues that helped lead to the passage of the Clean Air Act Amendments of 1990 (Waxman with Green 2009).

19. Indeed, according to Rep. Peter Welch (D-VT), "A major reason why Mr. Dingell was replaced as chairman was his go-slow view on auto issues" (Cohen and Friel 2009, 32).

## CHAPTER 2

1. Cap-and-trade is legislative shorthand for capping emissions of harmful air pollutants and establishing an emissions trading system through which market-oriented forces would be brought to bear on the management of pollution-reduction strategies.

2. Regarding the final vote, National Republican Congressional Committee (NRCC) spokesman Ken Spain said, "There's a reason why over 40 Democrats in swing districts voted against this. They realized that voting for Pelosi's bill wasn't worth the price of millions of dollars in TV ads that would be required to put up what will ultimately be a futile defense of this vote. The question is: What were the others thinking?" (Martin and Isenstadt 2009, 14).

3. Not all legislation is characterized by conflict, partisan or otherwise. Carson, Finocchiaro, and Rohde (2010) find that from the 96th to the 108th Congresses, a majority of bills that reached the House floor lacked conflict.

4. The transactional nature characteristic of some lawmaking emphasizes the importance of the distributive rationale in theories of legislative organization (Shepsle 1978; R. L. Hall 1987; Weingast and Marshall 1988).

5. The trade-off between policy and politics seems to be a "perennial dilemma" for members of Congress (Waxman 2009, 135).

6. In fact, cap-and-trade differed in important ways from the 1993 BTU tax fight. Waxman and Markey's cap-and-trade legislation was constructed with broad input and support from industry and environmental interests. Nevertheless, the narrative equating cap-and-trade with the earlier 1993 BTU episode fed fossil-fuel and opposition interests that stood to gain from stoking such perceptions in hopes of scaring off would-be supporters.

7. The others included David Obey (Appropriations), John Spratt (Budget),

George Miller (Education and Labor), and Barney Frank (Financial Services) (Cohen and Friel 2009, 30).

## CHAPTER 3

1. HR 3962 passed with support from a single House Republican, Rep. Joseph Cao from Louisiana's 2nd District (House passage, November 2009, *CQ Weekly*, 2660).

2. Some House members criticized the Senate bill as a poorly written legislative product that would lead to increased bureaucratic and judicial scrutiny, which, in turn, undermines Congress's legislative power. Indeed, the Senate version was less carefully crafted and more loosely written than the House version, more likely to encourage bureaucratic discretion from the Department of Health and Human Services and other executive agencies (e.g., "the secretary shall decide . . ."). And the imprecision of wording in fact invited intense scrutiny by the Supreme Court. There is a kernel of truth to the old adage that the House is the legislative work-horse and the Senate more of a show horse when it comes to expertise in writing legislation (Fenno 1973). The House reluctance toward the Senate bill was at least in part an institutional concern in that the inferior writing would lead to increased bureaucratic and judicial scrutiny that undermines the very nature of Congress's legislative power.

3. The White House demanded that all questionable provisions be removed from the reconciliation bill to minimize the chance that the Senate would make changes and then force the House to vote yet again (Wayne and Epstein 2010a). The leadership had included student loan provisions in the reconciliation to attract additional votes (Adams and Wayne 2010). Instead, two of the student loan provisions attracted points of order from Sen. Judd Gregg (R-NH), the ranking Republican on the Budget Committee. Their removal from the bill ultimately forced the House to run the gauntlet one more time to vote on the amended reconciliation.

4. Before President Obama even signed the ACA, Republican senator Jim DeMint (SC) and House Republicans Steve King (IA) and Michele Bachmann (MN) introduced repeal legislation. At the same time, Virginia's attorney general, Ken Cuccinelli, and other state officials filed lawsuits challenging the legislation's individual mandate (Wayne and Epstein 2010b).

5. A number of factors explain the increased partisanship in the Senate, such as growing ideological and partisan divides among constituents, and they are similar to forces at play in the House. However, the connection goes well beyond constituencies in that former House members elected to the Senate (i.e., "Gingrich senators") now contribute significantly to partisan voting in the upper chamber (Theriault and Rohde 2011).

6. For example, liberal Democrats had become so frustrated with Baucus's negotiation with the bipartisan group that some had advocated for a rule that would allow a secret vote on Senate committee chairs every two years—a not-so-veiled threat aimed at the Finance chair (Bolton 2009). The group included three Republicans (Chuck Grassley [IA], Olympia Snowe [ME], and Mike Enzi [WY]) and three Democrats (Kent Conrad [ND], Jeff Bingaman [NM], and Max Baucus [MT]).

7. July 20, 2009. https://www.youtube.com/watch?v=mHV4nDS501Y.

8. For example, evidence shows that the abortion issue has been used as a killer amendment to sink underlying legislation (see Finocchiaro and Jenkins 2008).

## CHAPTER 4

1. HR1256 was referred to two House committees, Energy and Commerce and Oversight and Government Reform. The bill was brought to the floor using a restrictive rule that allowed only one amendment, a Republican substitute. Restrictive rules like this can advantage the majority party by forcing members to choose between just two (or a few) policy alternatives, reducing the dimension(s) of choice (Riker 1989; Sinclair 2012). The nature of the special rule reflects a broader tendency toward restrictive rules in recent Congresses (Marshall 2005; Sinclair 2012).

2. The Senate bill, S982, was similar to the House version and was sponsored by Ted Kennedy, chair of the powerful Health, Education, Labor, and Pensions (HELP) Committee (Armstrong 2009).

3. A new and inexperienced agency would likely be more malleable in the face of potent tobacco interests (Cummings 2009) and would be more susceptible to funding restrictions that would undermine its mission. In contrast, the FDA was a much more difficult political target. Taking funding away from FDA meant taking money from regulation and safety of food, medicine, and medical products. FDA had a proven track record and reputation employing public health and scientific specialists to protect public interests in these areas.

4. Enzi had previously opposed tobacco-regulation measures because he preferred an outright ban on tobacco products—he was an antismoking activist. Both his parents had succumbed to smoking's deadly effects (Armstrong 2008a).

5. For another illustrative example, tax reform, see Birnbaum and Murray 1987.

6. According to House historian Robert V. Remini (2007, 270), William Howard Taft once warned Alice Roosevelt Longworth, the daughter of Teddy Roosevelt and wife of future Speaker Nicholas Longworth (R-OH), not to get caught between Cannon and a spittoon at a poker game.

7. Public outrage had been ignited by the 2005 Jack Abramoff scandal, which exposed lobbying tactics that included congressional golfing junkets to Scotland. As a result, Congress in 2007 adopted a package of ethics and lobbying rules that

largely banned travel with registered lobbyists and ended free travel on private jets (see Graham-Silverman 2008; Davidson et al. 2015).

8. Even the ban on advertising reflected the power of the tobacco lobby, as the law did not take effect until January 1971, after the New Year's Day college football bowl games (Glass 2009).

9. Preyer did not believe that tobacco use was harmful, and the change in sub-committee leadership thus was pivotal in terms of oversight (Waxman and Green 2009, 173).

10. The accumulation of evidence about the serious health risks associated with smoking and growing public support for tax legislation to cover health costs seemed to play an important role in legislators' change in attitude regarding tobacco interests, particularly among representatives who came from outside the tobacco region. For example, until roughly 1994, Rep. Charlie Rangel (D-NY) opposed higher cigarette taxes (Cloud 1994).

11. The settlement initially funded at about three hundred million dollars a year the creation of the nonprofit American Legacy Foundation to reduce smoking levels and ailments associated with tobacco use (Jalonick 2005). The foundation runs the national Truth Campaign, designed to reduce teenage smoking. Despite such efforts, the tobacco industry spends an estimated twelve billion dollars to market its products and thus significantly outspends antismoking efforts (Jalonick 2005, 702). And tobacco runs its own voluntary campaign ads to youth that are markedly softer/different in their approach than the Truth Campaign ads. The settlement also provided a major loophole for Big Tobacco in the requirement that the five largest companies would have to make payments only as long as they maintained 99 percent of the national market share, a situation that ended in 2004. Moreover, the American Legacy Foundation was forbidden from lobbying Congress for additional funding.

12. In 1995, the Clinton White House had exercised unilateral executive authority in directing the FDA to restrict sales and marketing to youth (Armstrong 2008b).

13. This was not the only bump in the road for the House bill. For example, Waxman worked out a compromise with the Congressional Black Caucus incorporating a provision to further study menthol flavoring in cigarettes (Zeller 2008b). The caucus had initially opposed the bill because its ban on cigarette flavoring exempted menthol, which has long been a favorite among African American smokers and a source of substantial industry profits (Zeller 2008a).

14. Dingell then exercised his discretion as chair, choosing not to yield back floor time to Boehner for a response. When the Republicans regained control of the House in 2011, Boehner became Speaker, serving until 2015, when he was replaced by Paul Ryan, Republican presidential candidate Mitt Romney's running mate in 2012. Ryan had to fumigate the Speaker's Capitol offices because of the stench from

Boehner's smoking. In retirement, the former Speaker joined the board of tobacco giant Reynolds American. As of this writing, he continues to smoke cigarettes.

15. In 2004, when he was a senator, Obama cosponsored similar tobacco legislation (Cummings 2009).

16. Altria's embrace did not necessarily make for a cost-free relationship for advocates of regulation in Congress. Powerful groups such as the American Association of Public Health Physicians remained opposed to Waxman's legislative effort, arguing that the bill compromised too much with Big Tobacco and that its regulatory scope did not go far enough (Zeller 2008b).

17. Indeed, Maura Payne, spokeswoman for R. J. Reynolds, seemed to flip the script in denouncing the 2009 legislation: "You worry there may be potential confusion for tobacco consumers that now that the products are FDA regulated, they must be safe or safer than before, and that may not necessarily be the case" (Cummings 2009, 23).

18. The whip and regional whips are relied on not only to collect intelligence on party support but also for many other critical roles—in this case, to disseminate information to the rank and file (Sinclair 1995; C. L. Evans and Grandy 2008; Marshall 2010).

19. The Senate's nongermaneness treatment of legislation on the floor greatly undermines committee autonomy and protection of committee products (Fenno 1982). Irrespective of committee membership, the freedom derived from nongermaneness allows senators to significantly shape bills on the Senate floor (Deering and Smith 1987; Sinclair 1989; Smith 1989; Oleszek 2004).

20. In 1994, the NFL created a concussion committee composed of researchers who analyzed a subset of 1996–2001 concussion data collected from NFL teams. The committee found no evidence of long-term harm from player concussions (Schwarz, Bogdanich, and Williams 2016). In 2013, the NFL paid a $765 million lawsuit settlement to retired players who claimed the league had covered up the risks associated with concussions. According to the *New York Times*, the NFL shared lobbyists, lawyers, and consultants with Big Tobacco but no other direct evidence indicated that the NFL took its strategies from Big Tobacco (Schwarz, Bogdanich, and Williams 2016).

21. Indeed, the committee system has many powerful tools to exercise influence over the executive bureaucracy, such as funding decisions, administrative oversight and reporting, and bureaucratic confirmations (Fenno 1966; Moe 1985; Sinclair 2000; Rudalevige 2009; Davidson et al. 2016).

22. Upton, like his immediate predecessors, aggressively defended Energy and Commerce's jurisdiction against those who sought to usurp it. When the chair of the House Natural Resources Committee tried to claim his committee's ascendency over energy policy, Upton warned party leaders of the potential institutional

calamity of such a move: "To diminish the authority of the Energy and Commerce Committee, is to weaken the power of the House—the people's body—and give an upper hand to the Democrat[ic] White House (Davidson et al. 2016, 187).

23. An increasingly important literature analyzes the mechanisms of interinstitutional influence between the courts and Congress (see, e.g., Eskridge 1994; Hansford and Damore 2000; Barnes 2004; T. S. Clark 2009; Pacelle, Curry, and Marshall 2011; Segal, Westerland, and Lindquist 2011).

24. *FDA v. Brown and Williamson Tobacco Corp.* (2000).

25. Hausegger and Baum (1999) find that the Court invites congressional action in its majority opinions fairly regularly, more than 10 percent of the time for the period they studied.

CHAPTER 5

1. President Obama issued an executive order (E.O. 13554) recognizing the Gulf Coast as a national treasure and declaring that the Deepwater Horizon spill was the largest in US history. The executive order also facilitated federal and state/local restoration efforts by creating the Gulf Coast Ecosystem Restoration Task Force.

2. It is estimated that nearly 1.8 million gallons of toxic chemicals were spread in the water to break down the oil before it reached the coast. This included Corexit, which was blamed for long-term worker illnesses resulting from the *Exxon Valdez* spill (Ferguson 2010; Harrison 2013).

3. An estimated ten million gallons of the spilled oil remains uncaptured (Magner and Dillon 2016).

4. Organizations such as the Sierra Club and the World Resource Institute suggest that the cost of correcting the environmental damage alone is at least sixty billion dollars (Magner and Dillon 2016).

5. Some of the more interesting examples of "environmental repair" projects include a baseball stadium in Biloxi, Mississippi, and proposed renovations to a coastal governor's retreat in Alabama (Magner and Dillon 2016).

6. According to an analysis by the Rhodium Group's Trevor Houser, the United States spends roughly six hundred billion dollars a year on oil, and even a one-hundred-billion-dollar spill every decade would not fundamentally change oil's cost (Cranford 2010). Moreover, the largest oil supplies available to the United States are in the Gulf of Mexico and the Arctic (Davenport 2010a).

7. About 80 percent of the Gulf's oil and about 45 percent of its natural gas comes from deep wells. In 2009, the year prior to the Gulf spill, BP extracted more oil from its deep Gulf wells than any other place in the world with the exception of Russia (Cranford 2010).

8. Soon after the spill, BP also committed a separate five hundred million dollars to fund independent research on the impact of the oil spill on the Gulf environment and the region's public health (Harrison 2013).

9. The 1990 Oil Pollution law passed after the Exxon *Valdez* spill capped *all* liability at seventy-five million dollars. This limit fueled conflict between Gulf Coast members of Congress, who wanted to protect small independent drillers, and environmentally friendly Democrats, who were pushing to raise the liability limit to ten billion dollars (Schatz and Davenport 2010).

10. S 3473, amending the Oil Pollution Act of 1990, was signed by the president on June 15, 2010, after passing the Senate via voice vote and the House 410–0 (Scholtes 2010).

11. During the 110th Congress, Speaker Pelosi had openly criticized the GOP's dramatic floor takeover to push for expanded drilling to lower gasoline prices, calling the tactic the "war dance of the hand maidens of the oil companies"; at the same time, however, she signaled an openness to more coastal drilling if the minority party could agree to a larger bundle of energy policy changes (Hulse 2008).

12. President Obama was committed to policy that would lessen the country's dependence on oil but recognized, as did congressional Democrats, that the suffering economy and peaking gasoline prices necessitated greater domestic production at least in the short term. Indeed, Obama said, "Producing oil here in America is an essential part of our overall energy strategy. But all drilling must be safe" (Davenport 2010a, 1335).

13. Indeed, with the failure to pass such comprehensive legislation, the Obama administration advanced its program of reducing carbon pollution and controlling the effects of climate change by imposing a series of sweeping regulatory controls on industry.

14. The lines of demarcation separating the subcommittees even dictated the sequence of questions asked during investigatory hearings (Ota 2010a).

15. For example, the House leadership allowed Rep. Charlie Melancon's (D-LA) amendment that exempted drillers from Obama's moratorium if they complied with new safety regulations issued by the Department of Interior.

16. Liberal coastal Democratic senators Menendez and Nelson sought to raise the liability cap from seventy-five million dollars to ten billion dollars. The original cap had been put in place under the Oil Pollution Act of 1990 (PL 101-380) following the *Exxon Valdez* oil spill. BP voluntarily waived this limit in its corporate response to the spill. The 1990 law also set up an oil spill cleanup fund financed through a five-cents-a-barrel tax that was allowed to expire from 1994 until 2006, when Congress reinstated the tax and raised it to eight cents a barrel (Schatz and Davenport 2010). The spill fund contained less than two billion dollars at the time

of the spill and was viewed as grossly insufficient, providing a rationale for senators who sought to raise the liability limit.

17. The top-kill operation literally shot junk into the leaking well—mostly shredded tires, knotted rope, and golf balls. The amassed junk would be held in place by injecting highly pressured cement and mud into the well.

18. Republican criticism of President Obama dramatically intensified, and the media coverage transitioned to what Johnston and Goggin (2015) have called the Accountability Phase .

19. Following the hearing, White House press secretary Robert Gibbs, added a broadside to the Barton apology: "What is shameful is that Joe Barton seems to have more concern for big corporations that caused this disaster than the fishermen, small-business owners and communities whose lives have been devastated by the destruction" (Schatz and Koss 2010, 1507).

20. The bitter partisanship that undermined Congress's previous legislative efforts seemed even stronger in the 112th. Indeed, Reilly commented that the commission's recommendations to Congress were met with "venomous partisanship" and that "we were treated as if we were the enemy" (Russell 2012, 798).

## CHAPTER 6

1. All numbers are in current dollars, not constant dollars.

2. Congress often reduces the duration of new borrowing authority so that members can claim a smaller debt-limit increase than the president has requested (Kowalcky and LeLoup 1993).

3. Early in the Reagan administration, House Democrats had OMB director David Stockton testify about the necessity of debt-limit increases. Ironically, as a member of the House GOP minority, he had routinely voted no on raising the debt ceiling. But Democratic support required more than Stockton's testimony: Reagan wrote personal letters to each House Democrat explaining the need to increase the debt ceiling (Sinclair 1983).

4. For decades, Congress relied on another sleight of hand in distinguishing between "temporary" and "permanent" increases in the debt ceiling. The former fostered political cover by implying that the ceiling would eventually be lowered (Kowalcky and LeLoup 1993, 17).

5. Commenting on the significance of the crisis, Steve Bell, a veteran Republican Hill staffer then serving as senior director of economic policy at the Bipartisan Policy Center, said, "This time it really was different" (Ferris 2016, 2).

6. Adopted in 1979 and named for Rep. Richard Gephardt (D-MO),the Gephardt Rule (House Rule XXVII) eliminated the requirement that the House hold a separate vote on the statutory debt limit. The rule required that when a concurrent

budget resolution was passed, the approved debt limit provision would be folded into a joint resolution "deemed to be passed" in the House. The resolution would automatically be sent to the Senate for consideration and if positively disposed of would then proceed to the president's desk for signature (Austin 2015, 16–17; Kowalcky and LeLoup 1993).

7. Ryan objected to a number of bipartisan plans in 2010–11. As a member of the Simpson-Bowles Commission, Ryan refused to support the commission's final proposal and sharply criticized the Gang of Six agreement. In addition, he and Cantor reportedly appealed to Boehner to reject the potential deal with Obama (Lizza 2012). Jackson's fears were realized in October 2015, when Boehner was effectively forced to resign as Speaker, a victim of ceaseless corrosion from within by Tea Party elements in the Republican House caucus.

8. For example, President Obama had shown a willingness to raise Medicare's eligibility age and structured care fees as well as to adjust federal payments under Medicaid (Kenen 2011).

9. The eighteen-member commission eventually passed a blueprint with support from both Republicans and Democrats, but the proposal did not gain the fourteen votes required to send it for congressional consideration.

10. On the need to raise the debt limit, Rep. Phil Gingrey (R-GA) said, "I do not look at it necessarily as Armageddon. I think Armageddon will occur if we raise the debt ceiling and don't do the things that I think we really need to do" (Schatz and Krawzak 2011, 1555).

11. The Gang of Six included four members from Simpson-Bowles and included cochairs Mark Warner (D-VA) and Saxby Chambliss (R-GA) as well as Dick Durbin (D-IL), Kent Conrad (D-ND), Mike Crapo (R-ID), and Tom Coburn (R-OK).

12. The new revenue in the Boehner counteroffer came from using a budgetary assumption known as "current law." Under current law, the baseline assumption is that any temporary tax changes (cuts or increases) take place as expected on their horizon. In contrast, current law budgetary baselines assume that any current tax policy in effect (temporary or otherwise) is locked in place (Sinclair 2012). Boehner's new revenue was somewhat hidden by the current law assumption.

13. The new revenue proposed by Boehner was generated through tax reforms such as lowering rates and ending loopholes (Bai 2012).

14. For example, Cut, Cap, and Balance's planned constitutional amendment would have required a two-thirds supermajority in both Houses and ratification by three-fourths of the states, a situation that was unlikely to occur. Moreover, some newer House members in particular began making unrealistic claims about what the legislation would accomplish. And Rep. Renee Ellmers (R-NC) suggested that President Obama could create a legacy by accepting the balanced-budget amend-

ment, but the president plays no role in the ratification of constitutional amendments (Cohen 2011, 1612).

15. For a detailed summary of the Gang of Six plan, see *CQ Weekly*, "Gang of 6 Focuses on Spending Cuts"(July 25, 2011, 1631).

16. About 74 percent of the Gang of Six's total savings came from spending cuts, while 26 percent came from new revenue. The $787 billion stimulus bill (the American Recovery and Reinvestment Act of 2009), which featured about 37 percent tax cuts and 63 percent spending, received zero GOP votes in the House prior to the arrival of the Tea Party Republicans after the 2010 midterm elections.

17. It was not a foregone conclusion the Speaker could rally enough GOP support to just raise the debt limit. Although the Speaker clearly understood that inaction on the debt limit would jeopardize the country's economy, many hard right members of Congress did not believe in the peril or preferred default to raising the debt limit (Krawzak and Goldfarb 2011; Schatz and Krawzak 2011; Ferris 2016).

18. Ironically, despite Cantor's efforts to firmly represent hard-line Tea Party views in these negotiations, he was defeated by a Tea Party insurgent in the June 2014 Republican primary in his congressional district, an immense shock to party leaders in Congress.

19. The framework placed the Senate in the spotlight again, making it a major player in the debt-limit debate. The Senate achieved consensus at least in part by cutting out hard-liner demands from the House GOP (Schatz and Krawzak 2011). Indeed, Rep. Jim Jordan (R-OH), chair of the powerful conservative Republican Study Committee, said, "The McConnell plan doesn't have 218 Republican votes—no way" (Schatz and Goldfarb 2011, 1629).

20. Sequestration allows the president to eliminate budget authority or other budgetary sources to reach planned budget targets (Austin 2015; Davidson et al. 2015).

21. Leaders from both parties generally agreed with the McConnell approach because most feared Congress could not (or would not) raise the debt limit on its own. McConnell and other supporters of the framework understood that the cataclysmic risk of default was too much to leave in the hands of Congress. Critics of the approach saw it as an extraordinary abdication of Congress's constitutional authority (Cranford and Schatz 2011).

22. The joint resolution of disapproval was also subject to presidential veto, so Congress theoretically could also entertain the added benefit associated with a public display of a veto override vote (Austin 2015).

23. The vote tally followed typical patterns during divided government, where the majority party provided the most votes but also relied heavily on the president's party, with 174 House Republicans and 95 Democrats supporting the measure. The Senate party margins tell a similar story.

24. Section 4 of the Fourteenth Amendment reads, "The validity of the public debt of the United States, authorized by law . . . shall not be questioned." Whether the president can unilaterally manage the public debt based on the Fourteenth Amendment has never been attempted or tested in court.

25. A material risk of impeachment would also arise if President Obama resorted to the Fourteenth Amendment against the clear views of the Republican leadership.

## CHAPTER 7

1. For example, Senate Democrats supported Obama's position on roll-call votes 96 percent of the time in 2013 (a post–World War II record high), while House Republicans gave their support only 12 percent of the time (a near-record low) (Ethridge 2014, 170)

2. Ten of Obama's twelve vetoes did not occur until the GOP took control of both chambers during the 114th Congress.

3. Party-unity votes occur when a majority of one party votes in opposition to a majority of the other party.

4. The 113th enacted 296 public laws, while the 112th enacted just 284 laws. Over the preceding thirty years, the next-lowest output was the 104th Congress (1995–96), with 337 public laws.

5. This trend continued into at least the first year of President Donald Trump's administration, with a Republican-controlled Congress unable to effectively legislate on some of Trump's signature issues, including the repeal of Obamacare, building a wall with Mexico, and an infrastructure program.

6. During 2015, 115 laws were passed, an increase of about 60 percent compared to 2011 ($n$ = 72 laws) and more than 40 percent greater than in 2013 ($n$ = 81 laws) (see *CQ Weekly* Feb. 8, 2016 "2015 Vote Studies," http://library.cqpress.com.proxy.lib.miamioh.edu/cqweekly/weeklyreport114-000004830476).

7. Ironically, this strategy ultimately added to rank-and-file conservative discontent and cost Boehner the speakership.

8. For example, the FY 2012 Interior and Environment spending bill provoked intense partisan conflict over spending cuts and featured several policy riders designed to undo Environmental Protection Agency regulations. According to the chair of the Subcommittee, "Wherever I go, the biggest complaint I hear about the federal government is how the EPA is creating economic uncertainty and killing jobs" (Gardner and Fuller 2012, 1321).

9. The Hastert Rule (really more of an informal doctrine) is critical to maintaining peace among party members and producing a valuable party reputation around policy.

10. Anne Wexler, who served in President Jimmy Carter's administration, was

fond of saying, "Congress does two things best: overreact and nothing!" We believe that Congress is getting even better at them.

Quoted material in the Wolpe journal is not footnoted. Wolpe obtained and used those quotes in real time from various sources—personal notes, emails, working drafts of memos and speeches, and contemporaneous published accounts from the news media, among others. The journal conveys the flavor of the days. The material quoted is integral to the account, and what was said by the principals and reported in the media, and used in the journal, was faithfully compiled by Wolpe as the events unfolded.

# Bibliography

Abramson, Paul R., John H. Aldrich, and David W. Rohde. 1995. *Change and Continuity in the 1992 Elections*. Rev. ed. Washington, DC: Congressional Quarterly.

Adams, Rebecca, and Alex Wayne. 2010. "Democrats Set for a Pivotal Week." *CQ Weekly*, March 15, 628–29.

Adler, E. Scott. 2002. *Why Congressional Reforms Fail: Reelection and the House Committee System*. Chicago: University of Chicago Press.

Aldrich, John H. 1995. *Why Parties? The Origin and Transformation of Parties in America*. Chicago: University of Chicago Press.

Aldrich, John H., and David W. Rohde. 1997–98. "The Transition to Republican Rule in the House: Implications for Theories of Congressional Politics." *Political Science Quarterly* 112:541–67.

Aldrich, John H., and David W. Rohde. 2001. "The Logic of Conditional Party Government: Revisiting the Electoral Connection." In *Congress Reconsidered*, 7th ed., ed. Lawrence C. Dodd and Bruce I. Oppenheimer. Washington, DC: CQ Press.

Anderson, Joanna, and Jennifer Scholtes. 2010. "House and Senate Advance Oil Spill Bills." *CQ Weekly*, June 28, 1580.

Applebaum, Binyamin, and Eric Dash. 2011. "S&P Downgrades Debt Rating of U.S. for the First Time." *New York Times*, August 5.

Armstrong, Drew. 2008a. "2008 Legislative Summary: Tobacco Regulation." *CQ Weekly*, December 8, 3284.

Armstrong, Drew. 2008b. "Tobacco Regulation Bill Passes House." *CQ Weekly*, August 4, 2123.

Armstrong, Drew. 2009. "Tough New Tobacco Rules Cleared." *CQ Weekly*, June 15, 1378–79.

Atkeson, Lonna Rae, and Cherie D. Maestas. 2012. *Catastrophic Politics: How Extraordinary Events Redefine Perceptions of Government*. New York: Cambridge University Press.

Austin, D. Andrew. 2015. *The Debt Limit: History and Recent Increases*. Congressional Research Service publication 7-5700. November 7.

Bach, Stanley, and Steven S. Smith. 1988. *Managing Uncertainty in the House of Representatives: Adaptation and Innovation in Special Rules*. Washington, DC: Brookings Institution Press.

Bai, Matt. 2012. "Obama vs. Boehner: Who Killed the Debt Deal?" *New York Times Magazine*, March 28.

Balla, Steven J., and Christopher J. Deering. 2013. "Police Patrols and Fire Alarms: An Empirical Examination of the Legislative Preference for Oversight." *Congress and the Presidency*, 40:27–40.

Barnes, Jeb. 2004. *Overruled: Legislative Overrides, Pluralism, and Contemporary Court-Congressional Relations*. Stanford, CA: Stanford University Press.

Beckmann, Matthew N. 2010. *Pushing the Agenda: Presidential Leadership in U.S. Lawmaking, 1953–2004*. New York: Cambridge University Press.

Benkelman, Susan. 2010. "Sui Generis." *CQ Weekly*, June 7, 1370.

Binder, Sarah A. 1996. "The Partisan Basis of Procedural Choice: Allocating Parliamentary Rights in the House, 1789–1990." *American Political Science Review* 90:8–20.

Birnbaum, Jeffrey H., and Alan S. Murray. 1987. *Showdown at Gucci Gulch: Lawmakers, Lobbyists, and the Unlikely Triumph of Tax Reform*. New York: Random House.

Black, Earl, and Merle Black. 2003. *The Rise of Southern Republicans*. Cambridge: Harvard University Press.

Bogardus, Kevin. 2009. "$2M Ad Blitz Launched by U.S. Chamber." *The Hill*, July 22, 1, 8.

Bolton, Alexander. 2009. "Dems Warn Baucus with Gavel Threat." *The Hill*, July 29, 1, 6.

Bond, Jon R., and Richard Fleisher. 2000. *Polarized Politics: Congress and the President in a Partisan Era*. Washington, DC: CQ Press.

Brady, David W., Morris P. Fiorina, and Arjun S. Wilkins. 2011. "The 2010 Elections: Why Did Political Science Forecasts Go Awry?" *PS: Political Science & Politics* 44:247–50.

Brown, Carrie Budoff. 2009. "Deal or No Deal? Baucus Casts Doubts, CBO Throws Cold Water." *Politico*, July 17, 1, 15.

Calvert, Randall L. 1987. "Reputation and Legislative Leadership." *Public Choice* 55:81–119.

Cameron, Charles M. 2000. *Veto Bargaining: Presidents and the Politics of Negative Power*. New York: Cambridge University Press.

Canes-Wrone, Brandice, and Scott de Marchi. 2002. "Presidential Approval and Legislative Success." *Journal of Politics* 64:491–509.

Carson, Jamie L., Charles J. Finocchiaro, and David W. Rohde. 2010. "Consensus, Conflict, and Partisanship in House Decision Making: A Bill-Level Examination of Committee and Floor Behavior." *Congress and the Presidency* 37:231–53.

Carter, Charlene, and Niels Lesniewski. 2011. "House Passes, Senate Shelves Balanced-Budget Legislation." *CQ Weekly*, July 25, 1629.

Chappell, Bill. 2016. "In a First, NFL Executive Admits Football Is Linked to Brain Damage." *National Public Radio*, March 15. http://www.npr.org/sections/thetwo-way/2016/03/15/470513922/in-a-first-nfl-executive-admits-football-is-linked-to-brain-damage

Clark, Jennifer Hayes. 2015. *Minority Parties in U.S. Legislatures*. Ann Arbor: University of Michigan Press.

Clark, Tom S. 2009. "The Separation of Powers, Court-Curbing, and Judicial Legitimacy." *American Journal of Political Science* 53:971–89.

Cloud, David S. 1994. "Tobacco Industry Losing Allies as Congress Eyes Health Tax." *CQ Weekly*, April 23, 985–89.

Cohen, Richard E. 2011. "Debt Limit Strife Tests Public Patience." *CQ Weekly*, July 25, 1610–12.

Cohen, Richard E., and Brian Friel. 2009. "Chairman Rising." *National Journal*, January 24, 22–32.

Conley, Richard S. 2011. "The Harbinger of the Unitary Executive? An Analysis of Presidential Signing Statements from Truman to Carter." *Presidential Studies Quarterly* 41:546–69.

Cooper, Joseph, and David W. Brady. 1981. "Institutional Context and Leadership Style: The House from Cannon to Rayburn." *American Political Science Review* 75:411–25.

Cox, Gary W., and Mathew D. McCubbins. 1993. *Legislative Leviathan: Party Government in the House*. Berkeley: University of California Press.

Cox, Gary W., and Mathew D. McCubbins. 2002. "Agenda Power in the U.S. House of Representatives, 1877 to 1986." In *Party, Process, and Political Change in Congress: New Perspectives on the History of Congress*, ed. David Brady and Mathew D. McCubbins. Stanford, CA: Stanford University Press.

Cox, Gary W., and Mathew D. McCubbins. 2005. *Setting the Agenda: Responsible Party Government in the U.S. House of Representatives*. New York: Cambridge University Press.

Cranford, John. 2010. "Oil, Water, Profit, and Peril." *CQ Weekly*, June 7, 1388–96.

Cranford, John. 2011. "Political Economy: Recovery at Risk." *CQ Weekly*, July 25, 1654.

Cranford, John, and Joseph J. Schatz. 2011. "Debt Ceiling: In Whose Hands?" *CQ Weekly*, July 18, 1546–50.

Cummings, Jeanne. 2009. "Trouble on Tobacco Road." *Politico*, April 14, 1, 23.

Dallek, Matthew. 2009. "The Power of the Liberals." *Politico*, July 17, 18.

Davenport, Coral. 2008a. "Waxman Claims a Premier Gavel." *CQ Weekly*, November 24, 3148–50.

Davenport, Coral. 2008b. "Waxman Quietly Pressured Colleagues to Support Change." *CQ Weekly*, November 24, 3149.

Davenport, Coral. 2010a. "Drilling Halt Heats Up Green Rhetoric." *CQ Weekly*, May 31, 1334–35.

Davenport, Coral. 2010b. "The Graham Effect on Climate Change." *CQ Weekly*, May 3, 1094.

Davenport, Coral, and Avery Palmer. 2009. "Climate Bill Rides Last-Minute Blitz." *CQ Today*, June 26, 1, 14.

Davidson, Roger H., Walter J. Oleszek, Frances E. Lee, and Eric Schickler. 2016. *Congress and Its Members*. 15th ed. Washington, DC: CQ Press.

DeBonis, Mike. 2016. "Obama's Legislative Legacy Comes Down to This Question: What If?" *Washington Post*, August 16.

Deering, Christopher J., and Steven S. Smith. 1997. *Committees in Congress*. 3rd ed. Washington, DC: CQ Press.

Dennis, Steven T. 2009. "Ross Is Blue Dogs' Bulldog." *Roll Call*, July 20, 1.

Dennis, Steven T., and Tory Newmyer 2009. "Blue Dogs See Signs of Hope: Democratic Leaders Clash over Bill's Timing." *Roll Call*, July 22, 1, 24.

Dionne, E. J. Jr., Norman Ornstein, and Thomas Mann. 2017. *One Nation After Trump: A Guide for the Perplexed, Disillusioned, the Desperate, and the Not-Yet Deported*. New York: St. Martin's Press.

Doherty, Carroll J. 1995. "Time and Tax Cuts Will Test GOP Freshman Solidarity." *Congressional Quarterly Weekly Report*, April 1, 916.

Dumain, Emma, Matt Fuller, and Paul M. Krawzak. 2015. "Crash Course: Leadership Novice Ryan Takes the Reins." *CQ Weekly*, October 26, 2–7.

Edwards, George C., III. 1989. *At the Margins: Presidential Leadership of Congress*. New Haven: Yale University Press.

Edwards, George C., III, and Andrew Barrett. 2000. "Presidential Agenda Setting in Congress." In *Polarized Politics: Congress and the President in a Partisan Era*. Washington, DC: CQ Press.

Eskridge, William N., Jr. 1994. *Dynamic Statutory Interpretation*. Cambridge: Harvard University Press.

Ethridge, Emily. 2014. "2013 Vote Studies: Presidential Support." *CQ Weekly*, February 3, 170.

Ethridge, Emily, Carolyn Phenicie, and Chris Wright. 2014. "The Contenders." *CQ Weekly*, June 16, 839–47.

Evans, C. Lawrence, and Claire E. Grandy. 2008. "The Whip Systems of Congress." In *Congress Reconsidered*, 9th ed., ed. Lawrence C. Dodd and Bruce I. Oppenheimer. Washington, DC: CQ Press.

Evans, C. Lawrence, and Walter J. Oleszek. 1997. *Congress under Fire: Reform Politics and the Republican Majority*. Boston: Houghton Mifflin, 1997.

Evans, Kevin, and Bryan W. Marshall. 2016–17. "Presidential Signing Statements and Lawmaking Credit." *Political Science Quarterly* 131:749–78.

Eshbaugh-Soha, Matthew. 2005. "The Politics of Presidential Agendas." *Political Research Quarterly* 58:257–68.

Eshbaugh-Soha, Matthew. 2010. "The Importance of Policy Scope to Presidential Success in Congress." *Presidential Studies Quarterly* 40:708–24.

Fenno, Richard F., Jr. 1966. *The Power of the Purse: Appropriations Politics in Congress*. Boston: Little, Brown.

Fenno, Richard F., Jr. 1973. *Congressmen in Committees*. Boston: Little, Brown.

Fenno, Richard F., Jr. 1978. *Home Style: House Members in Their Districts*. Boston: Little Brown.

Fenno, Richard F., Jr. 1982. *The United States Senate: A Bicameral Perspective*. Washington, DC: American Enterprise Institute for Public Policy Research.

Ferguson, Ellyn. 2010. "For Gulf Wildlife, an Oil and Chemical Cocktail." *CQ Weekly*, May 31, 1320.

Ferris, Sarah. 2016. "Showdown Scars: How the $4 Trillion 'Grand Bargain' Collapsed." *The Hill*, February 10.

Finocchiaro, Charles J., and Jeffery A. Jenkins. 2008. "In Search of Killer Amendments In the Modern U.S. House." *Legislative Studies Quarterly* 33:263–94.

Finocchiaro, Charles J., and David W. Rohde. 2008. "War for the Floor: Partisan Theory and Agenda Control in the U.S. House of Representatives. *Legislative Studies Quarterly* 33:35–61.

Fiorina, Morris P. 1989. *Congress: Keystone of the Washington Establishment*. New Haven: Yale University Press.

Fisher, Louis. 2000. *Congressional Abdication on War and Spending*. College Station: Texas A&M University Press.

Fleisher, Richard, and Jon R. Bond. 2004. "The Shrinking Middle in Congress." *British Journal of Political Science* 34:429–51.

Fortunato, David. 2013. "Majority Status and Variation in Informational Organization." *Journal of Politics* 75:937–52.

Friel, Brian, and Kerry Young. 2010. "A Trying Relationship," *CQ Weekly*, September 13, 2076–84.

Gardner, Lauren, and Matt Fuller. 2014. "Interior Bill Would Slash EPA Funding to 15-Year Low." *CQ Weekly*, June 25, 1320–21.

Gasper, John T., and Andrew Reeves. 2011. "Make It Rain? Retrospection and the

Attentive Electorate in the Context of Natural Disasters." *American Journal of Political Science* 55:340–55.

Gettinger, Stephen. 2011. "Return of the Floor Vote." *CQ Weekly*, May 2, 961.

Gilmour, John B. 1995. *Strategic Disagreement: Stalemate in American Politics*. Pittsburgh: University of Pittsburgh Press.

Glass, Andrew. 2009. "Congress Bans Cigarette Ads on the Air, April 1, 1970." *Politico*, April 1. http://www.politico.com/story/2009/04/congress-bans-cigarette-ads-on-the-air-april-1-1970-020715

Glover, Keith. 1994a. "Health: Latest FDA Tobacco Testimony Suggests Regulation Is Near." *CQ Weekly*, June 25, 1722.

Glover, Keith. 1994b. "Health: Subcommittee Votes to Restrict Smoking in Most Buildings." *CQ Weekly*, May 14, 1225.

Goldfarb, Sam. 2011. "Tea Partiers Build Capitol Credibility." *CQ Weekly*, February 21, 378.

Graham-Silverman, Adam. 2008. "Travel Decreases as Ethics Rules Complicate Privately Funded Trips." *CQ Weekly*, December 1, 3178.

Green, Matthew N. 2015. *Underdog Politics: The Minority Party in the U.S. House of Representatives*. New Haven: Yale University Press.

Greenstein, Fred I. 1994. "The Hidden-Hand Presidency: Eisenhower as Leader: A 1994 Perspective." *Presidential Studies Quarterly* 24:233–41.

Gruenwald, Juliana. 1997. "Regulation: Tobacco Industry Hands Over Subpoenaed Papers." *CQ Weekly*, December 6, 3029.

Hall, Andrew B., and Kenneth A. Shepsle. 2014. "The Changing Value of Seniority in the U.S. House: Conditional Party Government Revised." *Journal of Politics* 76:98–113.

Hall, Richard L. 1987. "Participation and Purpose in Committee Decision Making." *American Political Science Review* 81:105–27.

Hall, Richard L. 1996. *Participation in Congress*. New Haven: Yale University Press.

Hall, Richard L., and Molly Reynolds. 2012. "Targeted Issue Advertising and Legislative Strategy: The Inside Ends of Outside Lobbying." *Journal of Politics* 74:888–902.

Hallerman, Tamar. 2014. "Tapping Back in to Regular Order." *CQ Weekly*, April 7, 538–45.

Hansford, Thomas G., and David F. Damore. 2000. "Congressional Preferences, Perceptions of Threat, and Supreme Court Decision Making." *American Politics Quarterly* 28:512–32.

Harrison, R. Wes. 2013. "The RESTORE Act of 2012: Implications for the Gulf Coast." *Journal of Agricultural and Applied Economics* 45:331–37.

Hausegger, Lori, and Lawrence Baum. 1999. "Inviting Congressional Action: A

Study of Supreme Court Motivations in Statutory Interpretation." *American Journal of Political Science* 43:162–83.

Hilts, Philip J. 1994. "Tobacco Chiefs Say Cigarettes Aren't Addictive." *New York Times*, April 15.

Hixon, William, and Bryan W. Marshall. 2007. "Agendas, Side Issues and Leadership in the U.S. House." *Journal of Theoretical Politics* 19:83–99.

Hobson, Margaret. 2011a. "2010 Key House Vote: Offshore Oil Drilling Regulations." *CQ Weekly*, January 3, 59.

Hobson, Margaret. 2011b. "A Year after Oil Spill, Urgency Turns to Impasse." *CQ Weekly*, April 18, 852–53.

Hulse, Carl. 2008. "Some House Republicans Keep Up Protest." *New York Times*, August 4.

Jalonick, Mary Clare. 2004. "Thomas' Corporate Tax Bill Gambit Aims to Link Tobacco Buyout." *CQ Weekly*, May 22, 1212.

Jalonick, Mary Clare. 2005. "Loophole in Tobacco Pact Endangers Truth Ads." *CQ Weekly*, March 21, 701–2.

Jarlenski, Marian, and Richard Rubin. 2010. "Health Care Overhaul's Key Parts." *CQ Weekly*, April 12, 914–22.

Johnson, Haynes, and David Broder 1997. *The System: The Death of Health Care Reform in 1993–1994.* Boston: Little Brown.

Johnston, Travis M., and Stephen N. Goggin. 2015. "Presidential Confidence in Crisis: Blame, Media, and the BP Oil Spill." *Presidential Studies Quarterly* 45:467–89.

Kelley, Christopher S., and Bryan W. Marshall. 2008. "The Last Word: Presidential Power and the Role of Signing Statements." *Presidential Studies Quarterly* 38:248–67.

Kenen, Joanne. 2011. "It Takes a Crisis: Deficit Politics Focus on Medicare." *CQ Weekly*, July 25, 1613–14.

Key, V. O., Jr. 1949. *Southern Politics in State and Nation.* New York: Knopf.

Kiewiet, Roderick, and Matthew McCubbins. 1991. *The Logic of Delegation: Congressional Parties and the Appropriations Process.* Chicago: University of Chicago Press.

Kingdon, John W. 1989. *Congressmen's Voting Decisions.* Ann Arbor: University of Michigan Press.

Koss, Geof. 2010. "Fall 2009 Outlook: Oil Spill Response." *CQ Weekly*, September 13, 2098.

Koss, Geof, and Jennifer Scholtes. 2010. "Oil Legislation Spills Over into Fall." *CQ Weekly*, August 2, 1868–69.

Kowalcky, Linda K., and Lance T. LeLoup. 1993. "Congress and the Politics of Statutory Debt Limitation." *Public Administration Review* 53:14–27.

Krawzak, Paul. 2015. "Dynamic Scoring System Has Republicans Revved." *CQ Weekly*, January 12, http://library.cqpress.com.proxy.lib.miamioh.edu/cqweekly/weeklyreport114-000004599612

Krawzak, Paul, and Sam Goldfarb. 2011. "Debt Talks Move into High Gear." *CQ Weekly*, July 11, 1494–95.

Krehbiel, Keith. 1991. *Information and Legislative Organization*. Ann Arbor: University of Michigan Press.

Krehbiel, Keith. 1998. *Pivotal Politics: A Theory of U.S. Lawmaking*. Chicago: University of Chicago Press.

Kriner, Douglas L. 2010. *After the Rubicon: Congress, Presidents, and the Politics of Waging War*. Chicago: University of Chicago Press.

Krutz, Glen S. 2001. "Tactical Maneuvering on Omnibus Bills in Congress." *American Journal of Political Science* 45:210–23.

Lebo, Matthew J., and Andrew J. O'Geen. 2011. "The President's Role in the Partisan Congressional Arena." *Journal of Politics* 73:718–34.

Lee, Carol E. 2009. "Tobacco." *Politico*, June 23, 3.

Lee, Frances E. 2009. *Beyond Ideology: Politics, Principles, and Partisanship in the U.S. Senate*. Chicago: University of Chicago Press.

Lee, Frances E. 2013. "Presidents and Party Teams: The Politics of Debt Limits and Executive Oversight, 2001–2013." *Presidential Studies Quarterly* 43:775–91.

Lee, Frances E. 2016. *Insecure Majorities: Congress and the Perpetual Campaign*. Chicago: University of Chicago Press.

Lerer, Lisa, and Patrick O'Connor. 2009. "House Dems Strike Deal on Climate." *Politico*, June 24, 1, 15.

Liptak, Adam. 2013. "Experts See Potential Ways Out for Obama in Debt Ceiling Maze." *New York Times*, October 3.

Lizza, Ryan. 2012. "Fussbudget: How Paul Ryan Captured the G.O.P." *New Yorker*, August 6.

Magner, Mike. 2016. "Federal Study Tracks Health Problems in Gulf Spill Cleanup Workers." *CQ Weekly*, April 25, http://library.cqpress.com.proxy.lib.miamioh.edu/cqweekly/weeklyreport114-000004875433.

Magner, Mike, and Jeremy Dillon. 2016. "Gulf Environment Shortchanged in Chase for BP Settlement Dollars." *CQ Weekly*, April 25, http://library.cqpress.com.proxy.lib.miamioh.edu/cqweekly/weeklyreport114-000004875441

Maltzman, Forrest. 1997. *Competing Principals: Committees, Parties, and the Organization of Congress*. Ann Arbor: University of Michigan Press.

Manley, John F. 1970. *The Politics of Finance: The House Committee on Ways and Means*. Boston: Little, Brown.

Mann, Thomas E., and Norman J. Ornstein. 2006. *The Broken Branch: How Congress Is Failing America and How to Get It Back on Track*. New York: Oxford University Press.

Mann, Thomas E., and Norman J. Ornstein. 2013. "Finding the Common Good in an Era of Dysfunctional Governance." *Journal of the American Academy of Arts and Sciences* 142:15–24.

Marshall, Bryan W. 2005. *Rules for War: Procedural Choice in the U.S. House of Representatives.* Aldershot: Ashgate.

Marshall, Bryan W. 2010. "A Glimpse of History: Working for the House Majority Whip in the Early Days of the 111th Congress." *PS: Political Science & Politics* 43:183–88.

Marshall, Bryan W., Brandon C. Prins, and David W. Rohde. 2000. "Majority Party Leadership, Strategic Choice, and Committee Power: Appropriations in the House, 1995–1998." In *Congress on Display, Congress at Work*, ed. William T. Bianco. Ann Arbor: University of Michigan Press.

Martin, Jonathan, and Alex Isenstadt. 2009. "Energy Vote Aftershocks: Vulnerable House Dems Are Already in GOP Sights." *Politico*, June 30, 1, 14.

Massie, Thomas. 2015. "Speaker Practicing Legislative Malpractice." *The Cincinnati Enquirer*, January 5.

Mayhew, David R. 1974. *Congress: The Electoral Connection.* New Haven: Yale University Press.

McCarty, Nolan, Keith T. Poole, and Howard Rosenthal. 2006. *Polarized America: The Dance of Ideology and Unequal Riches.* Cambridge: MIT Press.

McCubbins, Mathew D., and Thomas Schwartz. 1984. "Congressional Oversight Overlooked: Police Patrols versus Fire Alarms." *American Journal of Political Science* 28:165–79.

Moe, Terry M. 1985. "The Politicized Presidency." In *The New Direction in American Politics*, ed. John E. Chubb and Paul E. Peterson. Washington, DC: Brookings Institution.

Moe, Terry M., and William G. Howell. 1999. "Unilateral Action and Presidential Power: A Theory." *Presidential Studies Quarterly* 29:850–73.

Newlin, Eliza. 2014. "Partisan Divide Is as Wide as Ever." *CQ Weekly*, October 27, 1344.

Newton-Small, Jay. 2011. "Congress: The Inside Story of Obama and Boehner's Second Failed Grand Bargain." *Time*, July 23.

O'Connor, Patrick. 2009a. "Moderates Bedevil Waxman—Again." *Politico*, July 20, 1, 12.

O'Connor, Patrick. 2009b. "Rank-and-File House Dems Resist." *Politico*, July 17, 1, 15.

O'Connor, Patrick, and Glenn Thrush. 2009. "Chaos and Arm-Twisting Gave Pelosi a Major Win." *Politico*, June 30, 1, 15.

Oleszek, Walter J. 2004. *Congressional Procedures and the Policy Process.* 6th ed. Washington, DC: CQ Press.

Olson, Mancur. 1961. *The Logic of Collective Action*. Cambridge: Harvard University Press.

Oppenheimer, Bruce I. 1977. "The Rules Committee: New Arm of Leadership in a Decentralized House." In *Congress Reconsidered*, ed. Lawrence C. Dodd and Bruce I. Oppenheimer. New York: Praeger.

Ornstein, Norman. 2009. "Obama and Allies Must Not Dawdle on Health Care Reform." *Roll Call*, July 22, 6.

Ornstein, Norman. 2011. "Worst. Congress. Ever." *Foreign Policy*, July 19. http://foreignpolicy.com/2011/07/19/worst-congress-ever/

Ota, Alan K. 2010a. "Black Gold for a Veteran Inquisitor." *CQ Weekly*, June 7, 1392–93.

Ota, Alan K. 2010b. "Keeping Cuts at Bay." *CQ Weekly*, November 8, 2528.

Ota, Alan K. 2010c. "Partisan Rift in Bipartisan Group." *CQ Weekly*, March 29, 744.

Pacelle, Richard L., Jr., Brett W. Curry, and Bryan W. Marshall. 2011. *Decision Making by the Modern Supreme Court: Creating the Living Law and Maintaining the Constitutional Shield*. New York: Cambridge University Press.

Parker, Ashley. 2015. "GOP Is Divided as Budget Bills Start Piling Up." *New York Times*, March 9.

Pearson, Kathryn, and Eric Schickler. 2009. "Discharge Petitions, Agenda Control, and the Congressional Committee System, 1929–1976." *Journal of Politics* 71:1238–56.

Peterson, Mark A. 1990. *Legislating Together: The White House and Capitol Hill from Eisenhower to Reagan*. Cambridge: Harvard University Press.

Polsby, Nelson W. 2003. *How Congress Evolves: Social Bases of Institutional Change*. Oxford: Oxford University Press.

Price, David E. 1972. *Who Makes the Laws? Creativity and Power in Senate Committees*. Cambridge, MA: Schenkman.

Rae, Nicol C. 1998. *Conservative Reformers: The Republican Freshmen and the Lessons of the 104th Congress*. Armonk, NY: Sharpe.

Reichard, John. 2010. "Health: After the Win, No Time to Lose." *CQ Weekly*, April 5, 814–17.

Remini, Robert V. 2006. *The House: The History of the House of Representatives*. Washington, DC: Smithsonian Books.

Riker, William. 1962. *The Theory of Political Coalitions*. New Haven, CT: Yale University Press.

Riker, William. 1986. *The Art of Political Manipulation*. New Haven, CT: Yale University Press.

Rivers, Douglas, and Nancy L. Rose. 1985. "Passing the President's Program: Public Opinion and Presidential Influence in Congress." *American Journal of Political Science* 29:183–96.

Robinson, James A. 1963. *The House Rules Committee*. New York: Bobbs-Merrill.

Rohde, David W. 1991. *Parties and Leaders in the Postreform House*. Chicago: University of Chicago Press.

Rohde, David W., and John H. Aldrich. 2010. "Consequences of Electoral and Institutional Change: The Evolution of Conditional Party Government in the U.S. House of Representatives." In *New Directions in American Political Parties*, ed. Jeffrey M. Stonecash. New York: Routledge.

Rohde, David W., and Kenneth A. Shepsle. 1987. "Leaders and Followers in the House of Representatives: Reflections on Woodrow Wilson's Congressional Government." *Congress and the Presidency* 14:111–33.

Rothenberg, Lawrence C. 1992. *Linking Citizens to Government*. New York: Cambridge University Press.

Rudalevige, Andrew. 2002. *Managing the President's Program: Presidential Leadership and Legislative Policy Formation*. Princeton: Princeton University Press.

Rudalevige, Andrew. 2009. "The Administrative Presidency and Bureaucratic Control: Implementing a Research Agenda." *Presidential Studies Quarterly* 39:10–24.

Russell, Pam Radtke. 2012. "Oil Spill Legislation Shows Signs of Slip-Sliding Away." *CQ Weekly*, April 23, 798–99.

Samuelsohn, Darren, and Robin Bravender. 2010. "Greens Desperate to Avoid Blame." *Politico*, November 4. http://www.politico.com/story/2010/11/greens-desperate-to-avoid-blame-044689?o=1

Sanchez, Humberto. 2013. "2012 Vote Studies: Party Unity." *CQ Weekly*, January 21, 132–40.

Schatz, Joseph J. 2010. "The Trials Ahead for John Boehner." *CQ Weekly*, November 8, 2520.

Schatz, Joseph. J. 2011. "Debt Deal Brings Relief, Frustration." *CQ Weekly*, August 8, 2011, 1756-58.

Schatz, Joseph J., and Coral Davenport. 2010. "Spill's Impact Spreads to Washington." *CQ Weekly*, May 10, 1132–35.

Schatz, Joseph J., and Sam Goldfarb. 2011. "No Grand Bargain on Debt Ceiling." *CQ Weekly*, July 25, 1628–31.

Schatz, Joseph J., and Geof Koss. 2010. "BP Pressed; Energy Bill Pushed." *CQ Weekly*, June 21, 1506-7.

Schatz, Joseph J., and Paul M. Krawzak. 2011. "Debt Plans Remain in Limbo." *CQ Weekly*, July 18, 1554–56.

Schickler, Eric, and Kathryn Pearson. 2009. "Agenda Control, Majority Party Power, and the House Committee on Rules, 1939–1952." *Legislative Studies Quarterly* 34:455–91.

Schickler, Eric, Kathryn Pearson, and Brian Feinstein. 2010. "Shifting Partisan

Coalitions: Support for Civil Rights in Congress from 1933–72." *Journal of Politics* 72:672–89.

Schoenberg, Tom, and Greg Farrell. 2013. "Obama Rejects Call to Use 14th Amendment to Fix U.S. Debt Fight." *Bloomberg*, October 9. http://www.bloomberg.com/news/articles/2013-10-09/obama-throws-cold-water-on-14th-amendment-to-fix-debt-fight

Scholtes, Jennifer. 2010. "Lawmakers Clear Legislation to Allow Quicker Release of Oil Spill Funds." *CQ Weekly*, June 14, 1460.

Scholtes, Jennifer. 2015. "A Piecemeal Strategy against Obama." *CQ Weekly*, January 12, 18.

Schwarz, Alan, Walt Bogdanich, and Jacqueline Williams. 2016. "NFL's Flawed Concussion Research and Ties to Tobacco Industry" *New York Times*, March 24.

Segal, Jeffrey A., Chad Westerland, and Stephanie A. Lindquist. 2011. "Congress, the Supreme Court, and Judicial Review: Testing a Constitutional Separation of Powers Model." *American Journal of Political Science* 55:89–104.

Seitz-Wald, Alex, and Zaid Lilani. 2011. "House Dems: If GOP Is Intent on 'Destroying Government,' Obama Should Use 14th Amendment to Raise Debt Ceiling." *Think Progress*, July 27. https://thinkprogress.org/house-dems-if-gop-is-intent-on-destroying-government-obama-should-use-14th-amendment-to-raise-debt-38a70df42c5a#.pqoeof84g

Shear, Jeff. 1995. "Force Majeure?" *National Journal*, March 11, 601–4.

Shepsle, Kenneth. 1978. *The Giant Jigsaw Puzzle: Democratic Committee Assignments in the Modern House*. Chicago: University of Chicago Press.

Shepsle, Kenneth A. 1986. "The Positive Theory of Legislative Institutions: An Enrichment of Social Choice and Spatial Models." *Public Choice* 50:135–78.

Shepsle, Kenneth A. 1989. "The Changing Textbook Congress." In *Can the Government Govern?*, ed. John E. Chubb and Paul E. Peterson. Washington, DC: Brookings Institution.

Shepsle, Kenneth A., and Barry R. Weingast. 1987. "The Institutional Foundations of Committee Power." *The American Political Science Review* 81:85–104.

Shepsle, Kenneth A., and Barry R. Weingast. 1995. *Positive Theories of Congressional Institutions*. Ann Arbor: University of Michigan Press.

Sides, John, Michael Tesler, and Lynn Vavreck. 2016. "The Electoral Landscape of 2016." *Annals of the American Academy of Political and Social Science* 667:50–71.

Sinclair, Barbara. 1982. *Congressional Realignment, 1925–78*. Austin: University of Texas Press.

Sinclair, Barbara. 1985. "Agenda Control and Policy Success: The Case of Ronald Reagan and the 97th Congress." *Legislative Studies Quarterly* 20:291–314.

Sinclair, Barbara. 1989. *The Transformation of the U.S. Senate*. Baltimore: Johns Hopkins University Press.

Sinclair, Barbara. 1995. *Legislators, Leaders, and Lawmaking: The U.S. House of Representatives in the Postreform Era*. Baltimore: Johns Hopkins University Press.

Sinclair, Barbara. 2000a. "Hostile Partners: The President, Congress, and Lawmaking in the Partisan 1990s." In *Polarized Politics: Congress and the President in a Partisan Era*, ed. Jon R. Bond and Richard Fleisher. Washington, DC: CQ Press.

Sinclair, Barbara. 2000b. "Republican House Majority Party Leadership in the 104th and 105th Congresses: Innovation and Continuity." In *Congress on Display, Congress at Work*, ed. William T. Bianco. Ann Arbor: University of Michigan Press.

Sinclair, Barbara. 2006. *Party Wars: Polarization and the Politics of National Policy Making*. Norman: University of Oklahoma Press.

Sinclair, Barbara. 2011. *Unorthodox Lawmaking: New Legislative Processes in the U.S. Congress*. 4th ed. Washington, DC: CQ Press.

Sinclair, Barbara. 2012. *Unorthodox Lawmaking: New Legislative Processes in the U.S. Congress*. 5th ed. Washington, DC: CQ Press.

Smith, Steven S. 1989. *Call to Order: Floor Politics in the House and Senate*. Washington, DC: Brookings Institution.

Smith, Steven S. 2007. *Party Influence in Congress*. New York: Cambridge University Press.

Soraghan, Mike, and Jared Allen. 2009. "Dems at Odds on How to Turn Tide on Health." *The Hill*, July 22, 1, 6.

Stewart, Charles, III. 2001. *Analyzing Congress*. New York: Norton.

Symes, Frances, and Sam Goldfarb. 2011. "Legislation Aimed at Expanding Offshore Drilling Passes in House." *CQ Weekly*, May 9, 1012.

Taylor, Alan. 2014. "Bhopal: The World's Worst Industrial Disaster, 30 Years Later." *The Atlantic*, December 2.

Teodoro, Manuel P., and Jon R. Bond. 2017. "Presidents, Baseball, and Wins above Expectations: What Can Sabermetrics Tell Us about Presidential Success? Why Ronald Reagan Is Like Bobby Cox and Lyndon Johnson Is Like Joe Torre." *PS: Political Science & Politics* 50:339–46.

Theriault, Sean M. 2008. *Party Polarization in Congress*. New York: Cambridge University Press.

Theriault, Sean M. 2013. *The Gingrich Senators: The Roots of Partisan Warfare in Congress*. New York: Oxford University Press.

Theriault, Sean M., and David W. Rohde. 2011. "The Gingrich Senators and Party Polarization in the U.S. Senate." *Journal of Politics* 73:1011–24.

Wallsten, Peter, Lori Montgomery, and Scott Wilson. 2012. "Obama's Evolution: Behind the Failed 'Grand Bargain' on the Debt." *Washington Post*, March 17.

Waxman, Henry, with Joshua Green. 2009. *The Waxman Report: How Congress Really Works*. New York: Twelve Hatchet.

Wayne, Alex, and Edward Epstein. 2010a. "Bill in Hand, Holdouts Weigh In." *CQ Weekly*, March 22, 690–93.

Wayne, Alex, and Edward Epstein. 2010b. "Obama Seals Legislative Legacy with Health Insurance Overhaul." *CQ Weekly*, March 29, 748–53.

Weingast, Barry, and William Marshall. 1988. "The Industrial Organization of Congress." *Journal of Political Economy* 91:132–63.

Weyl, Ben. 2014. "Business Not as Usual for a Divided Conference." *CQ Weekly*, June 16, 842.

Wilentz, Sean. 2013. "Obama and the Debt." *New York Times*, October 7.

Wright, John R. 1996. *Interest Groups and Congress*. Boston: Allyn and Bacon.

Zeller, Shawn. 2008a. "Client of the Month Club: Campaign for Tobacco-Free Kids." *CQ Weekly*, August 4, 2098.

Zeller, Shawn. 2008b. "Public Health Doctors Take on Tobacco Control Bill." *CQ Weekly*, July 21, 1952.

Zeller, Shawn. 2009. "All Smoke, Little Lobbying Fire, from Tobacco Giants." *CQ Weekly*, June 22, 1420.

Zeller, Shawn. 2014. "Rogers: Shutdown Is Out of the Question." *CQ Weekly*, November 17, 1384.

# Index

*Note*: Page numbers in italics refer to illustrations and tables.

CPSIA information can be obtained
at www.ICGtesting.com
Printed in the USA
LVHW08s0213110818
586531LV00001B/3/P

9 780472 053834